You'll See

A Story of Narcissistic Abuse, Survival,
and My Journey to Understand

Suzanne Groves

Black Rose Writing | Texas

First printing

This is a work of memoir, written according to the author's personal memory of actual
events and conversations of which she was part or to which she was privy. Names have
been changed for privacy purposes.

ISBN: 978-1-68513-403-7
PUBLISHED BY BLACK ROSE WRITING
www.blackrosewriting.com

Printed in the United States of America
Suggested Retail Price (SRP) $24.95

You'll See is printed in Sabon Next

*As a planet-friendly publisher, Black Rose Writing does its best to eliminate unnecessary waste to
reduce paper usage and energy costs, while never compromising the reading experience. As a result,
the final word count vs. page count may not meet common expectations.

This memoir was painful to write because it meant reliving experiences which left indelible marks upon my psyche. During the process, I received encouragement to be honest, brave, and comprehensive in telling my story, hoping it could validate and inspire others. As I began my quest for understanding, Noble Groves, my husband, best friend and rock, gave me the refuge of his unconditional love.

This book is for you. Forever and a day. Two, if we're lucky.

A NOTE TO MY READERS

This book recounts my lifetime of enduring psychological abuse and trauma at the hands of my father, whom I would ultimately discover to be both a narcissist and an addict. Some readers may find this memoir challenging because it includes stories about emotional abuse, eating disorders, alcohol abuse, and abandonment. Please engage in self-care as you read this book.

While the story I've written accurately represents my experiences, I have changed many names for the sake of privacy.

You'll See

"One day you will tell your story of how you overcame what you went through, and it will be someone else's survival guide."

–Brené Brown

PROLOGUE

The most lethal toxins are those undetectable to the innocents until the damage has already been done. Those who trust in a parent's fundamental goodness, despite experiences proving otherwise, stand to be the most harmed; the toxins keep attacking while the spirit keeps hoping. Until it stops.

Longing characterized my years with my father. If I could only meet his standards, ephemeral though they were, I would feel I belonged. That I was safe, shielded from outside dangers. I had been scarred long before I learned that the threats came from within, that they were his personality disorder and addiction. Make no mistake– I never lacked for food, clothing, or shelter. We took family vacations. I received a wonderful education. I enjoyed many achievements, academically, professionally, and personally. To an outsider, my life probably looked normal, if not privileged. The impact of psychological abuse can be just as damaging and traumatic as the scars caused by physical and sexual abuse. Possibly more, even, because the abuse is insidious. Invisible to detect. And the effects can outlive the abuser, almost in perpetuity.

It has taken time, distance, and death, but I have been gradually able to piece together the parts of this poisonous puzzle. I started from the very beginning and assessed each vignette as a significant clue in a mystery I've only begun to figure out.

It didn't have to be this way. But it was.

I chose December 21 for my father's interment at Dallas/Fort Worth National Cemetery because it's the winter solstice, the shortest day of the year, and marks the return of light after the darkest of days. My pastor met us there, along with my best friend, Margot, and Barry, my father's only real local friend. My daughter was unable to return to town in time due to her recent graduation from college, but I wasn't upset as I understood her ambivalence toward him. Mom wasn't there either; transporting her from her memory care facility would have been difficult, and she wouldn't have understood, anyway.

I had brought his medals to be interred with his urn. The coordinator from the cemetery placed them by his urn on a beautifully adorned table in a gazebo overlooking the acreage, replete with perfectly spaced white headstones as far as the eye could see. It was a beautiful, crisp day, for which we were thankful. The service began with the pastor and a perfect presentation of the flag by the color guard. They walked methodically to where I was sitting, with one officer kneeling to present the flag to me. I began to cry, clutching the flag to my chest. Next, a solo bugler played "Taps," which made me shiver with its haunting beauty. I continued wiping my eyes; I believe my father would have been pleased with me, perhaps for the first time.

Unbeknownst to us, the color guard had marched from the gazebo to the garden around the side. With the first command, they fired a shot. Then, a second, followed by the third, echoing through the hillside. They marched back, stood before me, and presented me with the three casings, which I rolled around in my hand like worry stones. Following the conclusion of our pastor's prayers, we proceeded to the columbarium, where my father's ashes and medals were placed under the guidance of the coordinator.

It was a beautiful, dignified send off for a man deeply committed to his country, yet disloyal to his own family. I had been so conflicted about honoring his wishes for this ceremony; as I told one of my friends, "He wasn't an honorable man. He doesn't deserve it."

"Suzanne," Eric said, "You don't have the right to make that decision. Your father was willing to lay down his life for this nation. He's earned this. Don't take it away." He was right, of course.

Despite my father's bravery in confronting external enemies, he lacked the courage to identify and overcome his internal enemies, namely mental illness and addiction. Despite our efforts to please, placate, manage, tolerate, and love him unconditionally, we couldn't conquer his demons, which still haunt me.

Chapter One: The Curb

We were a respectable-looking lot, the three of us, and that was my family's priority. My father, a thirty-five-year-old rising major in the United States Air Force, and my mother, the product of childhood poverty and abandonment, maintained a strict household. During the late 1960s, our Air Force transfer brought us to Biloxi, Mississippi, where we resided in a simple duplex on base, with a carport dividing us from our neighbors. Each day, my father donned his uniform–a crisp short-sleeved blue shirt adorned with his medals, immaculately creased navy-blue pants, and his spit-shined black patent leather shoes–before heading to his sterile office at the Military Personnel Center. My mother had a uniform of her own: beautiful sheath dresses she whipped out on her Singer sewing machine, kitten heels, and her perfectly coiffed chignon, shiny as a crow's wing. It was important to her and to my father that she represented him well at her weekly Officers' Wives Club luncheons; that's what officers' wives did in those days. I was the precious doll Mom dressed in homemade romper sets and, for special occasions, frilly dresses made even more formal with the requisite white gloves and dainty Mary Janes. By all accounts, we looked like the perfect family.

Appearances can be deceiving.

According to my mother, I was a bundle of enthusiasm and curiosity, prone to lying on my stomach to examine bugs up close, or peppering her with questions, or exploring the forbidden wooded area along the greenbelt behind our house with my best friend, Rita. I loved my tricycle and my Siamese cat, Jasmine, fiercely. Peanut butter and jelly sandwiches loaded with Lay's potato chips were my favorite food, which I could only eat when my babysitter was there. My special friend, Jennifer Acclisphere, knew all about my fantasy of being Samantha on 'Bewitched.' I can still see her swinging alongside me in the shared backyard. Her long blond hair and brilliant blue eyes made her radiant, and she listened attentively and nodded at all my four-year-old observations.

She wasn't real, my parents would say, teasing me and inquiring how I had come up with such an unusual name. But she was real to me, and in hindsight, I believe I needed her.

My father appeared aloof and enigmatic, even then, but my mother's moods were mercurial, and she would quickly become angry without warning. One summer afternoon, I apparently crossed some invisible line that triggered my mother's rage. With me close behind, Mom stormed to the kitchen on her delicate heels and picked up the rotary phone on the wall. She dialed a number and waited. I was afraid, but I didn't know why.

"Hi. We've spoken before, but I'm calling you because it's time. Can you be here in ten minutes? Yes, good. Okay. She'll be outside waiting." She calmly returned the phone to its cradle.

I looked up at her expectantly.

"Let's go pack your suitcase," she said, walking to her bedroom closet to pull my diminutive pink suitcase from behind her evening dresses. My bottom lip started quivering, and I remember plopping down on the floor hoping if I stayed still, the storm would pass.

She commanded me to rise, then swiftly entered my room and began extracting clothing from the dresser. Romper sets, panties, socks, and my good pair of shoes.

"Where am I going?" I whimpered.

"You've clearly shown you can't follow the rules of this family," she growled. Jasmine had sidled up to my legs and was rubbing her nose on my sandals.

"Your new family will be here in a few minutes," she said, leading me by the hand to the front door. "Say goodbye to Jas."

I became hysterical, crying, "No" and "Please, I'll be good." She shook her head. Jasmine had followed me to the door, protectively. I leaned down and gave her a ferocious hug.

"Let's go," she said, handing me my girlie pink suitcase stuffed with enough outfits to bridge the transition. We walked down the driveway. The neighborhood kids were playing nearby and stopped to watch what was unfolding with cautious interest. Mom sat me down on the curb.

"I'm sorry it had to be this way," she said before marching back up the driveway, into the house, and closing the front door.

Sitting on the hot cement and clutching my suitcase, I was terrified of what was coming and confused about what had just happened. Was I a bad girl? I wiped my eyes with my shirt, hiccupping and coughing and staring at each car that passed. Is this my new family? No one stopped, and the neighborhood kids had disappeared.

I'm not sure how long I sat under the brutal July sun; what seemed like hours was probably just ten minutes. Ten agonizing minutes. I heard my mother's heels and looked up to see her peering at me through shaded eyes. I tried to stop crying and sat up properly.

"Do you think you can be a respectable part of this family?" she asked.

I nodded enthusiastically.

"Will you obey the rules without backtalk, and do what you're told when you're told?"

"Yes, Mommy. I promise." I was still sitting on the curb, even as the backs of my legs were burning.

"Okay, then. Come on, let's go in."

I followed her into the house and went immediately into the bathroom, where I threw up.

Mom came in, wiped my mouth, and said, "Let's put you to bed. Oh, and you don't need to tell your father about this."

The moment she tucked me in, I remember dozing off quickly, but not without realizing (at some visceral level) that I was completely at their mercy. In hindsight, I believe after ten years with my father, she knew I would have to be tough to survive his behaviors. While rough in the execution, she conditioned me to be strong. It worked, at least a little.

I could be a Good Girl. My life depended on it.

Chapter Two: A Big Girl Bike

I like to say I have the Cold War to thank for my existence. My father and mother married in 1963, just before he was transferred to a base in West Germany, where he would be a radar station designed to keep watch over the East Germans. Mom had been married before to a man who treated her poorly, reckless with both their money and her heart. My father, in her eyes, was an "officer and a gentleman," a handsome man who owned a charming blue Corvette and appeared so polished, she felt lucky to be his choice.

It didn't take long for her to realize that he enjoyed having lots of choices. Particularly the pretty young fräuleins on base. Her job in the mid-sixties was to aid him in appearing more respectable, which would allow him to be on the short list for the next promotion. And so she did, becoming active in the Officers' Wives Club and befriending the locals. Living in West Germany afforded my parents the opportunity to travel frequently and absorb all Europe had to offer, which must have felt like heaven to a woman from humble origins in Reno, Nevada. She didn't want to lose him by questioning his dalliances, so she did the next best thing—she stopped taking her birth control pills. Nine-plus months later, I arrived. My job, from day one, was to be so enchanting, so perfect, and so lovable that my father would want to spend every non-working minute at home with us.

It worked for a little while. Or so it seemed from the "evidence." I have many photos Mom took in the wee dark hours when he would handle my late-night feedings after returning home from his shift. He looked like a father enamored as he held me to his chest while rocking me back to sleep. I wish I could remember how it felt and the uncomplicated love that must have once existed.

With his tour in West Germany ending, my father's next assignment called him to serve a year in Vietnam. We flew to the U.S. and headed for Corvallis, Oregon. This would be our new home for the year Dad ran a radar station near Saigon. Corvallis was equidistant from both sets of grandparents, chosen quite wisely because Mom needed all the support she could get.

Despite the impossible distance and an uncertain war (although it wasn't called that then), she and Dad exchanged daily correspondence, doing what they could to keep their connection alive. Many of the letters centered on the mundane–her search for furniture and his opinions on what she described, or a new recipe she had tried, or what he had for dinner and how he was getting along (or not) with his crew.

As I grew more precocious, her letters began focusing on funny anecdotes about me. She described my attempts to set the table at sixteen months and my putting Jasmine inside my toy box. She told him about my dropping a plate of beef stew on the floor because I didn't like it and convincing everyone I saw to give me a "cokie"– my word for "cookie." In one letter, she wrote,

"You said you'd enjoy 'studying' her–well, Honey, you might just as well plan on being thoroughly wrapped around her little pointy finger. She is truly an enchantress–and no one can resist her spell. She knows it, too, and the wiles she employs to get her way are clever–to the point of being diabolical. She's like quicksilver and stardust and the best Champagne. You'll see. As for her expressiveness, I'm not sure she got it all from you–and certainly I can't claim credit for it. A combination, perhaps? Because next to her we are both 'stone faced.' As I said, you'll see!"

Clearly, Dad wanted to claim my personality as his doing because that's who he was–a man who needed to be right, no matter what. But in that one letter, he must have realized his worst fear had come true: someone else had claimed my mom's heart, and accordingly, she was spoiling me with the affection better given to him. Himself an only child, my father wasn't one to share.

After his Vietnam tour, we moved to Biloxi, where we lived from 1968 to 1971. His return home each evening meant I was to leave them to their cocktails, cigarettes, and accounts of the day until he was ready to give me attention. I waited patiently each evening for my turn to tell him about my day. Four-year-olds don't tend to have exciting stories in grown-up terms, but I remember wanting his attention desperately. I did my best to be pleasing, not then knowing I was chasing an elusive concept.

Living on base had its benefits, not the least of which was a neighborhood full of children, mostly older, but enjoyable. Although I was limited to our front yard and the common greenway in back, I yearned to be a big kid. Her strict boundaries didn't keep me from getting hurt, though. In the space of about two years, I managed to break my collarbone, dislocate my shoulder, and run into the back of a parked car while riding my tricycle (with one arm in a sling) down the driveway, thus cutting my lip and earning a black eye. Mom used to say if that had happened today, someone would have called Child Protective Services. The emergency room staff at the base hospital knew us well.

I was exuberant and fearless and wanted nothing more than the freedom, at age five, that would come from my first Big Girl Bike. I knew the one I wanted, too–one just like my friend Rita had. Bright red, with a flower-adorned basket and a horn. I asked my parents if I could please, please, please have a Big Girl Bike–I said I was ready and I would be careful and anything else my five-year-old brain could conceive. They said they'd think about it.

A few days later, we had a family meeting. These always terrified me because they usually meant someone was in trouble. During this particular confab, though, Dad presented me with the "deal." He opened an envelope in which there were seven pieces of carefully cut paper, designed to look like coupons and adorned with his beautiful calligraphy. "These are Good Girl Slips," he said. "All you have to do is earn all seven of them and you will get your Big Girl Bike." He explained that to earn a Good Girl Slip, I had to get through an entire day without irritating or upsetting my mother, back-talking, or otherwise disrupting the peace. And I would have to complete my chores and eat what they served without complaint and, essentially, be perfect.

It seemed like the carrot, but in reality, it was the stick.

"If you want something, you must earn it." That was the lesson.

The first day, I nailed it. I didn't harass my cat or back talk my mother (though really, what she considered back talk was only me trying to understand the "whys" of what she told me to do). I made my bed. I brushed my teeth without being told. I offered to help in the kitchen. That evening, after my parents enjoyed their cocktail hour to recount their days, Dad congratulated me on MY day and gave me my first Good Girl Slip. Not only did I get the coupon, but I got his praise. I could almost see my Big Girl Bike in the carport.

The next day, something went wrong. Honestly what, I can't remember, but I imagine I gave the appearance of pouting, or perhaps I argued about what I was having for lunch. That evening, after cocktail hour, my father scolded me for whatever I did and told me to return the first Good Girl Slip. How I cried; it wasn't fair! I had already earned it! His rules, not mine. I handed over the first Good Girl slip–I had to start over.

This saga played on for nearly a year, with my earning the slips only to forfeit them. Adults could have bad days, but children apparently couldn't. Finally, either worn down or realizing the Good Girl Slips had humiliated me (or possibly both), I got my Big Girl Bike for my sixth birthday.

It had lost its magical luster. I would spend the rest of my life collecting metaphorical Good Girl Slips, hoping to earn love and praise, but the value never matched the rising cost of his attention.

Good girl, trained.

Chapter Three: A Lifestyle Disrupted

My life underwent a dramatic change in 1974, at the start of my fourth-grade year. Mom decided she was going to explore a new path. She had suffered from depression and anxiety, manifest through her growing fear of leaving the house and driving, so her therapist advised her to think about what she wanted for her future.

Interestingly, married women in 1974 still couldn't open bank accounts in their own name, but after hearing Dad tell her she was "no longer interesting," she concluded she might need to earn a living if he left her. While I was at school and Dad was at work, she put a plan in place to protect her (and my) future.

One evening, after Dad had come home from work and they had concluded their regular cocktail hour, Mom called me in from outside. I had been engaged in a lively game of yard football with the neighborhood boys, so I was reluctant to come in the house, but the look on her face was serious. She declared it was time for a Family Meeting. I joined them in the den, grabbing Jasmine for comfort before taking a seat on the floor. (My trousers were muddy from a few choice tackles.) I waited while fidgeting. They seemed anxious.

Finally, Mom took a breath and said, "Now that you've gotten older, I've decided I'd like to go back to school and complete my degree." She had dropped out of college after her freshman year at the University of Nevada at Reno before marrying her first husband. Not only did she plan to start at San Antonio Community College, but she said she planned to continue at the University of Texas at San Antonio. From there, she wanted to go to law school.

I burst into tears at this bombshell. Why didn't she want to keep taking care of me? "Who's going to make my clothes?" I wailed. I always had the most beautiful outfits, thanks to Mom's seamstress skills, and store-bought clothes just wouldn't cut it. Who would be there to greet me when I got home? The only mothers I knew who worked, and there were few, held jobs as secretaries or teachers. Why this, why now, and what else was going to change?

She assured me I would still have clothes and she would still cook our meals, but she acknowledged she may have to spend a lot of time studying. Dad sat stoically, sipping his Chivas. Mom had told Dad's mother about her plan, and in typical grandma fashion, she pledged any final support that might be needed to support Mom's dream. Mom had put all the pieces in place before she broke the news to Dad and then to me.

Mom was thirty-eight years old when she started at SAC, making her quite the anomaly given both her age and gender, but she took her studies seriously and began changing before my eyes. She became surer of her voice and more willing to disagree with Dad. Her style of dress evolved to become more modern as she developed friendships with her classmates. Her taste in music shifted towards groups like Santana. She cut her luxurious hair short, and she embraced her newly discovered feminism.

Albeit less frequently, they still socialized with Dad's military colleagues and their wives. Gone were the booze-laden bridge parties, but get-togethers still occurred on the base or at different families' homes. Mom had never been a "ladies of the club" personality, but now, infused with her resuscitated love of learning and the self-confidence college was giving her, she worked to persuade the other wives that they, too, could go back to school. They didn't have to be defined by their roles as wife and mother and volunteer, she preached. The world was changing, and it was time for women to get their chance.

One of Dad's superior officers clearly was displeased by Mom's lobbying efforts. She was putting dangerous thoughts in the minds of women who were only supposed to assist their husbands. Instead of defending Mom, Dad said he would talk to her.

And so he did. Loudly. She had just transferred to the University of Texas at San Antonio and was excelling in all her classes, reinforcing in her mind that if she could get into law school, she would succeed. Mom always had been a warrior for justice, and this discussion was no exception. She told my father women should have more options, women weren't chattel, and she knew he didn't understand why she was doing what she was doing, but she didn't care. She got to have a life, too, dammit, and too bad if he didn't like it. Too bad if other husbands felt threatened.

The last thing I heard before the front door slammed and my father sped away was, "You're a castrating bitch, you know that? A castrating bitch!"

He returned a few hours later. We ate dinner and pretended everything was fine.

I could feel the fault line of our family life shifting precariously. Luckily, I had the Robbins, our elderly neighbors, to visit after school and avoid being home alone. I had my neighborhood friends with whom to play various sports, and my best friend, Sophia, a few blocks away. I was finding security where I could and mostly, that didn't feel like my house.

One Saturday morning, while Dad played in a softball game on base and Mom talked on the phone, Sophia and I went roller skating. She had fancy lace-up skates; mine, of course, were the snap on variety, but I had become quite proficient. Until I hit a crag on the sidewalk and went flying, breaking my fall with my arms. I immediately knew something was wrong with my right forearm—it looked funny and hurt like nothing I could remember.

Sophia skated home, and I burst into our house, calling for Mom. She was still talking to Diana, Sophia's mom, on the phone and shot me a look, warning me about interrupting. "I fell and hurt my arm!" I told her, fighting back tears. She advised me to go soak my arm in Epsom salts and we'd see how it felt after. She returned to her conversation, laughing about how reckless Sophia and I could be.

I soaked my arm. It still hurt. Mom said we'd wait until Dad came home and figure it out from there.

Dad got home about twelve-thirty. I showed him my arm, and he said it didn't look too bad, probably just a sprain. Mom served lunch, and I ate my sandwich using only my left hand as the pain was intensifying in my right arm. Dad took his time eating while checking the television for any games that might be airing. The hours passed.

I went to my room to pick up a book, mistakenly doing so with my right hand. I dropped it as the pain seared up my arm. I yelled. Both parents came into my room to find me sitting on my bed, sobbing and in obvious distress. I told them what happened.

"Let me go take a shower first," Dad said. Around two o'clock, he and I made our way to the emergency room at Fort Sam Houston Army Base; Mom was studying. With military hospitals, one never knew how long the wait would be, depending on staffing, other cases, day of the week, and assorted other variables. This Saturday afternoon was extremely busy. I finally got an x-ray around five o'clock, which conclusively showed a nasty fracture. Dad seemed surprised, so sure it was just a sprain. The physician put the film on the light board, tracing the fracture with his pen for emphasis. I wasn't sure what was going to happen next.

It wasn't pleasant. The doctor snapped my bone back into place with a loud "pop" while my father held me down and I tried not to cry. They outfitted me with a massive cast and sent us home with child-appropriate painkillers.

We got home around seven. Mom greeted us at the door, got me situated in bed with a snack, and took Dad his cocktail because he had had a rough day. Differently said, I was supposed to be the center of attention at that moment, yet it was all about him. He never apologized for making me sit in pain for hours before it was convenient to take me to the hospital. I've never forgotten feeling like such an inconvenience.

After I finished my dinner in bed, doing my best to navigate the fork with my left hand, Mom took the tray. But before turning out the light, she leaned down and whispered, "I'm proud of my brave girl."

I would need to be braver still in the years to come.

Good girl, hurting.

Chapter Four: Work Ethic

"Saturday's child works hard for her living," as the adage goes. I was a Saturday child, and my father was insistent that anything worth having was worth working for, so I took my chores seriously in order to earn my allowance.

I also was born with a generous heart. Mom used to say I had a knack for finding the world's "strays" and doing what I could to help them find their way. I don't think that's such a bad thing, though I remember it feeling like a criticism as a child.

My elementary school had an interesting demography. Almost fifty percent of the students were from my mostly Caucasian working-class neighborhood, and the remaining half was from a primarily Hispanic neighborhood that required early morning busing.

Due to alphabetical seating, I ended up sitting next to Annette Ramos in third grade homeroom. She was a wisp of a girl, quiet and not particularly focused on school, but not disruptive either. Just…vacant. Winters were typically mild in San Antonio, but not that year. Fortunately, I had a very warm coat to protect me from the chill on my daily walk to school and during recess.

One day on the playground, I observed that most of us were wearing winter coats, but Annette was only wearing a threadbare sweater to keep her warm. It didn't accomplish the job. Without giving it a thought, I took off my red wool coat and gave it to her. She put it on proudly and gratefully. I told her she could have it since I had another coat at home (though it probably was too small). It felt good to help someone.

Before I had even gotten home that afternoon, walking the half mile or so without a coat, the principal already had called Mom to report what I had done. When I came into the house, Mom asked if it was true–did I really give away my winter coat? I explained that Annette was cold, that I had another coat and it seemed like the right thing to do. Mom said she informed the principal that it was my coat, and I could do with it what I wanted. The principal told Mom this sort of thing just wasn't done. It set a dangerous precedent, she said, and probably made Annette feel less-than; after all, there were social services that could help with such things. She had already told Annette's mother they must return my coat tomorrow. I was heartbroken that the principal turned my act of friendship into something divisive.

After my parents' cocktail hour, Dad had to verify the story–that I really gave a coat they had bought for me to a girl they didn't even know and whose parents had a responsibility of their own to keep her clothed. He was angry, and I was confused. He got angrier as I protested I had done the right thing. A good thing!

"Life is about decisions," he lectured. "Her parents clearly have made different decisions than we have about financial responsibility, but that's not yours to fix. You just can't save some people. That's why it's important to be smart with your money, so you don't need to have someone save you."

His degree was in economics, but still. I was eight years old.

His lecture reached its mark, though, and I learned one of my father's primary values: financial self-sufficiency. He admired it, so I would demonstrate it.

The following year, my friend Mary Ann and I decided we wanted to earn money so we could buy our own Christmas presents to give to family members. Ours was a well-established neighborhood with gazillions of trees, so we concluded the best thing we could do was rake leaves. Being in fourth grade, we didn't know how to write a business plan, but we understood we needed to charge a reasonable amount for our work.

Our first Saturday, we loaded up our bikes with trash bags in our baskets and rakes across our handlebars, then pedaled to our first house, its front yard covered with leaves from the now-barren tree. An older gentleman opened the door, and there we stood, in our "play clothes," hats, and mittens, offering to rake his yard and bag the leaves for one dollar.

We thought that sounded like a lot of money, not knowing how many hours it would take us to complete the task. He agreed, so we got going. Raking the leaves into manageable piles, then working together to get the leaves into the bags, we quickly realized this was hard work, but we could see the progress. After about three hours, we finished and rang his doorbell. He thanked us for our work and handed us three dollars. Three whole dollars! We were rich.

That same day, we finished another yard and not only received five dollars–five whole dollars–but the wife served us hot chocolate with marshmallows. This working thing wasn't so bad after all.

The next day, we got cracking early, buoyed by our early success. We tackled three yards in one day, clearing about twelve dollars and a few more cups of hot chocolate, then pedaled home to count our earnings. Two days, five yards, and we each had ten dollars to show for our weekend's work.

We were well on our way to having a good budget for our Christmas shopping spree at the local TG&Y dime store. My parents congratulated us on our industriousness, even as the neighborhood boys pedaled by and made fun of us. (We certainly could've broadened our territory if they had been interested in joining us). Mary Ann and I weren't so much entrepreneurial, though, as our independence simply intoxicated us.

After our second weekend working in much colder and wetter conditions, our spirits were a little less ebullient even though we each had twenty-plus dollars in our Christmas fund. We vowed to give it one more weekend and see if we had enough. I had two presents to buy, so my goal was thirty dollars. Mary Ann had a much larger family, but only planned to buy two presents for her parents. Our goal was within reach.

The last weekend was brutal, just shy of freezing but drizzling steadily. As we finished our last yard, both filthy and shivering to the bone, the kind family invited us indoors for much-appreciated hot chocolate and cookies. From there, we pedaled home.

Mom drew me a hot bath with Epsom salts and told me to soak until dinner. I may have nodded off once or twice, but finally got out, toweled off, and put on my warmest pajamas. After dinner, Dad said he wanted to have a talk, so I followed him to the living room.

"Have you done the math?"

I wasn't sure what he meant, so I said, "Well, Mary Ann and I made $64 over the last three weeks, so we each got $32." I waited for his congratulations.

"But have you done the math to determine what you really made?" I didn't understand.

"How many trash bags did you use, on average, at each house?"

I shrugged. "Maybe ten?"

"How many trash bags are in a box?" I shrugged. "Maybe twenty?"

"How many boxes of bags did you use in the last three weeks?" I shrugged. "Maybe three?"

"Try four," he said. "Do you know how much a box of trash bags costs?" I shook my head.

"Three dollars," he said. "Do the math. What's three times four?"

"Twelve," I answered confidently.

"Did you figure the cost of the bags into what you charged to rake leaves?" I shook my head.

"Well, why not?" I didn't have an answer, as this was a new concept.

"So, you owe me twelve dollars. You can ask Mary Ann to pay half, or you can just give me the twelve dollars now."

I wasn't about to ask Mary Ann to give back the money we had earned, so I stoically walked to my bedroom, took twelve dollars from my Holly Hobby wallet, and handed it to my father.

"Maybe next time, you'll ask for help before you start a new project," he said, then went to the kitchen for ice cream. I cried bitter tears, angry but unsure why. It just felt unfair.

The next weekend, Mary Ann and I pedaled our way to TG&Y, where I bought my mother a set of wooden spoons and my father a poster of a kitten clinging to a ledge with the words "Hang in There" across the top.

My mom liked her spoons. The poster never saw the light of day. And I had spent nearly all my twenty dollars.

Lesson: "You were wrong from the beginning, but I would not tell you unless you asked."

Good girl, silenced.

Chapter Five: Uprooted

While I was navigating middle school and my newfound social status as a cheerleader, Mom completed her bachelor's degree with honors at UTSA, then spent the next few months studying for the LSAT. Saint Mary's Law School accepted her, so she began her first year as a true oddity, suffering what only can be called "professorial harassment" as a nearly forty-year-old female attempting to become a lawyer. Meanwhile, I learned the nuances of the mean-girl world while being engrossed in a flurry of pep rallies, ball games, and plays (since I was also in drama). At least I was finally getting attention — sometimes good, sometimes bad. Dad continued going to work at the base each day, returning home to a family intent on pursuing their own individual dreams.

Things seemed to look up for all of us. At least for my mom and me. She and I had plenty we wanted to talk about each night. She shared stories about how she stood her ground while a professor grilled her, or the new friends she had made in torts class, or how she could never go into family law. I nattered on about my drama class, the new cheers I was learning, and how frustrated I was that I couldn't do the splits like Kimmie. Why hadn't I been more proficient in gymnastics so I could do the more complicated tumbling moves?

My father found fault at every turn. He would debate my mother about matters of law. He questioned my commitment to self-improvement and discipline whenever I expressed my age-appropriate insecurities. I could feel the tension building.

They only came to one or two of our games, seemingly disinterested in seeing me cheer and clearly having better things to do than watch seventh-grade boys playing ball. One Friday evening, after cheering at a basketball game then catching a ride home from one of the other moms, I walked into the middle of a raging battle.

"I don't like how you've changed," Dad bellowed at Mom. "You've put on weight. You ignore Suz. You've let the house go. You only seem to care about your god-damned law degree. This isn't what I signed on for." He took a gulp of Scotch.

"It's always about you, isn't it?" Mom hissed. "What you want. Not what anyone else wants. News flash: the world doesn't always revolve around you."

I sought cover in my bedroom, closing the door and turning on my stereo to let Stevie Wonder drown out the chaos. Soon, I heard the front door slam and knew that meant my father was taking one of his drives.

At that time, he had a beautiful white Datsun 260Z with cordovan vinyl interior–perfect for speeding away from his family to seek something, somewhere. And so, he did.

I cautiously emerged from my bedroom to find Mom in the kitchen, warming up my dinner. I wasn't particularly hungry. She was trying to hide the fact she'd been crying. She poured herself a glass of wine and sat down at the table.

"Your father packed a bag," she said tersely. "I don't know if he's gone for good, but I think it's time for you to think about who you'd like to live with should we get divorced."

Divorced. I didn't know anyone whose parents had gotten divorced. I didn't know what to say, so I poked at my tuna casserole while fighting back tears. Jasmine sat protectively under my chair.

"You need to eat," she barked. Why was she angry at me?

She went to their bedroom with her glass of wine, and I could tell from the conversation, she was on the phone with her best friend, Diana. I finished what I could of my dinner, putting the rest in the trash before retreating to my room for the night. After reading for an hour, I turned off my light and tried to sleep. My father hadn't come home.

I spent the next day in a fog, unsure of what was happening but trying to complete my chores and homework while waiting. Mom spent the day studying, unaware that she might have offered some comfort to me. My neighborhood pals and I had grown apart–a combination of my new social status as a cheerleader, and their own extracurricular activities–so I didn't know who I could talk to about my family falling apart. Besides, Mom always told me not to share the family secrets–not to "air our dirty laundry." Except this wasn't about me, even though it would surely affect me profoundly.

That afternoon, I took a long bike ride, pedaling through our extensive neighborhood until my legs were putty. When I got home, I saw Dad's Z in the driveway. I didn't know if I was relieved, scared, or a combination of both. It weighed me down with dread.

I came in quietly, for no other reason than wanting to be as unobtrusive as possible. I still didn't know the answer to the question my mother had posed the night before and didn't want to be put on the spot. They weren't in the living room or the den. I passed their bedroom on the way to my room and heard noises. I peeked my head in to find them in bed, doing something that seemed private and unintended for my viewing.

My stomach roiled, and I made it to the bathroom just in time to empty my lunch into the toilet. I sputtered and spewed and cried, confused and disgusted and something beyond. I went to my room to lie down.

I guess they heard me because my mother stormed into my room wearing nothing but her robe, even though it was nearly three o'clock in the afternoon, and demanded, "What's wrong with you?" I told her I was sick to my stomach. "I thought you were riding your bike," she said sharply.

"I was. I got tired. I didn't sleep very well last night," I replied.

"Well, take a nap then." And with that, she shut my door.

That night, Mom made my father's favorite meal–beef stroganoff–and they chattered away as if the previous night hadn't happened. She asked me why I was being sullen. He asked me why I wasn't eating. I didn't know how to express the feeling of having fallen down a rabbit hole with nothing making sense, especially in my 12-year-old brain. Yet, I had to be a good girl. So, I told them I was fine, finished my dinner, and went to my bedroom to read. When I came out to get a glass of water, they were canoodling on the couch. The happy couple. I felt like an outsider in my own family.

We made it through another Christmas, just barely, since Dad decided to "call it all off" one week before. He had asked for our wish lists then concluded we were being greedy and this, THIS is why so he hated the holiday. On December 23, he went by himself to get a tree, which we decorated that night. Two days earlier, my paternal grandmother had flown in from Olympia, Washington and soon had begun to express her concerns about my father being unkind and un-Christian to his family. He ignored her. The day after Christmas, she became seriously ill with a stomach virus, confining her to bed in my room while my father huffed around, angry that her sickness lengthened her stay. I adored my grandmother and was happy to have her there, sick or not, because she was interested in what I had to say and encouraged my pursuits. When she left, the house became darker and lonelier.

Soon, though, my focus turned to cheerleader tryouts. While I believed myself a shoo-in, other girls had been practicing all year to take a coveted spot from an incumbent. And those girls could tumble. I wanted to share my anxiety with my parents, but they were back in troubled territory and I didn't want to add to the family tension. So, I practiced my cheers and jumps in front of the Robbinses next door. Like surrogate grandparents, they beamed and applauded and said yes, of course, there's no doubt I would be on the squad once again.

On the afternoon of the May tryouts, they placed us in groups of three. None of the groups had more than one current cheerleader, which honestly helped the current squad look better in comparison–but it was still nerve-wracking. When it was my group's turn to audition, I turned on the charm, executed every move with precision, smiled until I thought my face would go into spasms, and yelled with unbridled enthusiasm. I was obsessed with making the squad, as if my very self-worth depended on it. And it did. My fiercest competition was my now-distant friend, Mary Ann, with whom I had raked leaves just a few uncomplicated years earlier.

Next day, they posted the list for the seventh- and eighth-grade cheerleaders. Mine was the last name on the list, done in alphabetical order. Below my name was Mary Ann's, designated as "substitute." I was relieved and secretly pleased I had outshone her blond-haired, blue-eyed beauty.

I wanted to spend my summer practicing, tanning, and preparing for my last year of middle school before high school. I also had signed up for journalism and looked forward to writing for the school newspaper, since I planned to be a journalist one day. The last day of school was full of hugs and promises and phone number exchanges, and then it was summer—glorious summer.

Until the day in early June when my father came home and called a family meeting. Nothing good ever came from family meetings except the expectation of conformity to, and alignment with, whatever edict the adult presented. My father was clearly agitated. Mom looked uncharacteristically unsettled.

"Well, it appears I'm getting passed over for promotion," Dad began, shaking his head and grimacing before taking a sip of his martini. Mom took a sip of hers. "After giving those miserable bastards everything I had to offer, with no genuine appreciation at all, it seems I won't be getting the promotion to full colonel."

Mom reached for his hand, and he pulled it away. I didn't know where this conversation was heading, but I sensed another seismic shift. "I found this out a few days ago, and I've been weighing my options," he continued. "And I've decided that I'm going to retire, effective next month. I've given my time, and I've had enough. They won't know what they had until I'm out," he said, finishing his drink.

I wasn't sure what any of this meant except that if my father didn't have a job and my mother was still in school, what would we do? We already lived on a tighter budget than I realized until much later in life. I knew, though, that asking about our security would be considered a provocative question, so I stayed unusually silent.

"Frank, may I ask what you're thinking you'll do for work?" Mom asked carefully. Apparently, he had discussed none of this with her.

He grinned and said he had it all figured out. Three of his former colleagues started a data security company in the Dallas area. He talked to them, and they agreed to bring him on staff.

"Looks like we're heading to Big D!" he said, lifting his glass in a toast. I froze.

Just like that. I looked at Mom, who gave me a look that clearly meant "Don't." "I don't want to move," I said, beginning to cry. "I made the cheerleading squad again, and I have journalism, and I have friends and the Robbinses next door. And I want to go to high school in ninth grade. I don't want to move! It's not fair!" The words kept tumbling through my tears. No matter what had happened in our household, I had an external support system that kept me distractedly optimistic and, dare I say, happy? My father poured another martini.

"Well, it's not your choice to make," he huffed. "It's mine. And I have made it. The end."

I was too stunned to say anything else, but in that moment, I recognized I was merely a prop in his life–someone to be positioned as it best suited him.

Instead of practicing my cheers, swimming at the community pool, and going to the mall with my friends–living the typical life of a middle-class 'tween, I spent the rest of the month helping Mom sort, pack, and clean. I tearfully called our cheerleading advisor to announce we were moving and that Mary Ann would finally get her coveted spot on the squad. I entertained the nostalgia of the neighborhood in which I had grown up by playing football and basketball and stickball with the guys. I visited the Robbins daily, and as July drew closer, I began dreading the inevitable goodbyes.

Tensions continued to grow like wild mint between my parents, and I could feel something akin to an amputation as I realized we really were moving, and my world would forever change without my consent. I also was just shy of thirteen years old, so some hormonal petulance was bound to emerge anyway, but still. I was miserable. My parents decided it would be a good distraction–I'm not sure for whom–to send me to my great aunt's and great uncle's house in New Jersey for two weeks while they sorted out some details. I had never met them, only spoken to them on the phone, but I was guardedly excited to be taking my first plane trip alone and getting the chance to see New York City, just on the other side of the Washington Bridge from their home.

The trip was an adventure, though Aunt Mary and Uncle Jim were older and never had children of their own, so they weren't always sure how to handle the mood swings and insecurities of a frightened tween about to be transplanted. Admittedly, I suffered a few pangs of homesickness along with bouts of self-loathing–my teeth weren't perfectly straight, I still was flat-chested, and how would I ever fit in at a new school in a place I'd never been? Aunt Mary assured me I would be fine and gave the same advice she apparently had shared with my mother when she was young: just keep doing your best, be kind, have faith, and everything will take care of itself.

When I returned to San Antonio, I saw the For Sale sign in our front yard.

It was really happening.

A week later, Dad's retirement completed with little fanfare, he packed his car and headed to the Dallas/Fort Worth area to get situated in an apartment, begin his new job, and start looking for our next house. He left Mom and me with the work of packing. I took on mowing the yard. She completed all the paperwork necessary to transfer to SMU Law School. I began saying my goodbyes.

He returned just once to close on the sale of our house and inspect our progress in preparing for the move. I gathered addresses and promised my friends I would write, and often. They did too.

We all probably knew that wouldn't really happen.

And then, with our household loaded into the moving van and Mom's red Datsun sedan laden with our clothes and cats, we departed for my father's apartment in Hurst. We would live there until the house my father had chosen (without my mom's input) in Arlington was ready for us to take residence. I kept quiet the entire trip, just petting both cats and trying not to cry. Why hadn't I asked if I could live with the Robbinses? They loved me—surely, they would have agreed.

We spent two weeks in the dreadful apartment before it was time to move into the new house. The neighborhood seemed nice enough, but I immediately felt its lack of soul, of life. Arlington was a bedroom community for both Dallas and Fort Worth, so it lacked any kind of culture, other than Six Flags (if you could call that culture). The neighborhood had no neighborliness to it, with just two girls my age down the street with whom I shared nothing in common but our gender.

It had been years since I had been the new kid in school, and it was definitely easier as a first grader than as an eighth grader. I was trying to adjust to a new world of affluent girls in designer clothes and Farrah Fawcett hair and heavy make-up and seeming sophistication. I didn't fit in, and I knew it from the start.

Mom was making her own adjustments to the pretension of SMU Law School and Dallas in general. Dad was preoccupied with his new corporate job, his new civilian wardrobe, and, as I would later learn, his new "friend" at the office. I got home from school around four; neither of them arrived until after six. Cocktail hour took priority until Mom started making dinner, usually around seven. Every day, I had three hours alone to process my misery.

I didn't really have any friends, though some of the popular girls invited me to go to the movies or to the mall, until they realized I wasn't one of them.

I had no one to talk to. My parents were absorbed with their own transitions and seemed to assume I was perfectly fine. I wasn't anywhere close.

Good girl, invisible.

Chapter Six: The Implosion

Within the first few months of my eighth-grade year, we settled into something resembling a routine, each of us adapting to our new lives, if not separately. Preoccupied as each of us was with our daily new challenges to navigate, we sought comfort where we could. For me, it was my bedroom, my cats, and my stereo. For my mother, it seemed to be the normalcy of cooking dinner every night before hitting the law books. For my father, it was…elsewhere.

Our new home wasn't a happy place, and though I had a nice bedroom with an adjoining bathroom, it still felt claustrophobic. My room was just a few feet from the living room, so even with my door closed and my stereo on, I was privy to arguments I didn't want to hear. I was privy to constant criticisms and accusations I didn't want to stomach. I tried to be seen and not heard, though I had so much I needed to say.

I hadn't known about Mom's suspicions because, at the time, she tried to protect me from life's uglies (even as I was quietly experiencing many uglies of my own, thanks to the mean girls at school). Until that day in late fall, not long before Thanksgiving break.

My father usually got home before Mom because she spent her afternoons studying in the SMU law library so she could focus, and her commute from Dallas took longer than his commute from Hurst. Because I typically arrived home first, one of my responsibilities was to bring in the mail, none of which was ever for me other than a periodic letter from my grandma in Washington. On that particular day, Mom opted to come home early, arriving shortly before I did. I was happy to see her first, because that meant a few tension-free moments before my father blew in and dominated the environment with his preferences and opinions.

Some moments become seared on your soul, so profoundly explosive that they forever changed your world. I wanted a snack since we always ate dinner late, so I headed toward the kitchen. Mom was standing in the dining room, still in her law school clothes, reading a letter. She swore, then she dropped to the carpet on her knees, sobbing and shaking. I began shaking too. I had never seen her like this.

I was only thirteen, but it felt like something evil had entered our home. I asked her what was wrong, and she just shook her head. I asked what I could do, and she just shook her head. I asked if someone had died, and she didn't respond. Finally, she said she was going to lie down. She poured herself a healthy glass of Dad's Chivas before heading to their room and shutting the door. I had never seen her drink Scotch.

I felt scared and helpless, but I didn't have anyone to turn to for help. So I went to my room, grabbed my earphones, and listened to the stereo while petting Jasmine. Ace, our other cat, was probably in with Mom. Sometime later, I heard my father pulling into the driveway in his sleek 260Z. I was afraid to greet him when he came in from the garage. I was equally afraid not to.

He came in, put his briefcase by his chair, said, "Hello," and asked why Mom was home. I didn't know. He started walking to their bedroom, and I stopped him, telling him something was really wrong and Mom was very upset in the bedroom with the door closed. I told him she had read something and began crying.

He brushed past me, marched down the hall with me in close pursuit, opened the door, and then ordered me to my room. And so I went, though I left my door open.

It was quiet at first, then the tornado touched down. Yelling. Profanity. More yelling. Silence. A door slamming. My father with an overnight bag. The garage door slamming. His 260Z speeding away. More silence.

I didn't know what to do. So, I sat quietly, alone, imagining him not coming home and what that would mean. Imagining him returning and what would that mean? A little while later, Mom emerged, went to the bar, and poured herself another Scotch. I cautiously asked about dinner. She told me to make a sandwich. And with that, she returned to their room for the night. I didn't make a sandwich, but I finished my homework.

The next morning at breakfast, which they wisely forced me to eat, my father wasn't at the table. I didn't want to ask. Mom sat down, looking like she hadn't slept, bleary-eyed from too much Scotch. She said she owed me an explanation. I didn't think I wanted to hear it. I absolutely needed to hear it.

"Your father is having an affair," she said flatly. With a woman he had known since high school, still living in Olympia, whom he saw every time he went to check on his mother. The letter apparently was quite explicit about their most recent activities in bed, how she couldn't wait to see him again, and other details Mom opted not to share. "She signed it 'Princess,'" Mom said. "He used to call me 'Princess.'"

I asked her what this meant. Were they going to divorce? Was he going to marry the other woman? My mom rose abruptly, poured another cup of coffee, and then yelled at me. "Dammit, Suzanne! Quit asking questions I can't answer!" She went to get ready for school.

My dreaded oatmeal was now cold, so I threw it in the trash and got myself ready to catch the bus. I really wanted to stay home, yet home wasn't safe. I made it through my school day, more sullen than usual, and came home to a blissfully yet regrettably empty house with nothing to do but wait.

Early evening, Mom came in and immediately poured a Scotch, then asked me blandly how my day had gone. I just shrugged. I wanted to ask how she thought it had gone, given the family implosion the night before, but I didn't want to antagonize her. "Fine. I got an A on my English paper." She nodded and went into the living room. I wasn't sure if I should follow her or leave her alone. So, I went to my room and shut my door.

A little while later, she came into my room without knocking–a rule they imposed on me but didn't follow themselves–with brown eyes ablaze. She told me I was making things worse. My attitude was adding fuel to the fire and pouting around the house wasn't doing anyone any good. I needed to pull myself together. Not everything in this world was about me.

Years later, at the start of my long-term counseling journey, I would learn about a concept called "projection." I didn't know it then, but I knew irony when I heard it. So, I just smiled. And then, out of nowhere, she slapped my face. Hard. I refused to cry.

Two hours later, my father drove in and joined Mom in the living room. Dinner was underway–probably spaghetti–and she was having another Scotch. I dared not join them, but I sat on the other side of my door to listen to what would come next.

It wasn't an apology. It wasn't a request for forgiveness. It wasn't her declaring he had broken her heart. It wasn't his promise this wouldn't happen again. Simply, it was my father stating he deserved to be happy too, especially given all the time she was spending away from the family to pursue her law school degree. His tone was clearly demeaning, as if her dream were just a passing fancy. He said he had needs that no one person could meet.

At that, I went to my bathroom and threw up.

I would later learn that this episode wasn't his first and definitely would not be the last. This wasn't how families were supposed to work, though. I couldn't wrap my young mind around the idea he would so easily betray my mother; I wanted her to stand up and fight for herself. She didn't. She served dinner; we ate in silence; they went to the den to watch television, and I retreated to my room.

My father came in later, knocking first. I looked up from my homework, expecting something–anything–that would help me understand. He let me know that my petulant attitude was getting old and that I would end up with no friends if I didn't change. And then he went back to the den. I heard them make small talk as if nothing had happened. As if my world hadn't been altered forever.

There were so many things I wanted to say but couldn't find words to express. Instead, I got ready for bed, with hopes for better days ahead.

Good Girl, alone.

Chapter Seven: Shifting Gears

At the end of my ninth-grade year, our family was in yet another period of transition. I was preparing for high school, my mother graduated from law school, and my father continued working his first corporate job while complaining that no one knew what they were doing there. Mom had been working as a law clerk for a small firm in Arlington while finishing her last year at SMU, and that summer, as I was at drill team practice, she began her law review classes in preparation to take the bar exam. She wasn't drinking as much, at least not at that time.

SMU held its law review classes four nights per week, meaning she wouldn't get home until well past nine. Meaning, she wouldn't be there to make dinner. My father didn't know how to cook anything besides scrambled eggs or what he could grill outside. So, the responsibility for dinner fell on my shoulders three of the four nights each week for six weeks. Thankfully, I had grown up watching Mom in the kitchen, so I knew quite a few things that were complemented by my year of home economics in eighth grade.

I'd put together shopping lists and do my best to make meals my father would enjoy. I experimented with new recipes, most of which he didn't like, then reverted to the standard fare he did like: spaghetti ("not as good as your mom's"), chicken cacciatore ("the chicken was a little overcooked"), chicken coated with melted butter then rolled in crushed Ritz crackers and baked ("not bad"), and beanie-weenie casserole ("I think it's missing something"), to name a few. On the fourth night, he either grilled hamburgers or ordered pizza. I don't recall him ever taking me out to dinner, just the two of us. And that was probably a good thing, since we had little to talk about other than his criticism of something related to my mother or me.

Some nights, my father got home later than usual, citing either a last-minute project or a cocktail with one of his colleagues as the reason for his delay. It wasn't until my twenty-year high school reunion that I put two and two together to realize he had been having an affair. It was with one of the office secretaries, who happened to be the divorced mother of one of my high school classmates. But back then, I didn't think it was possible he would cheat on my mother yet again, particularly after his exposure just a year or so earlier. In hindsight, my ignorance was my only bliss.

Except for drill team. Not quite like cheerleading, but good enough.

Finally, I was making some new friends and looked forward to starting high school where I'd meet new people from the other junior high that fed into it. While I had served as co-editor of my junior high school newspaper, I still didn't feel part of a group like I had in San Antonio. Making the drill team and practicing with girls in higher grades gave me the impression that my transition would be an easy one because I now had a "crowd." Relatively. I had a place I looked forward to going, even if it was the high school parking lot every morning in the heat of summer. I had girls who invited me to their homes to swim after practice. We'd binge on Taco Bell and McDonald's and Pizza Hut because we had been practicing for three straight hours, so surely, we had pre-burned the calories.

For six weeks, this was my routine: drill team practice, sometimes socializing, and more often, babysitting for the neighbor's children, coming home to tidy the house, and then preparing dinner and doing the dishes. Mom praised me for keeping Dad fed. I never told her about his late arrivals.

She and I were on the cusp of our life transitions. I didn't know my father was as well.

After she completed her law review class, she readied herself for the bar exam while continuing her work as a law clerk. It was the first time since she had married my father that she had made a salary, if not a rather small one. She walked a bit taller and was more inclined to argue with my father, particularly when it came to matters of law. He continued to believe he was an expert on all things. She would tell him otherwise. I would head for my room.

The night before the two-day bar exam, Mom went to a hotel in Dallas so she could focus exclusively on getting rested and ready. Both nights, I made dinner. She returned, exhausted and anxious. The exam was harder than she expected, and she worried she might have to re-take it—not an uncommon phenomenon, as she explained. She had applied for and gotten her first official position as an attorney with the U.S. government, yet her start date was contingent upon passing the bar. She wouldn't have her results for one to three months, so she continued clerking full-time while resuming her responsibilities in the kitchen. I continued going to drill team practice, babysitting, and getting ready for high school. We were about to shift gears, both of us, moving faster toward our desired destinations: hers, a law career that would allow her to put her keen intellect to good use; mine, to get the hell out of the house and away to college.

That August, just a few weeks before I would begin high school and a month before Mom received her bar exam results, my father returned home one afternoon and poured himself a Scotch. Something was wrong. I knew not to approach him, so I stayed in my room. Mom got home that evening, and by then, Dad was a little sloppy. He announced loudly, but with a strange snicker, that the sons of bitches had fired him. He didn't say why, only that they'd be sorry. My mom tried to explain carefully that Texas was a right-to-work state. He told her to shut up, that she didn't know what she was talking about. After all, she still wasn't a "real lawyer."

At least he was getting a pension from his Air Force service, and Mom was working as a law clerk, so we weren't going to starve. But I began to wonder if they knew what they were doing.

The week I started school, Mom received the good news she had passed the bar, so she began her official job as a federal litigator two weeks later. Shortly thereafter, Dad landed a position with another consulting firm, also associated with one of his former Air Force pals. I was happy being in a larger school with interesting classes, including my first year of journalism, and having a ball performing at pep rallies and football games.

I had stories to tell after school each day. My parents had resumed their pre-dinner cocktail hour discussions about their new adventures, each talking over the other and sometimes bickering but often just being enthusiastic about their new worlds.

They didn't ask about mine.

We usually ate dinner around eight o'clock, after which I'd go to my room to finish homework and get ready for bed, as I had to be at practice each morning by seven. I tried to be as inconspicuous as possible at home while trying to be as noticeable as possible at school.

It felt like having a split personality, but it was how I coped.

By being good. Until I wasn't.

Good Girl, struggling.

Chapter Eight: The Unraveling

In the early spring of my sophomore year, our drill team was invited to a national competition in Los Angeles. We were told that in order to help defray the cost of travel, we would work every weekend for a month painting house numbers on people's curbs. We were given paint and stencils. Our job was to pick our neighborhoods, go door to door selling our painting services, then quickly finish so we could move on to the next street. My experience raking leaves a lifetime earlier made this a fun proposition for me, except for the fact that every girl had to have one parent volunteer for at least one afternoon.

My father agreed, albeit reluctantly, to give up one Sunday afternoon to work with my group. He told me he would meet us on our designated street at one o'clock; we already had begun that morning. I wasn't looking forward to this because he never seemed able to interact with my few friends without it feeling awkward at best, embarrassing at worst. He didn't know how to relate to people as they were, only as he thought they should be. And because of his time in the military, his leadership style was "command and control," which meant things needed to be done the right way. His way.

He drove up and parked. I watched him walk toward us with a small bag in his hand. I was surprised and immediately sick to my stomach. He reeked of Opium, my mom's favorite perfume. Which could only mean they had made use of their morning alone, which I suppose was good for their marriage, but made me feel disgusted. Couldn't he have taken a shower? It was as if he wanted me to know, which was equally revolting. I didn't want to know anything about what happened in their bedroom or that anything had happened at all.

I properly introduced him to the other three girls, as I had been taught to do. I told him which houses we already had "sold" so we could get to work, as that had become our routine. He nodded, then walked over to two of my partners who had taped the stencils to the curb.

"Nope, not like that." He shooed the girls away, bent down, and proceeded to instruct them on using the measuring tape (from his bag) and pencil to properly align the stencils so they would be perfectly centered between the top and bottom of the curb. We'd only been doing this for three straight weekends and had yet to receive a complaint or request for adjustment, but here we were, watching my father making precise measurements, then drawing lines with a pencil where the stencils should be placed.

My partners giggled in the background, and I was sure he would be the subject of ridicule later. I was mortified. And that afternoon, we completed significantly fewer curbs (hence earning less money) with my father in charge.

The team met our collective financial goal, though, so we were off to Los Angeles for a few days, accompanied by our advisor and several parents. Fortunately, mine were not among them.

We spent our first day in Los Angeles at Disneyland, which was less exciting for me than many others because my grandmother had given my parents money to take me there when I was eleven. We split into groups, rode the rides, ate, and perused the stores until early evening. Then we returned to our hotel, practiced our routines, ate dinner, and readied ourselves for the first round of competition the next day. My parents hadn't given me much spending money. I brought what little I had made by babysitting before the month of curb painting, but there really wasn't much I wanted to buy. I saw my roommates emptying their purses onto the beds–T-shirts, Mickey Mouse ears, keychains, magnets, sunglasses!

While it mostly looked like junk, I was a little envious of the cute shirts, so I asked Michelle how much it had cost. She looked at me as if I was an idiot, then started laughing with the other girls before explaining she got it on a "five-finger discount." I already felt like a rube, but I wanted clarification, so I asked what that meant.

More laughter and shaking heads. They then explained they had stolen these items–who would pay twenty bucks for a T–shirt? I asked if they were afraid they'd get caught, or had they thought what might happen to the team if they got caught. More laughter, then an explanation that shoplifting was easy if you knew what you were doing.

These girls were from comfortable, if not wealthy, families. Why would they steal?

The night before our first day of competition, I decided this would be my one and only year on the team.

We competed in three different categories, moved on to the second day, and earned a trophy or two. The team was ecstatic; I just wanted to go home. I didn't want to be associated with them anymore.

Once we returned, we performed once more during half-time of a varsity basketball game. My parents came to watch, as they knew this would be my last time to dance with the team. After, my father commented that I seemed a little heavier than some of the other girls in my routine. Maybe I should lose a few pounds.

Mom said nothing other than that our performance was "interesting."

I vacillated in my decision to quit the team for a few weeks before official tryouts in May. My only other "team" was the rag-tag group of Journalism 1 students who would become writers for the school newspaper the following year. I had also decided I wanted to double-down on nerd status and join the speech and debate team, ensuring I would never be asked on a date by anyone at my school. I didn't care. I just wanted to find my path.

I skipped drill team tryouts and instead talked to my parents about going to a debate camp that summer hosted by Baylor University. They agreed and congratulated me for doing something more meaningful than dancing at ballgames and pep rallies. They didn't understand that drill team had been meaningful, at least to me, until it became clear that once again, I didn't fit in. They didn't understand me, plain and simple, because they chose not to.

During my two-week debate camp in Waco, I learned the finer points of cross-examination debate and developed a crush on one boy, only to end up making out with his best friend instead because my crush had a crush on a prettier girl. The boys were debate partners from a high school in Houston. I kept in touch with Chad for the first part of my junior year before realizing there was really no point.

After returning from camp, I took as many babysitting jobs as I could get and in between spent my afternoons slathered with baby oil and sunbathing in the backyard. One afternoon, while I was engrossed in a book, Dad surreptitiously snapped a picture of me. A few days later, he showed it to me and said, "Is this really how you want to look?"

I was incredulous. I didn't think I looked bad. He told me it was enough that my mom had put on weight once she quit smoking. After all, had he thought fat was beautiful, he would have married a fat girl. He didn't want me to be fat too, but I was heading in that direction.

I stopped sunbathing for the rest of the summer.

As I embarked upon my junior year, Mom was flourishing in her job as a federal litigator and traveled a fair amount for cases on appeal. Dad also traveled, but they managed to coordinate such that one parent always would be home. I dreaded him being out of town because that meant Mom would drink more than usual and she would go from being loving, praising, and indulgent to suspicious, accusatory, and unkind. I dreaded Mom being out of town because that meant I'd have to prepare dinner, attempt to make polite conversation, do the dishes, and retreat to my room. When they were together, they seemed to be fighting more than usual. My father had little interest in what she wanted to discuss about work, and conversely, it appeared she felt the same about him.

I focused on my homework, my writing assignments for the newspaper, and preparing for upcoming tournaments where I competed in cross-x debate, extemporaneous speaking, and oratory. For the first half of my junior year, I seemed to excel. I had made some guy friends from an all-male Catholic prep school in Dallas, one who became a boyfriend of sorts, and I had begun thinking about college. Just a short distance ahead, but soon, I could get out of the house–I could get out from under the microscope.

In early spring, I got a part-time job at an ice cream shop a few miles away. I still couldn't drive, having not yet taken driver's education because my father wanted me to wait. In hindsight, I believe he knew if I had a license and a car, I'd probably get into some kind of trouble. And that would reflect badly on them. Better to keep me under control.

On the few weekends I worked there, I rode my bike to the shop. The one school night I worked each week, Mom usually picked me up. One night, though, I was surprised to see my father waiting outside in his car. This meant either they had had a fight, or I was in some kind of trouble. I got in the car guardedly.

Our house was northeast of the ice cream shop; my father began driving southwest. I didn't dare ask. His radio was tuned to the jazz station, so we drove around for a few minutes, seemingly without any actual destination, before he turned down the sound. And from there, he began to explain why he had cheated on Mom. Arguably, why he was still cheating on her, though I didn't know it then.

I didn't want to hear that she didn't enjoy sex. I didn't want to hear she had become sexually unappealing to him because of her weight and how much she drank each night. I stopped myself from reminding him that her heavy drinking only began a few years ago, upon finding the letter from his mistress, Van. That he caused it all.

I didn't want to hear he had needs my mother couldn't meet, and it was only sex, after all. I didn't want to hear any of it because it all seemed so dirty, so sordid, so counterintuitive to the image we portrayed to the world. We were an upstanding family, weren't we?

I didn't say a word and just listened while looking out the window, fighting back tears. Is this how men really were, after all?

We got home to find my mother asleep in her recliner, her Waterford glass of Scotch on the end table beside her. I went to my room and petted Jasmine while listening to my stereo. I didn't want my warmed-up dinner. I didn't know what I wanted except to kill the pain.

They finally went to bed, so I went to the kitchen and pulled out the half-gallon of Blue Bell Homemade Vanilla ice cream. Despite working in an ice cream shop with a full assortment of fancy flavors, this was my favorite. I grabbed a spoon, ate nearly half of the ice cream in the brand-new container, put it back in the freezer, and went to my bathroom. I stuck a finger down my throat and immediately vomited all I had just consumed. It was easy. It was comforting. I wouldn't get fat, no matter what.

And so it began.

A month later, Jasmine–by this point, nearly sixteen years old–became unexpectedly ill. We never knew if she had gotten into some poison outside or if it was simply old age, but she began losing an alarming amount of weight to the point her bones showed. Dad took her to the vet; he had lost his most recent job, so he had time on his hands. The vet concluded there was no treatment that would save her. I came home from school that day to find my father digging a hole in the background. Next to him in a green garbage bag was the best friend I had ever known–my cantankerous Siamese I had had since I was two. I wasn't given the chance to say goodbye. I went to my room and shut the door. I didn't want to watch her being buried, and it wasn't as if he would offer any words of comfort other than "that's life."

Despite my grief over losing Jasmine and my attempts to steer clear of my parents and their chaos, I kept up appearances to the best of my ability. I wrote my articles, thrilling at seeing my by-line in the paper every other month. My new debate partner and I did well at our speech tournaments. My grades were good, and I continued talking to my prep school pseudo-boyfriend on the phone nearly every night. Yet, what had become my daily habit of coming home from school, bingeing on anything I could find in the pantry or the freezer, then throwing it all up before dinner, then throwing up my dinner before going to bed, wasn't helping me lose weight. Instead, I seemed to be gaining weight, according to Dad. So, one day I rode my bike to a drugstore about a mile away. I had quit my job at the ice cream shop and wasn't babysitting much anymore, so all I had was my weekly allowance–a pittance, really–for doing my chores around the house. I had heard about diet pills, so I meandered to the diet aid aisle and looked at the price for Dexatrim. Nearly twelve dollars for a box. I only had five dollars in my purse. I looked over one shoulder, then the other, and with the coast clear, I plucked the box from the shelf and buried it in my purse. Then, I went to look at lip gloss, found one for two dollars, and went nervously to the cashier to pay. She said it was a pretty shade. I thanked her, took the bag and swiftly left the store to pedal home quickly, lest I be found out.

I had gotten away with it. And I would get skinny.

The drill team girls were right. Shoplifting wasn't so hard if you knew how to not get caught. I got away with it! It felt liberating, and really, I didn't feel any guilt. Not then, anyway.

I started taking the diet pills the next day and realized within the first week that I could get by on a plain cheese sandwich for lunch and a few bites of dinner. The weight started dropping quickly, but it wasn't enough to make me feel better. One day after school, I walked to the convenience store around the corner and bought a pack of cigarettes; this was before an age limitation was imposed on tobacco purchases. I came home, sat on the back patio with a Diet Coke, and coughed through my first, my second, my third cigarette before putting them in my top dresser drawer, along with my diet pills and the syrup of Ipecac I had bought a week or so later to make the vomiting easier if I needed to binge. I believed I had it all figured out.

I was sixteen. I didn't.

In just a few weeks, my weight had dropped by more than ten pounds, such that it was visible. No one commented until one Saturday night after I returned home from my debate tournament. My mother had found my stash, and with Dad sitting beside her, began the interrogation. What was wrong with me, and didn't I know Dexatrim was basically speed, and why on earth did I have syrup of Ipecac, and when did I start smoking...the lashing continued while my father remained silent. I think he was just happy I had lost weight.

I promised I'd stop doing all those harmful things and would start counting calories instead. My mother relented.

I was lying.

The following week was Spring Break, so of course, I was home under the watchful eye of my unemployed father while Mom was at work. He was hoping to get his own consulting business started while working part-time for the new NBA team as a statistician–comparable to the work he did for the team in San Antonio while we were there. He didn't get paid, but we got free admission to the games we attended.

I didn't have any plans for the week, and as it turned out, that was just as well. On Tuesday, Dad invited me to join him on a quick run to the base in Fort Worth. We'd go to the BX ("Base Exchange") to pick up toiletries and other things he needed, then we'd go on to the commissary for groceries. Once inside the BX, I went in one direction, and he went in the other. I was keen on exploring the make-up to see if they were carrying any new brands since my last visit.

They did! I saw two shiny Lancôme displays, tauntingly beautiful with the promise of happiness for a price. I checked out the lipstick samples first and found a plummy color I knew would suit me. I held onto the box while exploring the eyeshadow. A duo compact with golden shades would really complement my dark brown eyes. I would return from Spring Break if not tan, at least with a fresh look. Happiness…for a price. And a steep one, at that. Both items combined totaled forty dollars. I only had ten in my wallet.

I walked around the store, holding both Lancôme boxes in my hand, wondering if I could persuade my father to loan me the money or just buy the makeup outright. Mom would have been a hard sell at that price. Dad didn't really understand makeup, so even though I knew he valued beauty, I was sure he wouldn't consider forty dollars–just for face goop–to be a good investment.

I had wandered to the ladies' clothing area, packed with round racks laden with clothes suited for a much older audience than I, but I flipped through the garments idly. I looked over one shoulder, then the other, and seeing no one around, I popped both boxes into my purse.

After finding Dad in the hardware section, where he was comparing prices of fertilizer, we proceeded toward checkout. I fidgeted a bit, ready to get to the car while he paid for his purchases. As was so often the case, he was in one of his sullen moods–likely because he hadn't found what he was looking for or perhaps because he was stuck with me–so he walked purposefully and quickly to the car. I was lagging behind when I heard a man call out, "Young lady, may I speak to you?"

Shit.

There we were, in the parking lot of the BX on a U.S. military base, as the man in plain clothes approached me from the store. Dad approached me from the car. I was trapped between the two. And I was more afraid than I'd ever been in my life, which says quite a lot.

"Did you, by chance, leave without paying for something?"

"No, sir," I said, hugging my purse against my chest.

I didn't dare look at my father, but I could feel his anger building. He asked, "just what, precisely," the man was accusing me of doing. He said it in his superior, I-was-a-Lieutenant-Colonel voice. The man simply asked us to follow him back inside, where he escorted us to a locked office in the back of the store. From there, he led us into his own office, which had a two-way mirror, though I didn't recognize it until later. He asked us to be seated. We sat.

He leaned into me, peering into my eyes, and asked again simply, "Did you leave without paying for a few items?"

I shook my head again. I couldn't speak. I kept a death grip on my purse.

My father was sitting deathly still, looking at me coldly with his steely blue eyes that had turned gunmetal gray.

The man sighed and told me they saw me on camera (I didn't think there was such a thing). He pointed to the mirror and said on the other side watching were two female military police officers who would take me to another room, ask me to remove my clothes, and ask me to empty my bag. I stayed quiet, thinking he may be bluffing.

He wasn't.

The minute he stood up, I started to cry, opened my bag, handed him the two precious Lancôme boxes with cosmetics promising happiness for a price, and said I was sorry. I couldn't look at my father.

The man sat back down and asked me to hand over my military ID, which gave me access to the base. My father let out a painful sigh. The man said we would be contacted by the base attorney for a hearing within the next few weeks. I apologized again. He handed my father some paperwork and escorted us from the store.

Speed walking to the car, Dad put as much distance between us as possible. I was uncertain if he planned to leave me there, stranded, so I picked up my pace, and though shaking uncontrollably, I got in the car. I started to speak, and he just held up his hand. He didn't want to hear it.

Once we arrived at the commissary, I moved to get out of the car, but he barked, "Stay!" as if I were a poorly behaved mutt. With that, he turned off the engine, got out, and locked the doors. I realized I wouldn't have been allowed entrance anyway, not without my ID.

I waited there for forty-five minutes, without air conditioning, sitting in the guilt of what I had done and the anxiety of what was to come. There really was no explaining, not then, because I didn't understand it myself. My world was spinning out of control.

We rode home with only the sports radio station to fill the void.

I immediately went to my room and began to shut the door, but he was right on my heels. And then he unloaded in a way I had never seen. He yelled about how I had embarrassed him, so emotionally that his bulging, reddened eyes were puddling with angry tears. He yelled he had no idea how they had managed to raise someone like me, a disappointment in most respects given my recent life choices, and that he didn't think he could ever, ever forgive me. I started to speak, and in a flash, his hand was around my throat. He shoved me back so hard my head hit the wall. I sank to my knees, crying. He left. I thought he had left the house, but he was waiting in the garage for Mom to get home.

She came to my room and told me Dad met her at the car, crying with rage, and told her what I had done. Did I remember she was an officer of the court? (I wasn't sure how that mattered, in this case.) Did I care about how my actions reflected upon the family? Was the makeup worth all this shame and humiliation? I stayed silent. One didn't argue with a federal litigator, especially one who's pissed.

I stayed in my room as they had a somber cocktail hour, though I heard the beginning of an argument that seemed to be Mom telling my father to give me a break. I was only sixteen. Teens do dumb things. I wasn't a bad person; I just made some bad choices. The discussion escalated, and I heard her yell, "Well, you never wanted her in the first place, so what should I expect?" I didn't hear him refute her claim. I didn't hear any response at all.

She brought my dinner to my room, where I ate what I could before flushing the rest down the toilet, then throwing up what little I had eaten soon after.

I wrote a heartfelt letter to the base commander the next day, asked for a stamp, and put it in the mailbox. I showed neither of my parents what I had written, but in essence, I explained I was an excellent student involved in many extracurricular activities, and I deeply regretted what I had done. I didn't want my actions to reflect poorly on my father, who had earned the Bronze Star for his service in Vietnam, or my mother, who was a federal litigator. I wrote I had learned my lesson and would never repeat it. I emphasized I was a good person who had made a bad choice.

By that Friday, the base commander had received my letter and called my father to schedule a formal hearing in the next two weeks. That would mean missing school, but it could also mean I would somehow move beyond this unfortunate predicament. The Mavericks played that night, so Mom and I sat and watched the game while Dad worked at the stats table. They both had softened toward me, a little anyway, and at the game, she told me while she wasn't proud of what I did, she was proud of how I handled it.

My father drove me to the hearing. I wore my best outfit, the one I saved for the second day of debate tournaments assuming an advance to the final round and tried to be more poised than my sixteen years really allowed. I wasn't going to cry, though. I wasn't going to cry.

The base commander's secretary ushered us to a conference room where he, the base's attorney, and the man who approached me in the BX parking lot sat on one side of the table. My father and I sat across from them. They thanked us for being there and asked how I was doing.

I started to cry. He nodded. Then he proceeded to read my letter aloud. It was the first time my father had heard my words. The commander asked if I had, indeed, written the letter. I nodded, wiping away tears.

"You seem like you've got a good head on your shoulders," he said. He then asked if I truly had learned from this experience.

"Yes, sir."

He asked if I would ever take something without paying, ever again.

I shook my head. "No, sir."

He looked at the attorney, who shook his head–I supposed that meant there were no further questions. "You'll be suspended from coming on base for six weeks, starting the day of the incident," he explained, then said they would return my ID after the suspension expired.

As we were nearing our house, Dad looked over at me and asked how I was feeling. "Okay, just really sorry."

He nodded. "I hope so," he said. "You should be. Don't ever embarrass me like that again."

And just like that, I was reminded yet again that my life was a reflection of him.

That April, I had an important paper due for my honors English class. Seems like it was a critical analysis of Edgar Allen Poe's "Hop Frog," if memory serves. I loved to read and loved to write even more, but I deeply disliked my teacher (which shouldn't have mattered) and was struggling with my math class homework, so I procrastinated until the Sunday before the Monday deadline. Since I didn't have time to read the material and write the paper, I called one of my classmates who lived nearby and asked if I could borrow her paper. She was an excellent writer. She agreed, so I biked to her house to pick it up for a few hours.

It was good. I mean, really good. I took her basic analysis and changed up some words to make it my own before returning it that evening. Monday, I turned in my paper. Our teacher said over the next few days, we'd each read our papers aloud to the class.

That Thursday, she asked me to stay after class. Once the bell sounded and the room cleared, she told me I wouldn't be reading my paper aloud. Clearly, she said, I had plagiarized another student's work, so I would get an F on the assignment. I couldn't lie since she was right. And I didn't have any reasonable defense for my actions. She said I had been an exceptional student, and she couldn't understand why I would do this. Had I been struggling, she said, I could've talked to her about it. No one had ever told me that, yet in this case, it was too late.

I couldn't tell my parents, though I knew they'd see a significantly lower grade on the next report card because this paper represented twenty-five percent of my grade. As it turned out, I didn't have to.

The following Monday, I was changing classes near the assistant principal's office. I looked up and saw my father, hard to miss because of his height, speaking with her before seeing me, some twenty yards away. I froze. He just shook his head and abruptly left the building.

That night, Dad called a family meeting. I threw up.

I was told to meet them in the living room, where he informed me I would not be taking honors English my senior year. He said it was bad enough I was a thief; now I was a liar and a cheater, too? My mother, well lubricated after her second Chivas, said at the rate I was going, it would be a wonder if I even made it to college. What in the hell was wrong with me? And why did I keep heaping scandal on the family? I didn't have the words then to say I was lost; I was miserable; I was lonely; I was afraid. I didn't have the words to say that nothing felt safe or stable. I didn't have words. I said nothing.

Mom told me I would start seeing a child psychologist the following week. Perhaps she could sort me out since they absolutely couldn't. Hadn't. Wouldn't.

Good girl, gone.

Chapter Nine: Redemption

I completed my junior year with no more significant incidents, other than having my heart broken when I was not selected to be editor-in-chief of the school newspaper. Our advisor told me while I was the best writer on staff, the student she selected to be in charge was better liked by the rest of the reporters. I knew he was a suck up but not serious about journalism. My parents always taught me that no matter the job, I was there to get results–not to win a popularity contest. They were wrong.

That summer, I decided I needed to re-make myself. This epiphany was not a result of my four unsuccessful therapy sessions, during which I spoke very little because anything I had to say would air family business that I was forever told need not be shared. I stopped seeing the therapist with nothing to show for the hours except the realization I could change if I so desired.

My transformation would begin with my appearance. I vowed to myself I would spend the summer losing weight–healthily–by becoming a vegetarian and running every night. Ironically, I had landed a job at the counter of a family run barbecue shop to which I rode my bike every day, but I was committed. I got a copy of Richard Simmons' book about not dieting and followed the menu plans to every detail. I also vowed to eat dinner earlier so I would have time for my food to digest before running for thirty minutes every night.

Mom said this was all well and good, but she had neither the time nor the inclination to prepare two separate meals each night.

She promised if I gave her my weekly grocery list, she would ensure I had what I needed.

Fortunately, I already had experience cooking dinner for Dad, but now I only had to please myself. And I did, whipping up vegetarian spaghetti and soups and salads and omelets that were healthy, nutritious, and satisfying. My weight was coming off safely and steadily. Mom started taking notice of my meals and asked if I would mind preparing the same thing for them periodically. I did. Dad took notice of my changing appearance by nodding with approval when I reported how many pounds I had lost. I finished the summer feeling more confident than I had since moving to Arlington, ready to take on my senior year, then flee, as quickly as possible, to college.

I had been appointed to the Executive Council of the Student Council, with my first official task being to welcome students to registration prior to the first day of class. When I showed up, my classmates immediately took notice of my new look. How had I done it? Anyone paying attention would have known my weight had fluctuated to extremes the prior year, but I was getting validation that my discipline had paid off.

Even from a few boys. They didn't interest me, though; I still had my guy friends from the Catholic prep school whom I'd see once debate tournament season began. Honestly, I didn't fit in with any one group at school, but definitely not the keg-party crowd who favored cheap beer and make-out sessions in a vacant hilltop lot nearby.

My sole focus was on making it a good year as features editor of the newspaper, president of the debate team, member of the Executive Council of the Student Council, and finally, taking drivers' education to obtain some semblance of freedom. I would commit to keeping my grades up so I could get into the school of my dreams–the University of Missouri at Columbia, considered the best school for journalism in the country.

Dad had begun consulting work for a handful of corporations that needed help to move data centers, which meant he was back on the road a fair amount. His travel sparked Mom's suspicions, particularly when he failed to call, so she drank more than usual. I bore the brunt of her rage.

One night, after we had eaten the dinner I prepared, and I had gone to finish my homework, Mom came into my room with a glass of Chivas in her hand. She said she was proud of how hard I worked to lose weight and that I looked good. She took a healthy sip as I watched nervously. She then said that if I were to get pregnant, they would completely disown me; I should not expect any help whatsoever. I had no idea why she would say that since I wasn't even dating anyone and had only ever kissed, certainly nothing beyond that. I told her she had nothing to worry about there. She took another sip and nodded. "Well, your father is concerned you're not dating anyone. He's worried you're a lesbian."

Unbelievable, except likely true. I shook my head in confusion and said they had nothing to worry about there, either. She left my room.

I put on running shoes, grabbed my Walkman, and left, running from two characterizations that were both untrue. Yet, that was what they thought–what he thought. Apparently, I had only two paths: be a slut or be a lesbian. When he returned home, I said nothing, yet kept a safe distance.

When I took the SAT in early September, I indicated they should send my results to three schools: The University of Missouri at Columbia, Northwestern University, and The University of Texas at Austin. I waited anxiously to find out where I'd be accepted. On October 11 of my senior year, I collected the mail and found a letter from Texas. My father was home, but I wanted to prolong the moment, so I stood on the front walk for a few minutes before opening the envelope.

The University of Texas at Austin was pleased to inform me I was being offered early acceptance. All I had to do was confirm by their deadline, and I was guaranteed a place in the freshman class of 1983. I let out an enormous sigh and punched the air with my fist. Yes!

Mom wouldn't be home for a few more hours, but I couldn't wait to tell her, so I ran into the house, grabbed the phone from the hallway, and called her from my room. Typically, I wasn't supposed to disturb her at work unless it was an emergency, but I couldn't wait. She answered, and I apologized for bothering her, but I got early acceptance at Texas! This was good, I acknowledged, but what if I accepted and then afterward, Missouri or Northwestern offered me a spot? She congratulated me and said we'd discuss it in more detail once she got home.

When I returned the phone to its hall table, my father was standing there, arms folded. "You couldn't have waited to tell both of us at the same time?" he glowered. I tried to explain that because I wanted to study journalism like Mom had done when she first went to college, that she'd appreciate my getting accepted by Texas. And early!

He walked away without offering any words of congratulations or anything else. Yet, he managed to put a damper on my sense of accomplishment and pride and the relief that I could now relax and enjoy my senior year. All because I told Mom first.

Later that fall, the Executive Council was tasked with coordinating the annual faculty-versus-student basketball game—boys and men only, of course. I proposed we make the event an opportunity for people to contribute toward a cause and suggested the price of admission be a toy. We would then donate the toys to an orphanage I had found in Dallas. What if we had our jazz band playing at half-time? We would take the event to a different level than prior years and help orphans in the process. The council agreed this was a fantastic idea. I agreed to coordinate the publicity and find a referee. It had to be a real basketball game, after all.

That evening, I waited until my parents finished their cocktail hour to approach Dad cautiously. I explained the event and what we wanted to accomplish. He listened patiently. I said that since he had played basketball at school and had worked for both the Spurs and the Mavericks as a statistician, would he have any interest in serving as our official referee?

He asked if there was money involved. I said there wasn't, which is why we didn't hire one of the professionals who refereed our regular games. He took a sip of his drink and looked over at my mom, raising his eyebrows. I didn't know what that meant. I waited, having learned much earlier in my life to not "natter" when he was contemplating something, else I'd incur his anger. "Sure," he said. "I'll do it."

And that was that. The last time he had been on campus was when he met with the assistant principal. I wasn't sure this was a good idea, in hindsight, as he wasn't very pleasant around young people. Yet, I had secured the last detail of the event.

I'm not sure where he bought the referee-like shirt, but he showed up thirty minutes before the game was set to begin. The bleachers were full to the brim, our jazz band was playing, and we had a mountain of toys stacked in the gym's corner. The vibe was full-on rowdy, and I was giddy with success.

I had lost sight of Dad amidst all the excitement, then saw him checking with the team at the score table to make sure the equipment was operating properly. I started to regret asking for his participation. Next, he went to the corner of the gym and began his elaborate stretches and other warm-up exercises that looked, from my vantage point, simply ridiculous. This wasn't the NBA. Hell, it wasn't even a real game! It was for fun and to help kids in need, right?

Not in his mind. When it came time to start the game, he walked slowly and authoritatively to the center of the court, bounced the ball a few times to ensure it was properly inflated, nodded to the score table team, and loudly blew his whistle. Next, the tip-off, and the game was underway–our boys' varsity team against coaches and other male faculty members who might have been basketball contenders, back in their day. It should have been fun, and to everyone else, it likely was. Yet, every time my father called a foul, the crowd booed, and I winced. He was in charge, and he made sure everyone knew it. When the game was over, I saw him approach our varsity basketball coach (who also was my drivers' ed instructor). Dread–that was all I could feel even as my Executive Council peers were congratulating me on a very successful event and asking when we'd get to deliver the toys to the orphanage. Teachers praised our efforts and said it was the best game they'd remembered in years, and we had raised the bar for years to follow. I waited for Dad to finish up so we could go home.

Mom was waiting for us when we arrived, handing him a drink so they could re-live their day, as usual. Dad talked at length about how much fun he had, how he probably made people mad by making all the right calls, how the varsity boys played well but needed coaching in certain areas, and that it felt good to be back in a gym. Not a word to me or about me regarding the overall event and how successful it was in exceeding our goal for donated toys.

He then said he had talked to the coach about refereeing future games and was given contact information for the local referees' association. He planned to contact them tomorrow because this was what he wanted to do. He was a natural, he proclaimed.

My event was all about him.

That spring, I was busier than I had ever been. I represented my high school in a statewide speech competition (having won at the local and regional levels) in Persuasive Speaking, ranking twelfth. I represented my high school in another state speech competition in extemporaneous speaking; I didn't clear the first round. As president of our debate club, I helped coordinate and host a debate tournament for junior-high students. My father agreed to be a judge for one and only round and was highly critical afterward that competitive debate had become speed-talking instead of genuine persuasion. I opted not to argue with him. I received several journalism awards from the Arlington Independent School District, which were highly coveted among those of us who competed. And my journalism advisor nominated me for a Women in Communications, Inc. merit scholarship.

I had officially accepted early admission to Texas. I knew where I was going. I knew I'd be in the journalism program. The end was near with my new journey on the horizon. A merit scholarship would prove the icing on the proverbial (non-caloric) cake.

A few weeks after my nomination was submitted, I checked the mail after school. Waiting for me was the official notification that I had been awarded the Abigail Van Buren scholarship and was invited, along with my sponsor, to accept it a few weeks later at a formal event at the Fort Worth Public Library. My awards and this scholarship served as a much-needed balm after losing the editor-in-chief role. To me, it was validation I was meant to write professionally.

My parents got home later, and I broke tradition by joining them during cocktail hour, nursing a Diet Coke as they sipped Scotch. I waited for a break in the conversation before reading them the letter I had received from WICI. Mom immediately congratulated me. Dad asked how much the scholarship provided. I explained it was a merit scholarship with numerous applicants. Of course, he asked about the money. I told him the scholarship was $300.

"That's not going to buy much," he said before getting up to pour another drink. From my perspective, it would at least go toward textbooks, but that wasn't enough. Once again.

I looked at Mom; I couldn't believe my achievement had been so summarily dismissed. She just shook her head and muttered, "I'm sorry." Yet she didn't confront him.

Good girl deflated.

Chapter Ten: Marking Time

Right after my father had Jasmine put to sleep, my mom's father called one evening, and I happened to answer. His tone was urgent; he asked for Mom. He informed her that my Great Aunt Mary and Uncle Jim–the ones in New Jersey — had been killed, along with another couple riding with them–in a head-on collision with an eighteen-wheeler truck. My mother was devastated, of course, since Aunt Mary had been more of a mother figure to her than my grandmother. They were childless, so their estate was divided between my mother, who inherited jewelry and furniture, and some of their nieces and nephews. My mother had a few pieces of furniture and the jewelry she inherited shipped our way. I don't recall there being any memorial services, at least not that we attended.

Among the beautiful pieces Mom inherited was a gorgeous strand of pearls with a delicate, pearl-encrusted gold clasp. I coveted them desperately–I didn't yet have pearls of my own, but the wealthier girls in debate from the Dallas private prep schools always wore theirs to the tournaments. It was, after all, the height of the preppie movement made popular by the book "The Preppy Handbook," the lifestyle Bible for all who wished to convey generational wealth (whether they had it or not). Pearls were critical.

After Spring Break, I was admittedly on autopilot, worrying less about tensions at home or even pressures at school because I knew my position at Texas was secure, and I only had to mark time for five months. Five short months before I could spread my wings and fly the hell away. There always was a lurking fear that at the eleventh hour, Dad would find a reason to rescind my tuition money (even as my grandmother had started my college fund), and I'd have to sort it out myself. Yet, I figured they wanted me gone as much as I wanted out, so standing in the way of my next chapter wouldn't be in their best interests.

I had learned my lesson about stealing my junior year. I didn't think borrowing was the same thing.

I was wrong.

The last debate tournament of the year, and my last tournament ever, was that April at a high school in Dallas. This was a big one, and I wanted to go out with a flourish and, hopefully, a win or two. I had stayed up all night Thursday sewing a new A-line black corduroy skirt to accompany the yellow lamb's wool cardigan I had recently purchased, the requisite Polo white oxford shirt, and the even more-requisite penny loafers. The only thing missing was a strand of pearls.

That year, Mom always drove me to school since my first class was at 7:30, giving her plenty of time to get to Dallas by her 8:30 start time. The morning of my last tournament, while she was in the shower, I went to her jewelry box, grabbed Aunt Mary's pearls, and stashed them in my purse. After she dropped me off at school, I sprinted to the bathroom to clasp the pearls around my neck. I immediately felt more worthy. A few hours later, the bus took us to the tournament. I walked taller than usual because my skirt was the bomb, my penny loafers were polished, and I was rocking Aunt Mary's pearls. A few of the fancy girls noticed, though they didn't say anything. Of course, they wouldn't.

I couldn't take the bus back because I had cleared to the next round, so I called Dad and asked if he could come get me. And he did. I chattered the entire way home about the judges, where we were in the rankings, and my nerves about making it to the finals in extemporaneous speaking so I could go to State once again. He remained silent. When we got home, Mom already had dinner underway. He motioned for us to go into the living room and sit down.

And then he just pointed at me. Truly, I had no idea. He looked at Mom and pointed at her neck. She moved her hand as if to brush something off her chin and neck, and he simply said, "No." He looked back at me.

"Did you ask permission?" He knew Mom didn't let me wear her jewelry. Any of it. No matter how much I implored.

I put my hand to my neck–literally grasping the pearls—and dropped my head. "No, sir." I tried to explain I just wanted to be as good as the other girls, to fit in, to have their approval. They all have pearls, I said, and it made me feel special to wear them. Maybe they had been good luck. My eyes welled up with tears. Why couldn't they understand?

My mother simply held out her hand, silently but glaring at me. I unclasped the pearls and handed them to her. "I just don't understand," she said in her courtroom voice. "Why? Why are you the way you are?" Is that a question anyone can answer, much less a seventeen-year-old?

"Apparently, you didn't learn a thing last year," my father said, taking a sip of his drink. "Life is about decisions, as I've always told you. Yet, you just keep making bad ones. I don't have high hopes for your future."

"Don't you ever, and I mean, ever, borrow anything of mine without asking," Mom said. "It's the same as stealing, young lady."

I chose not to ask why she didn't adopt that same approach when it came to the other women "borrowing" my father and stealing him from our family, especially since she was having her Scotch. Best not to throw gas on the fire. I apologized, said I wouldn't do it again, and retreated to my room.

By May of that year, things had begun to get real for me and my classmates–the end of high school was quickly approaching, ushering in a slew of milestone events. Kids who didn't even run together began blending–our class of nearly seven hundred students drew close after years of existing in social silos. We were no longer freaks or geeks or socials or jocks or misfits; we were simply rising graduates. I think we all could taste imminent freedom, and we were licking our collective lips at finally moving our lives forward. Even the teachers seemed sentimental. We were a very unusual class in many ways, including the choice of Van Halen's "Happy Trails" for our class song. Hardly a tear-jerker.

I was invited to prom by one of my platonic friends from journalism, who had been the closest thing to a bestie I had while in high school. My mother made my dress–a beautiful, cream moire silk number with empire waist, fitted bodice, and puffy sleeves adorned with emerald-green silk bows at the shoulders. She said I looked beautiful. Dad simply took the obligatory picture of me, my wrist corsage, my date, his boutonniere, and our awkward smiles.

He didn't tell me I looked pretty but told Mom the dress turned out well.

We triple-dated with two other couples, drinking cheap Boone's Farm "wine" before heading to the luxury hotel in Dallas in the limo someone's parents had rented, and made our pseudo-debuts as "grown-ups." I didn't plan to do the grown-up things I had yet to do, since my date and I were just friends, but I knew what others had planned for the after-parties at the nicest hotel in Arlington. Yet, I did enjoy the evening and, for the first time, allowed myself to dance and cut loose.

My date and his best friend had rented a room at the hotel in Arlington, as did a bunch of others, so it was a roving party. I had brought a bottle of Tanqueray gin I bought by myself. I looked a little older than my age, so I didn't get carded, which was good since I didn't have my driver's license - STILL. A few weeks before graduation and I still didn't get to drive. Anyway, my attempts at playing bartender were ill-advised and before long, I was zonked out on the bed while the party moved elsewhere. My date came to wake me around six that morning–none of us had curfews for prom–and he dropped me off with a chaste kiss before my parents were awake.

I slept the rest of the day, rising that evening with an epic hangover. Mom tried to make me eat dinner. I shook my head.

"If you're going to dance, you gotta pay the piper," she said with a chuckle.

Not the life lesson I wanted in that moment.

My graduation present was a used Honda Accord that reeked of cigarette smoke. It was a bilious metallic green with matching velour interior. It may as well have been a brand-new BMW–I loved it immediately. Dad allowed me to drive it, with him in the passenger seat, so he could correct my driving techniques while saying this was why high school coaches shouldn't teach driver's ed. Whatever.

The following weekend, he asked me to come outside because I wouldn't be allowed to get my license until I had mastered changing a tire, changing spark plugs, and checking and changing the oil. Seriously. I know now he was looking out for my safety–he wanted to be sure I could take care of myself if necessary–but it just felt like the carrot dangling in front of me...always moving just out of grasp.

I learned how to do all those things. The next week, he took me after school for my driving test. He took a seat in the waiting area as the Department of Public Safety official climbed into the passenger's seat, and off we went. I carefully maneuvered the car through the selected neighborhoods. I aced the parallel parking. I pulled into the DPS lot and looked at him expectantly.

He told me I had failed. I touched the center lane after turning right. "You're not supposed to cross the center lane." He may as well have been Dad, given his condescending tone. Which I got more of once my father got in the car. He asked if I really thought I was ready to own a car if I couldn't follow the rules?

Fortunately, my mother took me later in the week, and I passed with flying colors. Maybe not flying colors. But I passed. We celebrated with Dairy Queen chocolate milk shakes. They told me that evening, though, that I wouldn't be allowed to drive the car until I was officially out of school. Probably a very smart choice on their part since I was itching to get out of the house. But controlling, nonetheless.

I spent the next two weeks taking finals and preparing for graduation with the traditional Vespers service the night before. The real before the real-real. The service was beautiful, with the pastor praying we all make good life choices and serve God going forward; that our parents continue to hold us in their hearts and be patient with our journeys, never forgetting we would always need them; that we would carry our precious high school memories with us through our lives, and so on. It all was so close; I could taste it.

Mom asked Dad to stop at the grocery store on the way home—she just needed to run in for some lettuce or milk, not a major shop. We waited in the car; Dad turned down the radio.

"I've been thinking," he said, looking at me in the rearview mirror. "If you lost some weight and were a little nicer, you might actually have more friends."

Where the hell did that come from? I mean, I had gained back much of the weight I had lost the prior summer, but I wasn't fat. At least, I didn't think I was. But at that moment, having completed high school and one day before my graduation, he still found fault. He still found a way to expel the joy from anyone's moments but his. I had had enough.

I leaned forward and met his eyes in the mirror. "Why is it," borrowing Mom's turn of phrase, "Why is it that nothing I do is ever enough? That second place wasn't enough? That an A minus wasn't enough? That a $300 merit scholarship wasn't enough? That getting early acceptance to Texas—a difficult school to get into—wasn't enough? Why?" My voice was shaking; I don't think I had ever spoken to him this way.

He smiled, and I swear it was like looking at the Grinch but for the green skin. I squirmed slightly. "Here's why. If I think you're seven-eighths perfect, I'm going to focus on the remaining one-eighth it will take to get you there."

And just like that, I realized that for him, perfection was an attainable goal...one he seemed to believe he had mastered. I sank back, my shoulders slumped, and stared out the window.

My journalism crew decided we would throw a graduation party at a nice local motel and had been making hasty arrangements in the days leading up to graduation. I boldly offered to secure the room reservation–a suite that would give us plenty of room to party. Two of the guys with fake IDs said they'd buy the booze, including a huge keg. The morning of graduation, I drove to the motel–yes, I finally got to drive my car–paid in cash, got the keys, and gave one to the guys. We were allowed to check in at three, and here they came with a keg and a ton of bottles of alcohol (plus mixers and cups) loaded into the back of the truck. We got the room set up before heading home to change for graduation.

The plan was simple: we would charge a three-dollar cover for everyone who came. Yet, other parties had been planned, so we assumed it would just be our small group, plus ancillary friends. We couldn't wait to get through the graduation ceremony so the party could start!

Just like Vespers, the ceremony was held at the local college's auditorium, which felt quite fancy at the time. We listened to all the speeches. We each crossed the stage as our names were called and brandished our diplomas like hard-fought championship trophies. For many of us, they were. We sang the fight song and then the alma mater (choking back sentimental tears as we swayed in unison). Finally, our class song came on– "Happy Trails"–and the beach balls started flying. It was quite a spectacle, quite a giddy celebration, even as the administrators admonished us. For the last time!

Mom and Dad knew about our graduation party and asked that I at least come home for a glass of Champagne before embarking upon the festivities. I don't believe I told them the room was in my name. My father popped the cork on the bottle of Piper-Heidsieck and filled our glasses. It was so much better than the sparkling Boone's Farm my group drank before prom! Knowing it was likely my last time to see many of my classmates, I wasn't terribly concerned about what to wear to the party. Everyone in journalism was kind of grungy. So, I put on my scraggly old jeans that I had frayed at the hem, a pair of huarache sandals I had bought in Dallas over Spring Break, and for reasons I still don't understand, one of my father's short-sleeved work shirts. It had multi-colored stripes, and I thought it was anti-preppy. I was Boho before Boho was a thing, at least in my mind.

Having learned at least one lesson, I asked him if I could borrow it before putting it on. He raised his eyebrows, shrugged, then nodded. I hugged them both goodbye, as they seemed uncharacteristically sentimental. I wouldn't understand until decades later what high school graduation signals for the parents, but I was glad to feel a moment of warmth.

And with a wave, I jumped into my Green Machine and drove purposefully to the motel.

By the time I got there, the party was in full swing, and it wasn't just my crew. Apparently, at graduation, everyone heard this was the place to be. Imagine, the geeky journalism students throwing the graduation bash of the year! It was so crowded, I had a hard time getting in the door. The guy playing bouncer, one of my prom date's friends, waved me by, and I made my way to the bathtub where the booze was kept. I didn't really like beer.

Someone had brought a boom box, so the walls were reverberating with the music of the early eighties–a few hair bands mixed with some Prince mixed with some punk and all points in between. The eighties were nothing if not diverse! The party grew by the hour; people drank and found places to make out. I was called out by the general manager, with a row of three police cars watching us from the perimeter, and told I needed to make the guys get off the roof. Already a bit drunk, I called them down without incident. Over the course of the night, I was approached by four different guys, all of them jocks, who proclaimed they had had crushes on me throughout high school but were intimidated to ask me out. Would

I go out with them over the summer? I politely declined each of the invitations; if I wasn't good enough to ask out while we were in school, why should I go out with them now? I didn't say that, of course. That wouldn't be nice. I felt a little smug.

The party began winding down around five in the morning. Our core group got busy cleaning up the suite, with only one pink mound of vomit on the carpet and a broken towel rack to betray our revelry. Someone brought donuts, and we counted our money. Taking out what each of us had invested, we each made a tidy profit of about seventy-five bucks. It made me think of the lessons I learned about the business side of raking leaves and thought, surely, my father would be proud of my business acumen.

I opted not to tell him.

Instead, I finished high school with a slightly different perspective on myself.

Good-enough girl.

Chapter Eleven: Responsibility

One of my mother's friends and former colleagues had left her role with the U.S. government to go across the street and join her attorney husband's private practice. I had known Mary from my years of going to work with Mom on school breaks. She and her husband were kind enough to offer me a job as an office clerk the summer before I left for college. My job wasn't particularly clear-cut–really anything that needed doing in the office including filing, copying, answering the phone when the receptionist was out, running files to the courthouse down the street–it was a swell job in a high-rise building, paying five dollars an hour plus an unlimited supply of Diet Coke. I got to dress nicely, with what I had, and ride to and from work each day with Mom, who I was beginning to realize I would miss terribly once I left for Austin.

Mom had several law clerks that summer who became my pre-college mentors, of sorts, often inviting me to lunch or occasionally even to happy hour, though I wasn't yet of legal drinking age. The thought of these future lawyers encouraging a seventeen-year-old to drink while underage is amusing, in hindsight, but they treated me as if I was a friend. On the days I knew I'd be joining them, I opted to drive myself to work and kept my drinks to two tidy glasses of chilled Chardonnay. That's what the female clerks were drinking, and they were very sophisticated in my eyes.

Sometimes, I just wanted to drive to Dallas in my new car to practice navigating highways before heading off to Austin. I'd blare my radio with favorites from Prince, Madonna, the J. Giles Band, A Flock of Seagulls, and more. It was exhilarating, glorious freedom. I was earning more than I ever had and planned on using that money for my college wardrobe. Despite Mom's light pressure, I decided at the end of my senior year that I would not go through sorority rush at Texas. Not only was it ridiculously cut-throat, but it was also expensive, and besides, I was going to be a bohemian journalist. I didn't have time for frivolity if I were to be the next Barbara Walters (my secret desire). During her one year of college in Nevada, Mom defied the odds and pledged Kappa Alpha Theta, which was one of the top houses at UT. I didn't think I could compete, so it was better not to try at all.

However, Mom had an office clerk that summer named Tildy, who was a rising sophomore at Texas. She was in a sorority, and as we became close quickly, she persuaded me to go through rush. I was late to the Panhellenic party but submitted my paperwork just the same and soon was invited on rush "dates" by local girls representing the houses interested in me. It was a good list and included Gwyn's sorority, Theta, and a few others. As Tildy and I hung out, she explained all about rush, showed me pictures of her pledge year, and advised me what clothes I'd need. It was equally exciting and terrifying, but Mom was there to help with clothes we would buy, and clothes she would make.

My summer was full of promise as the countdown began. I already had a built-in friend at Texas in Tildy, which was good since only six other people from my graduating class were enrolling there and none of them were anything but acquaintances. I planned to start my life anew!

In late June, I was driving home from Dallas, jamming to the radio while daydreaming about my big move. Dad was out of town, so I had invited Tildy to spend the night. Our plan was to get Geppetto's pizza and cheese bread–the local gold standard at the time–and watch MTV. Mom didn't leave work until 5:30, so she'd arrive home after I did.

Within a mile of my exit, something distracted me, and when I looked back to the highway ahead, I found myself barreling down on the car in front of me. Traffic had come to a dead stop, and though I slammed on my brakes, I still rear-ended the car in front of me. I had been driving for not quite a month. I started to cry, and not knowing what to do in this situation, I exited my car to check on the driver in front of me. He was okay. My car wasn't, but his car definitely wasn't. We exchanged information while waiting for the police, who arrived quickly. As it turns out, the other driver was the father of my high school's former star quarterback. I was mortified and prayed he wouldn't tell his son who hit him, though he probably wouldn't have known me, anyway.

I was inconsolable while talking to the police officer. The only thing I could say, beyond my "I'm sorry" mantra, was that my father would absolutely kill me when he got home. He. Would. Kill. Me. Probably not the wisest thing to say to a police officer, but hey, I was in shock. Genuinely.

With paperwork completed, the officer deemed my car safe to drive. The highway was backed up for miles and miles, but the route to the exit ramp was clear, so he followed me off the highway and then followed me home to ensure I arrived safely. I was in terrible shape emotionally; physically, I was fine enough.

I pulled around back, parked my car, and examined the damage. It looked even worse than it had on the highway. My beautiful new-to-me car, crumpled in front with part of the bumper dangling. They would both kill me. I just knew it.

Shortly thereafter, Mom pulled into the driveway, leaped out of the car, took one look at the car and one look at me and simply said, "Oh, Suz…what have you done?" We went inside, and each had a glass of wine. She said she was listening to talk radio when they gave a traffic report about a two-car accident on 1-30 in Arlington, and she had a feeling–she had this visceral feeling–that it was me. Mom could be clairvoyant at times, but this felt more like a referendum on what a disappointment I was. I started crying again. She said I'd have to tell my father when he called. I was hoping he'd call before Tildy arrived; I wanted to at least enjoy my pizza later.

The phone rang, and Mom answered. They chatted briefly before Mom told my father I needed to speak with him. I took a deep breath, took the receiver, and asked how he was doing. He said he doubted that's why I wanted to talk. As calmly as possible, I explained that I had rear-ended someone on the highway just before the exit. I knew from drivers' ed that I was legally at fault, though I didn't really know the details of auto insurance because Dad had never explained it. He asked why I rear-ended the man and wasn't I paying attention? I told him I was briefly distracted, though I couldn't remember why, but that I had asked the other driver if he was okay, and he said he was fine.

At this point, Mom yelled at me to never, ever, ever do that again. I looked at her in surprise. What, don't check on someone whose car I had just hit? Dad said she was right. My question could be interpreted in court as an admission that the accident could have inflicted serious injury that would be very expensive for us if proven. That it could wipe out the family, even. I said I was sorry and handed the phone back to Mom before waiting in my room for Tildy.

Neither asked if I was okay. They were in "circle the wagons" mode. Dad would head home in the morning.

Tildy arrived, we pigged out on pizza, and she did her best to console me before heading back to Denton. We both agreed that with my father arriving the next morning, it might be better to reschedule. She had met my father and seemed to sense it would be an awful scene.

Surprisingly, it wasn't. While he remained aloof, as was typically the case with me, he said the car likely wouldn't be totaled. I didn't understand what that meant, but I elected not to ask. At least he was talking to me. Kind of. He spoke with the insurance company, and we made arrangements to drop it off at the collision repair they recommended the following Monday. My neck had begun to hurt, most probably because I had whiplash, but I wasn't taken to a doctor. I laid on the heating pad instead.

Two long weeks later, my car had been repaired and was ready for pickup. Dad drove me early in the morning so I could get to work on time. He signed all the paperwork, examined the car to ensure the repairs were to his satisfaction, then he walked me to my car. I thanked him for helping me, for forgiving my mistake.

He held up his hand. "Don't thank me yet. This is going to cost you one thousand dollars," he said breezily.

"What?"

That's when he explained, for the first time, the concept called "deductibles" and that he had set mine, like theirs, at one thousand dollars. He explained that insurance covered everything but the deductible. And I was responsible for paying for it if I planned to take the car to college.

I made five dollars an hour, which meant I'd be turning over five weeks of my earnings to cover my debt. There went my college money. Most of it, anyway. I drove to work, seething.

Later, he would explain that his philosophy in this area was that you don't insure your own stupidity. He could have set the deductible lower, but that would have meant higher monthly premiums for him to cover. He hoped this taught me a lesson or two about responsibility.

In reality, it taught me that once again, I had to err before being taught. At least no one was hurt, and we weren't being sued by the high school football star's dad.

I've only had two other car accidents since then–one my fault, one not. In both instances, I asked if the other driver was okay. That, to me, is the responsible thing to do. The kind thing to do. Paranoia be damned.

The final few weeks before my big move were a blur of rush dates, kind of dating my former debate partner who was a year older, getting fitted by Mom for the clothes I'd wear during rush, and assembling what I would need for my dorm room. Dad took me to the bank to establish my checking account so he could deposit a small monthly allowance for "incidentals" since my room and board were already covered. Mom agreed to pick up sorority dues, assuming I made it through rush.

The fateful day arrived. We packed Dad's truck and my car with all the belongings I could take, I said a tearful goodbye to our cat Ace, and we convoyed to Austin. My dorm was co-ed, so I wasn't sure what to expect there, but we took my things to my room and met my roommate. Then we headed to Wendy's for a quick lunch before I was to attend a convocation for all girls going through rush. The restaurant was packed with beautiful girls sporting their letters–meaning they already were active in their sororities and were required to display their affiliation during rush week. Sorority candidates weren't allowed to talk to them, nor were they allowed to talk to us. I just stared in awe, then panicked because honestly, I didn't think I stood a chance. Mom clearly saw the concern in my eyes and just patted my hand. "You'll be fine."

I finished up the convocation along with about twenty-five hundred other girls. We learned how the process would go and were told by the Panhellenic chair, not without a degree of attitude, that there were only sixteen sororities on campus. Each sorority capped their pledge class to fifty girls. Of the twenty-five hundred going through rush, only eight hundred would find their sorority home. Choose carefully!

No pressure.

My parents took me to Bombay Bicycle Club for an early birthday dinner; my birthday was the following day. I think I was in too much sensory overload to make much conversation, and my throat felt constricted by the emotions involved in saying goodbye. I had been working toward this moment since eighth grade! I should be reveling in the fact that, in an hour, I'd step into my shiny new chapter. I felt terrified.

Dad drove us to the parking lot in front of my high-rise dorm. They both stepped out of the car. I slowly did the same. Mom took off her prized 14k gold shrimp hoop earrings. Like the pearls I had "borrowed," they were another prop indicating social success, especially among sorority girls. She handed them to me and said they would give me luck, though I had to return them on my first visit home, and that I would do just fine. I could call her anytime. Even collect if I needed to. (Dad grimaced at that.) She hugged me and quickly got back in the car.

After my father gave me a rare hug and a breezy pat on the back, he stepped back and said one last thing before getting in the car: "Don't let school get in the way of your education." Then they drove off. It wasn't until many, many years later that Mom told me she cried non-stop during their three-hour drive back to Arlington.

My roommate and her boyfriend were waiting in our room with a cheap bottle of Chianti and an extra glass to spare. She was a sophomore and didn't plan to go through rush but would be there rooting for me. She even loaned me her lapis-bead necklace, another critical prop in Sorority World. I was grateful.

Rush was exhilarating, and while it was against the rules, I talked to Mom every night about what house I liked and how conflicted I was because the Thetas were rushing me hard, but so too were the Alpha Chis (Tildy's house). The Thetas all were perfect and rich; I was afraid I wouldn't be able to keep up. The Alpha Chis were an eclectic mix of beauty queens and intellectuals and bohemians—I felt like I could find my place with them. And so I did, though I'm sure Theta would have given me a bid if I hadn't listed them as my second choice going into the third round.

Though I had read this in an essay published in the late 1970s, I didn't really believe there were girls who had been groomed since birth to pledge a sorority of which they were a legacy–the daughter, sister, niece, or granddaughter of a member in good standing. Bid day arrived and yes, I was invited to join Alpha Chi. I was thrilled! Leaving the church where we picked up our bids, I heard girls on the pay phones crying as they told their parents they hadn't gotten the house they chose, so they wanted to transfer to SMU or TCU or any other school where rush was held in the spring. They simply couldn't bear not being a Kappa or a Theta or a Pi Phi. I couldn't believe someone would leave the University of Texas at Austin–a prestigious institution–because of a sorority.

I had a lot to learn.

By my second month, I already had attended about eight frat parties, drunk my weight in trashcan punch, made friends both in the sorority and in some of my classes, and realized that college courses were hard. Really hard. After my first two journalism classes, I became so intimidated by the competition and the sheer beauty of so many of the girls who planned, as did I, to go the broadcast route that, without telling my parents, I changed my major to English. I'd find a different way to break into the field.

Through one of my new friends, I landed a coveted job as a runner for a big-deal law firm downtown, making five dollars an hour. When we weren't on errands or making copies for the attorneys, we were allowed to study in one of the many conference rooms. I was finding a way to keep everything balanced. I even opened a second checking account so I could easily deposit my biweekly pay. Life was good!

My first visit home, I was Chatty Cathy the entire weekend, regaling my mom with stories of the frat parties and the cute boys and the new lingo I was learning and the clothes I would need for upcoming events. We pored over patterns and examined her fabric stash. She made all my favorite meals—fried chicken and meatloaf and lasagna and pork chops with fried rice–and washed my clothes. It was clear she missed me.

Dad asked me how I was doing in class–I wasn't there just for the party, after all. (But I wasn't letting college get in the way of my education!) He then lectured me about my questionable choice of getting a part-time job when they were sending me a monthly allowance. They were paying for college, and I should be focused on my studies. He didn't understand that almost every one of my sorority sisters had unlimited use of their parents' credit cards. It was a competitive environment, and you had to look just right. My part-time job would help me do just that.

He told me I was being frivolous, and he didn't understand who I was becoming.

In my mind, I was becoming responsible.

Not so much.

While I wasn't allowed to drive my car until Dad was assured I knew how to change a flat tire, replace spark plugs, and change my oil filter, he didn't apply the same preventive training to my checking account. Little did he know I had two accounts to manage, having opened the second one in Austin to make depositing my paychecks easy.

A few months later, one of my sorority sisters called me in my dorm and said to come to the sorority house. My father was waiting for me in the parlor.

He was there, unannounced. I had a flashback of seeing him outside my assistant principal's office my junior year in high school. This couldn't be good. Had something happened to Mom? Were they divorcing? I sprinted the two blocks from my dorm to the House and found him waiting at one of the mahogany tables.

His greeting was cool, and I could tell from the set of his jaw something was wrong. He looked me up and down, then invited me to sit.

Seems that balancing a checkbook wasn't part of my life skills training. He had been contacted by the bank and told I had bounced checks. A lot of them. Each bounced check meant a twenty-dollar penalty fee on top of the deficit, which seemed counterintuitive to me–I mean, if the bank knows I'm overdrawn, why charge me for money I clearly didn't have?

He had obtained a copy of my account records along with my canceled checks and developed a comprehensive spreadsheet to show me how many ways and places I had gone wrong. I nodded dutifully. He asked why I couldn't understand the simple process of immediately entering the amount of a written check into the register and immediately subtracting it from the running balance. I didn't have an answer because really, it was that simple? Can I mention I was a few months into my eighteenth year, and obviously, my frontal lobe wasn't fully developed? I didn't know such things back then, but it would have made for one hell of an argument.

He finished up by saying he had made a deposit of one hundred dollars in my account and had paid around one hundred and twenty dollars in penalty fees. Before leaving (yes, he drove three hours just for this thirty-minute meeting and would drive three hours back to get home for dinner), he suggested I save the money I was making at my office runner job because he expected me to pay him back. In full. Not just for the penalty fees, but for the emergency loan to put my account in the black. I thanked him, told him I wouldn't make the same mistake again, and apologized.

Turns out, I would make that same mistake again a few years later. After that, though, I didn't turn to my father for any kind of financial help until much later in life when I found myself amid an unexpected divorce.

Watching him drive away, I felt conflicted. Yes, he had gone out of his way to "help" me. And yes, his response was reasonable by most standards. But why did it feel like it was a form of emotional blackmail, too? Every time he "helped" me, there were impossible strings attached...most of which were designed to remind me just what I disappointment I was. Yet, for as long as I could remember, asking him to teach me, help me, advise me, or coach me was an exercise in futility. He would condescend, scold, or mock and I would withdraw, shrink, and retreat. I was forever in a no-win situation with him that would only get worse.

Good girl, wrong. Again.

Chapter Twelve: Emerging

There were only three differences between the summer before my senior year in high school and the summer before my sophomore year in college. I had my first true love, an Austin native, to whom I wrote letters daily from work. I was now on the sorority side of rush season, so I accompanied my local sisters on numerous rush dates and gloried in the fact I didn't have to be on the other side of things again. And I could save some money for my sophomore year.

Otherwise, I returned to my healthy weight-loss regimen, as I had gained the predictable freshman fifteen. I went to work. I went running. I picked out patterns so Mom could whip up some new outfits, which my sorority sisters believed were made by my "little dressmaker in Dallas"–this seemed posher than saying, "My mom made it." And I counted the days until I could get back to Austin.

I moved into the sorority house one week before rush began–one of only a few sophomores given the opportunity to live there. We spent the week, from dawn until well after ten each night, learning every candidate's name and data points, practicing skits, practicing songs, practicing formal introductions (I already knew that part), and gearing up to score the best pledge class possible. What little free time I had, I spent with my boyfriend Adam, though his time also was limited due to fraternity obligations and soccer practice. I had lost all the weight I gained freshman year, plus a bit more. My bobbed hair had grown out, and I felt truly confident. It would be an exceptional year.

Because I was his girlfriend, I was invited to Adam's fraternity's rush parties–so much easier than ours! Just milling about, drinking, and being charming to the guys they wanted to recruit. Our process was five days. I think theirs might have been two. Anyway, I was credited with helping win over many of the guys they wanted. The first month of school, his entire fraternity showed up during our formal sorority dinner hour, stood in a circle around the room, serenaded us with the fraternity song, presented me with a yellow rose, and invited me to become a Little Sister. It was quite the moment, especially having felt all but invisible in high school! His house was not considered one of the top frats, but I didn't care; I loved him, and most of the guys were great fun.

Adam was at soccer practice that evening, so he wasn't there to present my rose. It wasn't the first time a man I loved let me down. It certainly wouldn't be the last. I chose not to dwell on it and, instead, went to the frat house with the other newly tapped Little Sisters for photos and a celebration. To this day, I can't exactly tell you what our official duties were, other than to set guys up with our sorority sisters, to help recruit, and to help our "little brothers" survive their Hell Week replete with hazing rituals that would be illegal today.

Adam was an exceptional student, so thanks to him and our nightly study dates at the student union, I got the best grades of my college career that sophomore fall semester. I was spared going to mixers and matches with other fraternities since he and I were a couple, but I went to Adam's frat parties nearly every weekend. By the end of fall semester, I had become bored with the entire scene.

Having taken two classes in the American Studies department my freshman year, I decided to pursue that as my major instead of English. I also joined The Daily Texan newspaper team, which required all newbies to serve a semester as copy editor before receiving writing assignments. Copy editing there meant writing headlines and cut lines for stories written by Daily Texan writers, as well as stories coming across the AP and UPI wires. That was a heady experience–to create headlines for articles written by professional journalists! I returned from winter break with a new focus, one that felt it would bring me closer to who I was meant to be.

That process would take nearly thirty-seven more years, but who's counting?

I worked two nights per week on the copy desk, requiring me to leave formal dinner at the house early and netting me glares from our housemother, Elaine. She maintained ridiculously high standards and expected us all to stay through dessert. I had better things to do than worry about her haughtiness. Nonetheless, in addition to my work on the newspaper, I studied hard in all my classes.

And I had a few lessons learned from my father confirmed by two other men.

One of my professors and mentors, for whom I worked as a research assistant, thought my intellect was greater than the field in which I had set my sights. As I helped him with his dissertation–mostly editing–he began talking to me about life in academia. He said I had the chops if it were something I wished to explore. He encouraged me to talk to the department head, a crusty older man with his bachelor's from Harvard and both his master's and doctorate degrees from Yale. He wasn't particularly approachable, but I followed my mentor's suggestion and made an appointment during his office hours.

I arrived in a nice outfit, hair and makeup done, bringing a few of my better papers with me for his review. He asked me to be seated and inquired about the reason for my visit. I explained I might wish to pursue graduate degrees in the field but wondered what that involved. I was hoping he'd advise me about things such as scholarships, fellowships, the length of the programs—something, anything that would be helpful! He told me he was familiar with my name from a few of the instructors, and I had a reputation for being an excellent student.

However. He stopped, looked me up and down, and with a flick of his hand said, "Problem is, as long as you spend as much time as you apparently do on your clothes, your hair, your makeup, and your nails, you'll never be taken seriously as a scholar."

I was flabbergasted! A woman couldn't be smart and attractive in equal measure? Seems I'd learned that lesson earlier, yet the world required women to try, anyway.

I thanked him for his time, went back to the sorority house, and called Mom to tell her about the conversation. Instead of hearing the outrage in my voice about his comments, she simply said, "Well, well, well–seems like we've made a scholar out of you, after all." I didn't know what to make of that then, because it seemed like she was almost mocking me for finally showing I was smart! In hindsight, I believe she was encouraging me to quietly give the old man the finger and just go for it.

I didn't ask for clarification.

Toward the end of my spring semester, I was required to meet with a liberal arts adviser to review my degree plan and select classes for the fall semester. I showed up at the appointed time and sat across his desk as he reviewed my progress, ready for what he would advise I take next to stay on track.

He asked if I'd come sit on his lap while we reviewed my options. Getting the desired classes and the optimal schedule really required intervention by the advisers, he explained with a lewd smile. I felt disgusted, but all I could do was politely thank him, leave the office, and request an appointment with a different adviser. I never explained why, and I never saw him again.

Instead, I changed my major back to English, with American Studies as my minor. My mentor was taking a position at another university, and I really didn't want the department chair further denigrating my aspirations. Plus, I really loved the class offerings, knew I wanted to write for a living, and greatly respected the faculty.

From my first semester at Texas, my father told me I was making a mistake. I should major in business instead of anything in the liberal arts. He was sort of okay with my initially majoring, for a few weeks, in journalism because at least that would be a tangible degree. But liberal arts?

During my next visit home, I told my parents over dinner I had changed my major back to English with my minor in American Studies. Mom nodded approvingly–she spoke often about how the critical thinking skills she gained in her liberal arts program served her well in law school, as they continued to serve her now. She said if I were so inclined, the rigor of writing inherent in a liberal arts program would prepare me well for law school. (I never wanted to go to law school.) I looked at my father, who was chewing methodically–as was his habit–thirty-two times per bite. I waited for him to say something.

"Well, Suzanne, all I can say is, I hope you either plan to marry well or become a teacher, because that's about all an English degree will get you."

Confined, once again, by a man's opinion. I should have been used to it by now, particularly since that perspective was reinforced by other men in my periphery. Everywhere, really.

I quietly vowed I'd prove him wrong, and within a few short years, I did.

The month before the end of the spring term, I had gone to Adam's fraternity formal, I had changed majors, and I had found an apartment near west campus since I planned to move out of the sorority house. I had had my fill of estrogen and petty bullshit, quite honestly, and was morphing into my new, bohemian, angst-filled writer persona, so perhaps I'd be taken more seriously as...whatever.

Active sorority sisters were required to attend every Monday evening meeting unless ill, out of town, or in class. One April Monday, after going through our chapter and committee updates, the chapter president said an important topic needed to be introduced for our votes. This should be good–to redecorate? To ask for fresher vegetables and leaner meat at dinner? To dig up the parking lot and install a pool to help with recruitment?

Seems that one of my pledge sisters, Jennifer, had been brought before the standards board of the sorority house. She pledged as a junior and was soon to graduate; she alone helped raise our chapter grade point average and already had been accepted to medical school. She moved out of the house at the beginning of the spring term and, gasp! She moved in with her boyfriend. That. Simply. Wasn't. Done. Do you agree, ladies?

Jennifer was sitting there proudly, stoically, knowing she was well on her path to a medical career but that she had to endure this kangaroo court to become an alumna in good standing. I looked over at her and smiled before raising my hand. The president invited me to speak, and boy, did I.

Invoking all my speech and debate skills, as well as a pinch of Mom's courtroom tone, I stood and gave my searing oratory. "If we as a chapter vote Jennifer out, we're hypocrites. YOU'RE hypocrites. And here's why. Those of you living here, in this house…many, if not most of you with boyfriends, have slunk back to the house at six or seven in the morning, having spent the night elsewhere. At least she," and I pointed to Jennifer emphatically, "at least Jennifer is being authentic. Her last semester before she goes to medical school, and she wants to be with her boyfriend instead of wasting time or money here, and you want to condemn her for that? C'mon, it's 1986. What's wrong with you people?"

I sat down, garnering a few feeble claps from some of my more empathetic sisters. Jennifer gave me a wan smile.

The president called for us to vote, writing "in" or "out" on a slip of paper we each placed in a box. Our Sergeant-at-Arms left the room to tally the votes. A few minutes later, she returned and said yes, most of the chapter had voted to remove her from the sorority.

I got up and left before the meeting was over, having made a clear decision based on my own moral compass, such as it was.

A few days after moving out of the house and returning home for the summer, I told my parents about the incident. I told them how wrong it was, with Mom nodding enthusiastically. "Good for you," she said, taking a sip of Chivas. They already knew I had signed a lease on my apartment, where I would live the next two years free of roommates or external drama.

What they didn't know was before moving out, I had informed the sorority president that I wanted to go "inactive," meaning I wanted to keep my national membership but wanted out of the chapter. I was brought before the standards board, just weeks after the Jennifer debacle, and was interrogated about my choice. Apparently, I had to meet one of the requisite reasons to stay in good standing with national.

"Is it because of financial hardship?" No. "Is it because you are leaving the university?" No. "Is it because your academic and extracurricular load is such that you can't meet the time commitments required by the chapter?" Okay, sure. That one worked. They told me I could think about it over the summer. I didn't have to participate in rush, but I would need to sign the formal documents when we returned for fall term.

After sharing my Norma Rae moment with my parents, I concluded by telling them I was leaving the chapter. Mom said while she could understand, maybe I should give it some time? I shook my head and said no, it's like what happened with the drill team. These women had shown me who they were; I didn't want to be one of them. She nodded.

Before refilling his drink, my father looked at me and said, "You quit drill team. You quit your journalism major. You quit your American studies major. Now, you're quitting your sorority. Seems like you have a pattern of quitting, doesn't it?"

Reduced, yet again, to a dumb girl who doesn't make smart decisions.

Good girl, judged.

Chapter Thirteen: Experimenting

There's something about me and junior years.

What would be my last summer home with my parents, I landed my first waitressing job at the brand-new Tex-Mex restaurant in town and learned I had a gift for gab that enabled me to make a boat-ton of money in tips. I also learned the importance of completing my degree, though there was never a question I wouldn't, because so many of the wait staff had either not gotten a degree or never tried. This was their livelihood. I also learned that the wait staff liked to party.

My relationship with Adam was on shaky ground; I had grown bored, and he had grown distant. So, I went out on a few dates with older guys at work. Nothing to write home about there. My parents came to the restaurant a few times and sat in my section; I was proud to show off how I handled my tables. Some days, I pulled a double shift, and though exhausting, it was profitable. Dad said he was proud of my work ethic. Mom deposited my money at the credit union at work, and over the course of the summer, my savings were nicely padded. I couldn't wait to get on with my junior year.

That August, my parents helped me move into my new furnished apartment. With ghastly wooden paneling and putty-colored shag carpeting, it was outdated by decades, but I was on the second floor in the corner, and my balcony overlooked a lovely greenbelt. It was like living in a treehouse!

Two weeks before we left Arlington, my father had a transient ischemic attack (TIA), or mini stroke, in the middle of the night, fainted, and broke his jaw, which required his mouth to be wired shut for six weeks. He still found a way to express himself through clenched teeth, mostly sounding like he was growling. Come to think of it, he growled most of the time anyway, so this wasn't new.

The air conditioner was out in my apartment unit, and moving day was mercilessly hot as only Augusts in Austin can be. As Dad grew more frustrated at moving load after load from both our cars (Adam was not available to help since he was at soccer practice), he began yelling–as best he could through a mouth wired shut–at my mother and me to hurry up and get this over with!

Moving into my first apartment to live by myself represented another important milestone worthy of celebration. So much for that. Again, the center of attention belonged to my father.

After getting my stuff into the apartment, my parents made the drive back to Arlington. I began unpacking and wondered how I would get through the steamy night. It was so hot, the vanilla candles I had bought for my living room were softening, emitting a delicious aroma but slowly melting, nonetheless. I invited Adam over, but he was tired from practice. I spent that first night by myself, windows open, while praying for relief. An inauspicious beginning to my next chapter, but it was a new chapter.

Classes started the next week, and soon thereafter, I got my first features assignment from The Daily Texan. I had formally gone inactive in my sorority and eased out of my Little Sister responsibilities–such as they were–with the fraternity. I began hanging out with some of the artsier students I met through the newspaper and through my classes. I cleared out the preppy clothes favored by sorority girls and moved toward a style that can only be described as "girl has no idea what she's doing," but at least the look was my own-ish. Maybe I would be taken more seriously.

It took many years to understand that you can have freedom, or you can have security, but you can't have both simultaneously. With the constraints of sorority life–the expectations, the rules, and the rituals–I had security, but not much freedom. Living among others, I had watchful, if not judgmental eyes keeping me in line. Having severed those bonds and now living by myself, I had all the freedom to make my decisions–to the degree anyone can while still on their parents' payroll–but no real security. I was too young to realize that. So, despite nineteen years of my father's lectures about life being a series of decisions, I definitely made some poor ones.

I suppose I was growing, but pains cropped up along the way, starting with my first official break-up with my first true love…the last vestige of my college security. His friends had become my friends, and so, loyalty being what it is, they broke up with me, too. Thankfully, I still had a few friends from The Daily Texan, as well as people I ran into, and drank with, from my freshman dorm.

Shortly after my break-up, I was walking down the west mall of campus and came face-to-face with Joel, who had lived down the hall in my dorm. I'd had a crush on him before Adam and I became an item. Joel was handsome, a year older, and very much out of reach. At the time, he had a serious girlfriend, but mostly, I believed he was simply out of my league. We chatted for a few minutes, and then he asked if I'd like to go out for a drink the following evening and might he get my phone number? It was a true Dear Diary moment, and I said of course, that would be fun.

I didn't expect he would turn into my next big love, but within a few weeks, that's exactly what he became.

We clicked along for several months, and for reasons I can't remember, we abruptly stopped seeing each other. I didn't seem to be very good at relationships–years later I would learn from one of many therapists that I not only had serious trust issues when it came to men, but I hadn't had a healthy relationship modeled for me by my parents. All I knew was that I was single, yet again. That should have propelled me into a deeper focus on my studies.

It didn't.

But it did send me into the arms of my best friend at the time, Shelly, who welcomed me to her apartment and handed me a glass of white Zinfandel–the three-dollar-a-bottle kind. I cried, she listened, we sipped, and repeated. I asked if she had any junk food–

I was ready to eat my feelings! She was perpetually on a diet, so she said she didn't have snacks, but would I like a cigarette? I hadn't smoked since my junior year in high school because it was disgusting, though I smoked a few one night in a Sixth Street bar with my friend Gina. I felt miserable the next day.

"Sure," I said, blowing my nose. I coughed through the first one, coughed through the second, and by the third, I had mastered the art of smoking. She laughed because I kept shaking the lighter as if I was trying to extinguish a match, but I had stopped coughing. I crashed on her couch that night, heading back to my apartment the next morning. Over my first cup of coffee, I took the pack of Benson & Hedges Menthol Lights she had given me from my purse and lit a cigarette. It didn't taste that good, but I had another. After finishing my coffee then heading to class, I realized I felt kind of buzzy. Awake. Not hungry. This was good!

I came back to Arlington a few weeks later for Thanksgiving break. Mom was in the kitchen that Wednesday afternoon, already beginning meal prep for the next day's feast. It was, after all, Dad's favorite holiday. I sat in the kitchen chatting with her, then leaned back and asked, with every bit of insouciance I could muster, if she would mind if I smoked in the house.

That scene from the Exorcist where Linda Blair's head spins around–that was Mom. She slowly approached me, almost predatory, hands on hips, and said, "What?" I asked again. She shook her head. "After all the haranguing you did to get your father and me to quit smoking when you were little, and now...you're smoking?" It was a rhetorical question. "I'll go outside." And so, I did.

That evening, when she told Dad I had taken up smoking, he simply said, "You'll regret it. Decisions, Suzanne, decisions. You keep making bad ones. Someday, you'll learn."

What I didn't say then, but told him a few decades later, when I still couldn't kick the habit, was I had learned that the combination of cigarettes and coffee enabled me to focus. And it suppressed my appetite, meaning I would lose weight...always the priority. Being heavy meant being unworthy of respect or admiration in his eyes. Earning his praise was my priority. Why did I keep getting it wrong?

Thanksgiving was as predictable as ever, not just with the traditional food, but the requisite squabbling before the mandatory family photo sitting in front of the massive spread. Proof positive that we were a normal, upstanding family having a Norman Rockwell moment. Dad was a creature of habit–actually, borderline OCD in a way that would only intensify as he got older–so we had to eat by two thirty at the latest so we could have the traditional turkey sandwich by seven thirty followed by pumpkin chiffon pie at eight. Fortunately, my friend and high school prom date called late afternoon and asked if I'd like to go watch what was then the traditional Texas versus Texas A&M football game. I didn't ask my parents so much as tell them I'd be out for the evening. They told me to have fun because, clearly, they weren't.

We went to a local sports bar to watch the game–I think Texas lost, sadly–then went to his friend's apartment for an impromptu party. One of his friends, Joe, had been in my biology class and was an all-around, fun guy, so it was no surprise the place was rocking! Simple Minds blared on the stereo, pot smoke permeated the room, and a full bar was lined up. My friend Mark got me a beer, then Joe offered me a joint. I had only tried pot once before and wasn't terribly impressed, but I took a few hits, then sat down on the couch to sip my beer and take in the scene. Joe appeared a little while later and asked if I had ever tried Ecstasy–then a legal drug favored by the nightclub crowd. I said I hadn't, wasn't sure I should. (My friend Tracey had told me I didn't need drugs because reality was enough for me, and I can say she was completely accurate.) Decisions, right? He said he'd just give me half to see how I handled it. I agreed and swallowed the pill.

After about thirty minutes, I wasn't really feeling different and said as much. He gave me the other half, and within thirty minutes, I was dancing without reservation and having, truly, a high old time. The happy lasted for maybe twenty minutes before I ran to the bathroom, closed the door, dropped to my knees and threw up Thanksgiving, threw up the drinks, threw up bile, then threw up nothing. Panting, shaking, and sweating, I laid my head on the toilet seat and cried. Something was wrong. I prayed and begged: Dear Lord, if you let me live through this, I'll never, ever do it again!

A short time later, Mark banged on the door. I told him I was sick, desperately sick. He went to get Joe, and I heard them conferring about whether they should take me to the ER. I yelled NO! That would push my parents over the ever-loving edge. I washed my face and walked out, green and unsteady, apologized (a lifetime habit), and asked Mark to take me home. I was beyond embarrassed; I was supposed to be the cool chick from Austin who knew how to hang.

I wasn't, apparently, and I didn't, obviously.

It was well after midnight when I quietly entered our house; all the lights were off. Even though my bedroom was just a few paces to the right, it felt too hard to navigate. So, I crawled onto the couch instead and covered myself with a blanket.

I awoke late the next morning with a headache unlike any I had experienced and feeling like I needed to puke yet again. After finishing in the bathroom, I came back to the sofa. Mom came in to see how I was, and taking one look at me, she said, "You and Mark must have tied one on!" She brought me some aspirin and a cup of coffee. I survived the experiment, and true to my promise, I never repeated it.

My drive back to Austin later that day was grueling since I couldn't shake my headache and didn't want to eat, but I made it safely and gave myself a quiet weekend to recover before resuming classes that Monday. The rest of the semester passed rather uneventfully; my grades weren't particularly good, yet I made it through the term with a handful of articles published in The Daily Texan. I was getting paid for them, even!

What I wish I had known then but didn't learn until graduate school nearly thirty years later was the pure correlation–unique to education–of applying myself completely to master concepts and getting rewarded with good grades. I also didn't see my college career as anything more than a prerequisite for landing a respectable job that would allow me to live indoors and buy groceries. As an undergrad, the simple gift of learning new things, full time, every day and all day, was lost on me. I was just trying to fast forward to the next chapter without really enjoying the one I was reading.

Winter Break of my junior year, my college grades arrived at the house a few days after I did. Back then, grades were sent to the student's parents unless otherwise instructed. I never otherwise instructed. Dad got the mail as I was sleeping in, and I heard him banging around the kitchen—his way of getting me out of bed. I groggily walked to the kitchen for coffee, which already was cold since it was nearly eleven o'clock in the morning. Mom was at work.

He sat down at the table, eyeing me coldly.

"Why do you think we're paying for college?" he asked. My first thought was, um, because not attending college was never an option? Because you want me to have a better life than you had? Because Grandma paid for much of it? Because you love me? Because that's what parents do, if they can? Just because?

I warmed up the coffee in the microwave and said something vapid like, "Because you want me to get an education so I can get a job?"

He nodded, then added, "And to prepare you for life. It's a competitive world out there." Yes, I knew this.

"How on earth did you get an F? God dammit, Suzanne, I thought you were smarter than this."

An F? What?

I had made a few Cs that semester–again, junior year apparently wasn't my thing–but an F?

"How. Do. You. Get. An. F. In. Swimming?" he thundered.

And then I remembered. I was going to get in tip-top shape, so I had enrolled in a one-hour swim class on the other side of campus at Texas' famed natatorium. But when the semester started, amidst writing for the Texan, the two science-for-non-science-major classes that were impossibly difficult for me, my upper-division courses in my major plus romantic turbulence, I had forgotten I had registered for it. I never went.

Shit.

"We won't continue paying for this level of irresponsibility," he said. "I won't have our money wasted like this. Decisions, Suzanne. Decisions. You need to get your head back in the game."

I wasn't sure which game he was referring to, as there were so many from which to choose.

I apologized and vowed I would do better. He left to run errands.

I was lost once again.

The last semester of my junior year began with my decision to take a part-time waitressing job at a twenty-four-hour deli and bar favored by the late-night crowd wrapping up their binge-drinking on Sixth Street. I worked Fridays, Saturdays, and Sundays from six at night until six the next morning. The schedule was hell on my sleep cycle, but the job itself was lucrative, and I met Jay, another soccer player. For the month I worked there, we were "a thing." He was smart enough, decently attractive, and a lot of fun–particularly when we just hung out. We lasted as long as my job there–one short month. I already had dropped a class, unbeknownst to my parents, because the job was making it hard for me to focus on studying. I got fired for refusing to save the uneaten kosher pickles and rye bread, placed on every table as a pre-meal nosh. We were supposed to return pickles and bread from the table back to the bins in the kitchen once the table was cleared. At some level, I knew this likely was a health code violation. And seeing the condition of many of the patrons, I also knew it was simply gross. After two warnings, I was fired the third time the manager caught me dumping the pickles and bread in the trash.

Around this time, I met Ralph, a lanky, scraggly guy who was the lead guitarist in a band. The lead guitarist! They played on Sixth Street–Austin's then hotspot–and his on-stage presence mesmerized me as he transformed into his character, "Richie Lather." You can't make this stuff up. This was the mid-eighties, and the band followed the pop culture trends, big hair and all. For a month, I got to tell the bouncers, "I'm with the band." I received free drinks and the chance to sit with the other groupies and to feel for a moment that I was an "it" girl. Richie Lather opted to cheat on me with a more enthusiastic groupie, and shortly thereafter, they became a thing. She got to say she was with the band. I stopped going to see them play. Really, they weren't that good.

By April, I felt frazzled, and my grades were tanking. Because I had dropped a class and had changed majors a few times, the only way I could graduate on time would be summer school. I briefly thought about taking a semester off and earning as much money as humanly possible waiting tables. I didn't voice this to my parents, obviously, but I was seriously off course and didn't know how to ask for help.

That seemed to be one of my life's themes that didn't really change in the years to come.

The only course I enjoyed that semester was creative writing because it gave me permission to tell stories, to find a voice. I used my short stories as therapy to express the many hurts I already had experienced. Yet, the stories didn't change anything other than to help me see that I might be a little crazy. My instructor thought I was gifted.

I only got one A that semester. It was in Creative Writing.

Convincing my parents to let me take summer school was a task unto itself. Dad sent me a lengthy letter—the style of which Mom and I always called his "poison-pen letters"—blasting me for my continued bad choices. My grades would be better if I spent more time studying and going to class than slinging burgers and Reuben sandwiches in a deli. Did I really expect them to keep supporting this nonsense? Would I ever grow up and learn some responsibility? "Remember, if you don't graduate by next May, you're on your own."

He signed these types of letters and later, emails, with "Your Father."

What I had failed to tell them, because I wanted it to be a surprise, was that I had applied to and been accepted for a summer internship with Texas Monthly Press. Surely, that would be something good to have come from a terrible semester?

I dreaded coming home but did so before beginning a full summer of courses to put me back on track. At dinner that first night, I proudly told them about my opportunity and how competitive the selection process had been. Dad put down his fork and asked, if I was going to summer school to get my grades and degree track where they needed to be to graduate on time, why on earth would I take an internship? I tried to explain that I needed the experience, and perhaps it would open some doors post-graduation.

"How much does it pay?"

It didn't. The payoff was having Texas Monthly Press on my resume. I had landed the coveted position. My father told me how foolish it was and once again, said I was not making good life choices.

Meanwhile, my mother had finished three glasses of wine during dinner, following a few glasses of Scotch beforehand, so she wasn't much help other than to glower at Dad as his tirade continued. I excused myself to put some laundry in the wash, then retreated to my room to read.

The argument began, starting with why my father couldn't ease up on me for just a second? It quickly turned ugly, with Mom yelling that the only women he didn't seem to criticize were those with whom he was having, or had had, affairs. In an instant, she was on the phone slurring at Van, his lover in Olympia, whose sex-filled letter had broken Mom's heart (and fueled her drinking). Now standing in my doorframe, I watched him grab the phone away from her, hang it up tenderly, then drag her down the hall and into their bedroom.

That was the one and only time I ever saw him use physical force with her, though I had been on the receiving end of it myself. He seemed unhinged, and I was afraid.

Then he came to my room and asked me to follow him. I was nervous but obeyed. He went to the wet bar and pulled out the bottle of Scotch. "See?" He pointed out the subtle horizontal marks he had made with a black Sharpie. Every night, he would examine the bottle to see how much she had drunk and make a hash mark to track the progression.

Not much different from the handwritten dossiers he wrote, enumerating the myriad ways Mom and I disappointed him, which I found in his desk drawer years before when looking for other clues about his secret life. Not unlike the hash marks he made on the ice cream containers when I was at the height of my binge-purge habit. But disturbing, nonetheless. He was tracking our "badness" without trying to understand or help. Just more fodder for his contempt and more justification for his philandering.

"You've got to get her to stop drinking," he said. When did this become my problem? I just looked at him.

"I can't get her to do anything," I said calmly. "Besides, I'm heading back to Austin the day after tomorrow."

He told me he didn't understand my selfishness. I only cared about myself, and it was obvious.

Well, someone had to, right?

Good girl, wrong.

Chapter Fourteen: Bitten

With one exception, that summer was the most extreme I've ever had. My Austin apartment complex had a pool, and nearly every day, people worked on their tans and drank whatever they could find. I went to my classes, mostly, then off to Texas Monthly Press, frequently, and then poolside to party with my neighbors, usually. I had begun dating a guy who lived in the same complex, a grad student named Bob who was shorter than I, but still interesting. He was from Minnesota and had an accent I hadn't heard before. He was a cyclist and urged me to ride my bike to class.

I wondered if that was a jab about losing weight.

He, his roommate, and his roommate's girlfriend liked to go out and hear local bands, so once we started dating — really dating — the four of us would hit the bluesy scene. Mostly small, hazy bars, where we saw Timbuk 3 several times before they landed their big record deal. We went to the live recording and filming of Stevie Ray Vaughan's "Live Alive" album and video, standing so close that some of Stevie's sweat hit my face as he rocked out on his guitar. We went to the second Farm Aid concert, hosted by Willie Nelson at Manor Downs, and saw the Grateful Dead, among other legends, while standing in the sweltering July Fourth sun. I was approached by a leather-clad biker who, looking at my bikini top, asked if he could bite my breast. I kept walking.

I had two literature classes, an anthropology class, and a biology class over the two-term summer. Again, I had taken on more than I could manage. I couldn't fail, though, especially going into my senior year. Focus, I needed. Fun, I wanted. Usually, I opted for the latter.

One afternoon in mid-July, I was taking my trash to the dumpster when I saw a cute tabby cat, as skinny as he was friendly. Having grown up with cats, I sat down on the curb and coaxed him my way so I could pet him. I scratched his back and ears; he came and sat in my lap. Maybe, just maybe, I should bring him to my apartment? He purred as I continued petting him until I began patting his rump like I always did with Ace. In a flash, he spun around and bit me hard on the inside of my left wrist, leaving a significant puncture wound unlike any I had experienced. Then he ran away. I didn't chase him.

I had little in the way of first-aid supplies, so I simply rinsed my wrist in warm, soapy water. Surely, that would be good enough. The next day, the wound was swollen and looked moderately infected to my untrained, non-Mom eyes. I called my mother and told her what had happened. She said I needed to get to the military hospital immediately because cat bites can be dangerous.

I thought she was suggesting cat scratch fever, but I didn't say that because the reference would have been lost on her. I also thought she might be overreacting. So, while I asked her for advice, I didn't take it.

Until the next day, when the wound began oozing. I drove to the hospital at Bergstrom Air Force Base and waited to be seen. A nurse evaluated the wound before telling me the doctor would see me shortly. When he came in and examined my wrist, he asked if I had seen the cat since the incident. I shook my head. He told me Austin was experiencing a rabies outbreak that summer for reasons unknown and I would be required to undergo rabies shots "just in case." I had no choice. That first day, I received four shots: one gamma globulin shot at the site of the wound, a shot in my hip, and a shot in each arm. He handed me my injection schedule, which required I return at three-day, then seven-day intervals, at the same time for the next four weeks to complete the treatment. Failure to miss a shot or stop them altogether would cause my death.

That's a lot to process and, given how sore and deathly ill I was over the next two days, compliance would be a challenge. I called my parents when I got home and, of course, Dad answered. Mom hadn't told him about the cat bite, so I explained what had happened and how I would get regular shots for the next month. I assured him my doctor had given me a note explaining any absences from class to my professors. He said nothing, and finally, I asked if he was still there.

He told me he couldn't understand how utterly stupid I had been to pet a feral cat. I didn't mention that Ace had been a stray. I brought him home from the nearby grocery store parking lot in the basket of my bike while we were in San Antonio. I didn't mention that story because, of course, he wouldn't find it relevant.

He didn't ask how I was feeling but said if I planned to use this as an excuse to drop summer school and, subsequently, would need to tack on an additional semester to graduate, I'd be doing so without their help.

I completed the full month of rabies treatment and never saw the damned cat again, but my professors were understanding, and I managed to get two Bs in the second summer term. Along with eight stitches in my left pinkie, the pad of which I nearly lost prying the lid off a partially opened can of kidney beans, and the return of Joel. He had missed me, he said, and would like to get back together.

Senior year was off to a good start.

While we had our share of arguments, Joel and I had an abundance of fun, too. I began imagining what it would be like to share my life with him, and we would daydream about a future in which I was a Pulitzer-winning journalist, and he would drive home in his Porsche. At the time, he knew what he wanted materialistically, but didn't know what career path would take him there. That semester, I took a part-time waitressing job at another restaurant on Sixth Street; he worked as a driver for a food delivery service. We had money to go to concerts and to movies and to "our place" for the best strawberry-swirl margaritas in town. We felt like grown-ups.

That winter break, I told my parents I would only be home for a week or so. I needed to get back to Austin to work, but mostly I wanted to get back to Joel. Dad questioned my priorities. While he never talked about the importance of family as related to his extracurricular activities, he made it clear my loyalties were displaced. After all they had done for me, weren't they worth a few more days of my time? The man who married his first wife right out of college (only to divorce her less than two years later) seemed to have forgotten what young love felt like.

I acquiesced, tacking three more days onto my visit, but was uncomfortable the entire time. I had to become a different person to avoid criticism. Yet I watched them carefully, trying to understand what kept them together. He had his "errands" and she had her Scotch.

A few nights after Christmas, Mom had drunk more Scotch than usual and, after dinner, began her verbal thrashing. Had I spent more money on presents for Joel than for them? Did I appreciate all they had purchased for me? Why was I only nice when I wanted something? On and on it went. I couldn't take it anymore, and in an unusual move, I fought back. I reminded her of the stories about Grandpa and his drinking and how she brought him out of a blackout so he could get to work by hitting him over the head with a table lamp. My father watched, quietly. She told me it was different, that I didn't understand. Oh, I understood all too well about certain holes in our heart we try to fill however we can.

I went to the bar, pulled out the Scotch and gin bottles, walked to the powder room, and emptied the booze into the sink. Returning to the living room, I held them in front of Mom, shaking, and said simply, "Stop. No more." She looked at me so coldly, I thought she would strike, but she didn't. She just seemed dumbfounded. I took the bottles to the kitchen and threw them away, turning around to see Dad standing in front of me.

"Why in the hell did you do that? Do you know how much money you literally poured down the drain?

I was confused. "You said you wanted me to help."

"Not like that."

The next morning, I packed my car early, thanked them for a nice visit and all my presents, and drove to Austin as fast as I legally could.

Good girl, done.

Chapter Fifteen: Finishing

I still dream about my last semester in college and all its associated stressors. First, in order to graduate, I had to take five classes–a fifteen-hour load. Three of the classes were upper-division literature classes, one of which was an intensive Shakespeare class. I took The History of Soviet Philosophy with Joel and, the worst of the worst that I kept putting off, a comprehensive math course. The workload was extreme, but on top of my waitressing job and spending time with Joel, I did the best I could.

The clock also was ticking, and I knew I needed to find a post-graduation job. That pressure alone exacerbated my anxiety. There was no way, absolutely no way, I would move back with my parents. So, I put together my first resume and submitted it to the career center on campus. I hoped to land a job with either a newspaper or a magazine. I wasn't picky.

I wasn't one of those students who paid much attention to the national economy–I had had no need–but I would graduate in 1987 as a major recession loomed in the U.S. Seems there weren't too many publications recruiting at The University of Texas, or anywhere, really. I did get a few invitations to interview; it felt like sorority rush all over again.

First, I interviewed for a position with a public advocacy organization with offices nationwide. This position interested me because it would enable me to make a difference, which I deeply craved, having felt powerless for so long. I got a call-back for a second interview, and then a third.

The second entity to request an interview was a federal intelligence agency; I received notification for an appointment immediately following Spring Break. The idea of being an agent intrigued me–serving in an exotic location and adopting different identities appealed to my desire to escape, to become someone different. Mom took me shopping while I was home for Spring Break and bought me a beautiful navy wool gabardine dress with a snappy belt — equally elegant and professional — along with my first pair of professional pumps. I already had a navy Coach bag, so my look was complete. I was ready!

The intelligence agency wasn't well-regarded by most of the students at Texas and protests were expected. Accordingly, my interview was a mission unto itself. I had to report to the career services offices at my appointed time where I was given an envelope directing me to the next location. There, I received another envelope with the destination at another area of campus. I wasn't used to walking in heels, but I made it to the designated location just five minutes before my thirty-minute interview began.

The gentleman interviewing me wore a solid black suit, white shirt, and a solid black tie, yet what really distinguished him was the four-inch vertical scar down one of his cheeks. He told me he was a counterintelligence agent in the Dallas office, focused on Soviet activities. I leaned in, my enthusiasm growing. He asked about my interest; I told him both of my parents worked (or had worked, in my father's case) for the federal government, and I felt this was the best way I could serve, too. He asked about my studies and what foreign language, if any, I could speak and read. I said I had taken nearly three years of French in college. (Apparently, they wanted people who were fluent in Mandarin, Russian, or Japanese.) He asked if I had any foreign experience whatsoever, and I told him I had lived in Germany. He took note, with interest, and asked for more details. I told him I was born there and moved to the States when I was about two years old. He sat back. Then he said if I was really interested in becoming an agent, I should get my master's degree in something relevant (more so, I suppose, than English) and learn one of the "in-demand" languages. As we were wrapping up, though, and I was doing my best to hide my disappointment, he advised me I may not be suited for this line of work because he didn't think I could "blend." I found this rich coming from a man with a gruesome scar on his face, but perhaps that's why he had an office job. And his comment felt ironic since I had felt invisible for so long.

My third interview request came from a retail apparel chain to become a management trainee. Why not? I liked their clothing and management sounded impressive; finally, my father would be proud that I was doing something business-y. I had a single interview, which went well given my prior experience in the service industry...I had some relevance–and was told they would contact me by mail in a few weeks.

Heading into the last month of college, I had interviewed to be a community activist, an intelligence officer-in-training, and a retail manager. I just knew I needed a job to pay the bills, since Joel and I decided we would live together once we moved to Dallas. He wanted to be close to his mother there, and I didn't want to be without him. But to say I didn't have a plan beyond that would have been the understatement of my young life.

I received an offer from the public advocacy group for a post in Boston, making poverty wages. I knew my parents wouldn't help support me–my father had made that point resoundingly clear–and while I was told many of the young activists lived in communes, that wasn't my idea of a good time. I politely declined the offer, which they countered with an opportunity to work in San Marcos, Texas, just a short drive from Austin. Still, the money wasn't enough, and I didn't want to wait tables to supplement a meager salary. Again, no thank you.

The letter from the retail corporation arrived just a few weeks before graduation, offering me the position of Assistant Manager-in-Training at the mall location in Plano—just north of Dallas—for a whopping $14,000 per year (plus benefits!). I accepted and told them I would report for duty in mid-June (assuming I graduated) once Joel and I found an apartment, moved, and got situated. I was on my way!

I called my parents, with whom I had already discussed my options, and told them I had accepted the offer. Silence. Then my father said if I had wanted to go into retail management, I didn't really need an expensive college degree from a prestigious university to do so, and really, did I waste four years of their money on tuition, room, board, books, etcetera? I thought he would be proud of me for trying to be fully self-sufficient and make good decisions. Yet in that moment, I only felt ashamed I had once again disappointed him.

Despite several borderline panic attacks, I finished all my courses with grades allowing me to graduate. I had crossed the finish line! After the College of Liberal Arts graduation ceremony, my parents took me for margaritas at my neighborhood bar before we walked through campus, taking pictures of the place I had called home for four years. It was more emotional than I expected; I had been so focused on "the rest of my life" that I took most of what I would immediately miss for granted. I began pining for Austin well before I packed my car to drive back to Arlington. If only I had made better plans, better decisions, I wouldn't have had to settle for a job choice I didn't really want but took out of necessity. Oh, well.

They took me to a fancy restaurant for graduation dinner, where I ate pheasant for the first time and felt quite grown up. Expecting a special graduation gift, my eyes lit up when my father handed me a card. Maybe it contained a big check, or one of his notorious IOUs for a future something of my choice. Mostly, these IOUs never materialized, but still.

Instead, it was simply a card from him, signed in his signature green ink, with a P.S. that said, "Congratulations! You're officially off the family payroll."

No expressions of pride, encouragement, love–just a termination, of sorts. Message received, loudly and clearly.

Good girl, dropped.

Chapter Sixteen: Jumping

Interestingly, possessing a college degree did nothing to help me navigate my first eight months out of college. Joel and I found a nice, two-bedroom apartment near Plano which we decorated with an odd assortment of furniture, all hand-me-downs from our families, and did grown-up things like making dinner every night and renting movies from Blockbuster. Joel had yet to find a job. From my first day as Assistant Manager, I realized what a mistake I had made. I didn't have an office, for starters, though there was a desk in the stockroom. No, I had to be on the floor, selling, stocking, and folding, folding, folding the damned shirts and sweaters and jeans in just the right shape so everything would be orderly in the retailer's famous way.

On my lunch or dinner breaks, I would wander to the food court and get popcorn and a Diet Coke; on desperate days, I'd eat a corn dog. And the real kicker: no one informed me during the hiring process I could only wear clothes from that retailer, and they had to be in season–full-price, though we got a discount. The minute an item went on the sale rack, we couldn't wear it anymore. Quickly, I accumulated a hefty balance on my first credit card; it didn't occur to me to just buy two outfits and wear them every other day.

Within a few months of starting, they transferred me to the brand-new children's concept store at The Galleria. I was pleased to have been chosen and looked forward to working in a more prestigious location. I used to enjoy babysitting, so how hard could it be dealing with children and their anxious parents on a daily basis?

Hard. Very, very hard.

Unless you've been called to the retail industry, as many lovely people have, you're pretty much ruined once you get through the Back-To-School season. Every day, I returned home exhausted and resentful, especially since Joel had only landed a part-time job, also in The Galleria. To feed my creativity, I'd style the front windows, putting together adorable ensembles on the little-bitty mannequins. When the regional manager surprised us with a visit, I was quickly told I had to follow the merchandising book to the letter. No freestyling.

I continued looking for writing jobs while bracing for the holiday season — this time, not because of my traditional family drama, but because of the retail frenzy. My brain was twitchy from no creative outlet, so I started a regional newsletter for the company, putting together stories, typing them on my electric typewriter, cutting the stories into columns, laying them out, taping them down with transparent tape, using press-on letters with interesting fonts for the headlines, and taking it to the regional office to copy and distribute. (I did all of this on my own time, incidentally.) After seeing my first edition, the regional manager was impressed and encouraged me to continue.

It was my only means of maintaining my sanity, especially when the holiday push began in early November.

Neither of my parents came to see me at work, nor did they visit our apartment, nor did they invite us to dinner except that Thanksgiving. Mom was traveling more frequently; Dad was refereeing high school basketball games. They were busy, I guess, but I felt untethered…I was so accustomed to being bound that once free, I felt abandoned.

When I spoke with them, after hearing their stories, I'd try to share some amusing anecdotes of my own–usually about the high-school and college students I was "managing" or a particularly awful encounter with an entitled Highland Park parent. They weren't really interested. Sadly, neither was I.

My relationship with Joel started to crumble, but I didn't know how to fix it, and my parents had hardly set an example of peaceful cohabitation. I didn't have any friends locally, and I had little in common with the other area assistant managers with whom I'd occasionally grab a drink. In short, I was miserable everywhere, just like in high school. My life didn't fit me. At least, it didn't fit the idea I had of myself.

Predictably, my attitude became negative, and that was most manifest at work. One evening, shortly after Christmas, my store manager and the district manager who originally hired me pulled me aside and confronted me. I wasn't exhibiting values inherent to the brand, though they weren't that eloquent. I was impatient with the customers and the employees, and something needed to change.

I agreed. Something needed to change quickly. So, I quit.

How good it felt! I had made a huge life decision without discussing it with anyone. Freedom!

That evening, I told Joel, and he sat quietly before asking where I thought I might work since we had bills to pay. I had no savings, nor did he. I was too naïve to worry, so I just said I'd figure it out. I called my parents, and my father completely lost it, reminding me again of my track record of making poor decisions, and this time, he would not bail me out. (When had he, actually?) He hoped I had incurred little debt–I had–and that I had taken his advice to always have cash savings on hand–I didn't. I chain-smoked while he lectured, feeling every bit the failure he always seemed to believe I was.

A few days later, Mom invited me to lunch, so we met at her downtown office, and she asked if I would mind if Emmitt, one of her fellow attorneys whom I'd known for nearly ten years, joined us. He literally watched me grow up, and I always liked him, so I agreed happily. We went to my favorite casual restaurant at The Adolphus Hotel, and honestly, I was relieved to be around real adults. He asked me about my plans, and I told him I was desperately trying to find a writing job. I had a solid portfolio of my articles from The Daily Texan. I just needed someone to give me a shot.

He asked if I had ever considered public relations, and Mom immediately perked up, saying she had worked in public relations for Pacific Bell before she married my father, and of course, I'd be a natural! I asked what all it entailed, and upon hearing that I'd be writing newsletters and coordinating press events and beyond, it felt right. I nodded hopefully. Emmitt told me his cousin worked for one of the big PR/advertising agencies in town — actually, one of the biggest in the Southwest — and said I could use his cousin's name as a reference. The minute I returned to my apartment, I sat down to create the cover letter of all cover letters, introducing myself and writing that "Harry Bell said the agency often takes people off the streets if they have the right talent; while I'm not quite on the streets yet, I'm ready to make a difference," or something to that effect. I put it in the mail along with my one-page resume and crossed my fingers.

(P.S. I learned after the fact that Harry Bell was the sandwich-cart man. My earnest reference to him likely gave the execs quite a laugh.)

Two days later, the PR vice president called me and said, "You give good letter." I'll never forget that line! He asked me to come in the next day for interviews–four hours' worth, as it turned out. I think I spoke with every ranking person on the PR side of the firm. I was in love! The office was at The Crescent–a timeless, European-inspired property near downtown Dallas–and everyone there was so chic, sophisticated, successful...or so they appeared. As the evening drew to a close, I was asked to return the next morning for a writing test. Of course!

I chattered at my mom for an hour, convinced this would be my big career move! I hesitantly told my father, and he wished me well, but said not to get my hopes up. By this time, I had moved into our apartment's spare bedroom, but Joel kindly offered polite encouragement.

As I've long since learned, public relations requires more than an ability to write. There is a style and a flow that is expected, whether it's a press release or a public service announcement or the official response to a crisis or an executive speech. The test I took included all of these and more. I fumbled my way through, and when the allotted four hours concluded, I had finished to the best of my ability. Everyone was friendly and wished me good luck as I left.

The next morning, the phone rang, and it was the president of the PR division. I held my breath. He said while everyone loved me and I had an upbeat presence and clearly, I could write, it was also clear I didn't know squat (my word) about PR. My writing test scored a C, he said, but he saw potential and would be happy to connect me with some of the smaller agencies in town where I could learn the craft.

I felt crushed. And unemployed with the clock ticking and my debt growing. Decisions–life is about decisions, right? There and then, I made one of the most important decisions of my life. I told him if I was to learn, I wanted to learn from the very best. This agency managed some of the most coveted accounts in the nation, including a major packaged foods company, a leading beverages corporation, and more. Might he consider letting me work as an intern?

I stopped talking. He paused, cleared his throat, and told me he hadn't considered that. He'd make a few inquiries and would call me back. And he did, just fifteen minutes later, offering me an internship for twenty hours a week at five dollars an hour, no benefits. I immediately said yes, and he told me to be at the office the following Monday.

Mom was already at work, so I called her first, nearly screaming with joy that I had gotten my break! She asked if we needed to go shopping because my clothes from my retail wouldn't be adequate– far too casual for an up-and-coming PR maven! I told her I couldn't afford it, and she said this was her treat. We went shopping that Saturday, and she helped me get my first professional wardrobe together but asked that I not tell my father.

No problem there.

When I called him to share my good fortune, he said he hoped I'd be able to pay the bills on eight-hundred dollars a month; wasn't my share of the rent four-hundred and fifty? And are they taking out taxes? Always about the money. Pfft. I'd think about that later.

Who could have predicted that within the first three weeks, my hours would grow to forty per week? By the second month, I was averaging fifty hours a week and was assigned to the team managing a new product rollout for the global packaged foods client. By the third month, I had found an apartment closer to work and told Joel we needed to split. By the fourth month, I was in New Orleans managing the two-day press event for the packaged foods giant, with my first professional Account Coordinator position at a rival agency waiting for me upon my return. While my initial salary would be just $15,500 per year (plus benefits), I no longer felt invisible.

Good girl, rising.

Chapter Seventeen: Losing

Shortly after starting my new agency position and breaking things off with Joel, Dad planned a trip to Olympia, Washington, to begin the process of selling Grandma's house. He had recently moved her into a nursing home. I hadn't seen her since her last visit to Arlington when I was in high school, though we still exchanged letters. So, he invited me to fly up for a brief visit; he would pick me up at the airport since he had arrived several days earlier. It wouldn't be until after his death that I learned on each of his visits, he carved out time to spend with his long-time and long-distance mistress, Van. I had wrongly assumed he had ended the relationship.

Grandma had an exceptional gift, borne either from a fundamental aesthetic or financial limitation, of scouring rummage sales and thrift shops to find hidden treasures. With love and attention, each could once again become useful, relevant, and often, quite valuable. Her home was a veritable museum of antique furniture and unusual art pieces that seemed mismatched individually, yet in aggregate, exuded a humble elegance. If one looked closely, her careful repairs–to the upholstery, the veneer, or the accessories–could be detected, but never detracted from the effect. Born and raised during the Depression, my father viewed such items as nothing more than second-hand junk and could not understand my mother's and my fascination with, and even longing for, pieces with "history." He preferred new and shiny; we preferred old and imperfect.

His preferences never changed.

Growing up, I didn't get to see her often because she lived across the country, but when I visited, I loved accompanying her on her treasure hunts. She taught me to look past the obvious and see the underlying beauty in everything. The key, she always said, was to evaluate an item's fundamental character — its "bones," as she called it. Under all the paint, behind the chipped veneer, or peeking from beneath a poor finish might await a chair, a dresser, or a table that, with careful rehabilitation, could become a showstopper. "You have to see its potential," she explained. My mother had a close relationship with Grandma, and she eagerly absorbed every lesson. With time, Mom had acquired an eye for antiques too…much to my father's chagrin.

My grandfather died in 1974, and while she missed him, I believe Grandma also enjoyed living independently. She was a devout and active member of her church, yet I think she found her greatest comfort in the home she had created. It wasn't until I was in my early twenties–some sixteen years after Grandpa died–that my father recognized the need to move her from her home and into an assisted living facility. I wasn't privy to any discussions they may have had, and I can guess that she may have objected, but at eighty-eight years of age, she needed greater care than she could provide for herself.

After Dad met me at the airport and while driving to her facility, I remember feeling torn. Of course, I would want as much of her furniture as I could fit into my small apartment, yet the finality of what had yet to become final felt like a veiled betrayal. Was I a modern-day carpetbagger, benefiting from her loss?

Turns out, she was already gone, mostly. We arrived at the center to pick her up and take her to her house for one last visit. I was ill-prepared for the sights, smells, and sounds of what was purportedly the best assisted living center in the area. The halls were lined with people in wheelchairs, moaning or sleeping or staring at the walls; others wandered, wringing their hands and wearing confused expressions. The desk nurse greeted my father by name, and as I watched in horror, she bellowed for my grandmother–my elegant, beautiful grandmother—using only her first name and with a tone one might take with a misbehaving child. I looked at my father, prepared to voice my indignation, but he just shook his head.

A few moments later, I saw Grandma peek around the corner as if she were a shy child, then slowly walk toward us wearing a dirty housedress and fraying slippers. Her hair, still more naturally brunette than gray, was unkempt and in dire need of washing. Out of context, I'm not sure I would have recognized her. She looked at my father, then looked at the nurse who reminded her she was going to see her house. She nodded wordlessly, and we walked to the car.

With time and maturity, I've learned not to chatter incessantly when nervous. "Nattering," Mom always called it. In that moment, though, I couldn't contain myself. As we drove toward her home, I tried to tell her about my first "real" job working for a major advertising agency. She would nod, then call me by my mother's name. I would explain who I was, and she would nod, then ask about how our other sisters were doing (she had six of them). I would explain I wasn't her sister, and she would nod, then she would ask me how my husband–her father–was feeling. I finally fell silent, and a few moments later, I looked up to see my father giving me a gentle look in the rear-view mirror. In an uncharacteristically tender move, he reached his hand around to pat my leg in assurance that it wasn't me whom Grandma had forgotten. It was everything.

Dad pulled up to her house, and I waited for him to help her out of the passenger seat before climbing out of the car. I had forgotten how beautiful her home and garden had been, though both now showed signs of neglect. It was late spring, and the apple trees in her front yard already had begun to bud, promising a generous crop in the fall. The blackberry and raspberry bushes along the drive, though clearly untended, were bountiful with fruit that wouldn't be harvested, and a taunt of Grandma's signature jam that wouldn't be made. I wondered if her cellar was still stocked with the jams and apple butter she put up each year before my father moved her. I wanted to go inside. I was afraid to go inside. I decided to smoke a cigarette instead. My father was walking her carefully up the steps, and he turned to look, but for once, did not admonish me for my bad habit...one he had kicked when I was eight. I heard my grandmother telling him the farm sure seemed small and asking when these other houses had been built. Grandma had grown up on a farm on vast acreage. In her mind, she was still there.

I stubbed out my cigarette in the street and walked slowly to the door, entering a home I hadn't seen in nearly fifteen years, but that would be indelibly etched in my brain. Everything was as it had been, though covered in a thin shroud of dust. I watched as she wandered through each room, wringing her hands nervously. She would look back at my father for reassurance before venturing into the next room, pausing to run her fingers across a table or peer curiously at a vase she seemed afraid to touch. I followed them into the small kitchen, then into the room that had been my grandfather's workroom, then back into the kitchen. I didn't know what to do.

"Mother, would you like Suz to fix your hair?" my father said a little too loudly.

She looked up at him, then looked at me and said softly, "Who?"

I bit my lip to keep from crying. I wanted to hug her, to tell her who I was, but I simply stood quietly. Dad pulled out the kitchen chair and helped her sit down. Then he went upstairs to her bathroom and returned with a comb, a brush, and a pair of scissors. He set them all on the table and told me he was going to check the backyard.

My freshman year in college, when I lived in a co-ed dorm, was in the early eighties, and most of the non-fraternity boys wanted to sport the whole "Fast Times at Ridgemont High" look, down to the ridiculously spiked hair. I had watched my stylist enough to know the basics about cutting hair, so I used my sewing scissors to provide haircuts for beer money. The good news about that style was it wasn't terribly exact, so my novice skills weren't an issue. I never thought I would have to recall even the basics, yet here I was.

I took the brush and began gently to untangle Grandma's hair. Then I ran the comb under warm water before beginning the task of restoring her lifelong hairstyle of neat bangs and a chin-length bob. I had only cut a few strands when she asked me if my new job gave me the chance to write. I nearly dropped the scissors.

"You always wanted to be a writer, so I hope your boss is giving you every opportunity," she said quietly. "Do you? Do you get to write?"

"Not as much as I would like, but hopefully as I get more experienced, they will let me," I said, my eyes moistening.

"And what about that boyfriend of yours, Joel? Wasn't that the boy you went with in college?"

"Yeah, that didn't really work out," I said as I carefully measured each section of her bangs to ensure my line was even. She looked me in the eye and smiled.

"You know, your grandfather and I didn't marry until, by all accounts, I was considered a spinster," she said. "I had the chance to have a career and make my own living, and I never regretted it, not once," she said proudly. She had attended a "normal school," a college of sorts where she earned her teacher's certificate but had elected to become a bank teller instead.

"I like to think I was better off, once your grandfather passed, for having learned to live alone when I was young. Don't be in too much of a hurry, my dear," she said. "You have plenty of time for everything."

We continued to chat for the next ten minutes. I finished her hair, then asked if she would like a neck rub. She nodded, so I gently massaged her neck and shoulders until my father returned, raising his eyebrows in a question I could only answer with a smile. My grandmother remembered me after all.

Until she didn't. As we helped her upstairs to see the rest of her home for one last time, she began asking about the farm and if my husband could still find trustworthy help. The curtains had closed yet again.

We drove her back to the center in time for her to have dinner, promising we would return in the morning. I was scheduled to fly out that following afternoon. I hugged her and told her I loved her. She nodded before turning and shuffling into the dining room.

"Up for dinner? Or maybe a drink first?" Dad asked after we had been driving silently for what seemed like hours. I nodded, still sorting my thoughts.

A few minutes later, we pulled into the parking lot of a waterfront restaurant along Puget Sound, where my father ordered us each a dirty martini, a dozen oysters, and a healthy platter of Dungeness crab. I nibbled at my food but gulped my martini, ordering a second and then a third. I can't remember what we discussed and, knowing us, it probably wasn't that deep. When we got back to Grandma's house, I was a little woozy and a lot weepy. My father handed me a pad of sticky-notes. "Put one on any piece of furniture you'd like to have," he instructed. "Just know that it must fit in your place because we don't have room. I'm not paying to move furniture just to put in storage." I imagined they could have made room but, well, antiques. He went to pour himself a Scotch as I carefully surveyed each room.

The camelback couch upholstered in a sage velvet was my first choice, followed by a beautifully handcrafted escritoire in the traditional Swedish style–a wedding gift, he told me, from Grandma's father. I selected her walnut dining room table, two mahogany end tables, her delicate coffee table with clawed feet, and another occasional table. Then I ventured upstairs to her bedroom, closing my eyes to breathe in the smell of her powders and soaps permeating the air–a clean and simple scent. I looked at her double bed, carved from mahogany, the matching vanity with a mismatched bench she had upholstered, and the dresser–as unique as anything I had seen–and knew these would become among my most cherished pieces. I attached a sticky note to each before going back downstairs.

"Do you remember falling down those stairs when you were little?" Dad asked from the couch. I shook my head, then looked back at the wooden staircase. "I did?"

"You had this game you would play," he said, stopping to take a sip of his Scotch, "and we kept telling you not to do it, but Grandpa thought it was adorable. You never wanted to go to bed when everyone was still awake downstairs, so you would run up the stairs yelling 'night' then you would run down the stairs yelling 'morning!' Over and over and over again. Except the one time you slipped and tumbled down about six stairs. That broke you of it," he said, chuckling.

"Oh my God, Dad! That's terrible! Did I need stitches? Did I have a concussion?" I started laughing.

"No stitches, just a nice little goose egg," he responded, tapping the back of my head.

"No wonder I'm bad at math," I said, getting up for a glass of water.

"I'm pretty sure it wasn't a traumatic brain injury, Suzanne," he said, still chuckling.

We talked for a few more minutes before he handed me a stack of photo albums. "You might want to go through these," he said. "You want to sleep in Grandma's room?"

I simply nodded; my attention was now fixated on the books. We said our goodnights, then I spent the next hour looking at pictures of my grandparents, great aunts and uncles, my father and others I could never identify before finally giving in to exhaustion. I walked carefully up the stairs with my overnight bag, changed into my nightgown, brushed my teeth, and then slipped into Grandma's bed for the very first time. While the feather mattress would need replacing, everything else about the set was perfect, exactly as it was.

It had good bones.

The next morning, I took one last walk through the house before saying my goodbyes. I didn't want to think about who would buy it and if they would love it as I had. We got into the car and headed to see Grandma.

When we got to the room she shared with a woman whose name I can't remember (but whose angry countenance I'll never forget), Grandma was sitting up in her bed, wearing her brocade bed jacket adorned with a brooch, matching clip-on earrings and two bobby pins in her neatly brushed hair. We asked if she would like to sit out in the garden for a few minutes, and she nodded, but when she got out of bed, she was unstable on her feet. Dad went to get a wheelchair from the front desk staff. I told her she looked pretty.

"It's so nice of you to visit me. How I've missed your stories about law school," she said, taking my hands and squeezing them. Looking at me, she saw my mother.

"You know I always love seeing you," I said softly. My father came in with the wheelchair, and together, we helped get her situated before going outside to breathe in some fresh air and sunshine. She blinked and blinked as she looked at the flowers. I'm not sure she had been in this garden before.

We sat together for about fifteen minutes as she asked about her father, asked me how my work as an attorney was going, and how her now deceased brother, Henry, had been feeling lately before her eyes closed. I thought she was falling asleep. Then she opened them and looked me in the eye, smiling.

"You promise you'll remember what I said yesterday," she said. "Everything in its time. You don't need to be in a rush for anything. Trust God and He will lead you," she said, taking my hands and kissing them. I reached down to hug her, tears cascading down my cheeks.

"I love you, Grandma," I whispered into her ear. "I will always remember what you said."

My father told me we needed to go so I wouldn't miss my flight; I had to go back to work the next day. I didn't want to leave because I knew I would never return. We took Grandma back to her room where the television was blaring, and her roommate stared defiantly at the screen. I opened my mouth to say something, as Grandma had covered her ears, but my father shook his head. Grandma sat down gingerly on her bed.

"I think it's time for my nap," she said.

I didn't know what to say.

"Would you like some lunch first?" my father asked her.

"I think it's time for my nap."

I sat next to her and gave her a hug. Her eyelids were drooping; we didn't make eye contact. I told her again I loved her and would see her soon. She nodded. I hugged her again, gave her one last look, then we departed for the airport.

Grandma died five months later, two days before she would have turned ninety.

I was in my apartment that Saturday afternoon, having just returned from the grocery store before it started raining. My windows were open, and I was listening to music while deciding what I might cook for dinner. The phone rang. In those days, people either answered their phones without fear they were about to be scammed by a telemarketer, or they let their answering machine take the message. Caller ID didn't exist.

I turned down the stereo and answered. The caller asked curtly if I was Suzanne, Emily's granddaughter. I confirmed my identity, and she introduced herself as calling from Grandma's nursing home. I sat down. She then said, quite formally, that she was sorry to inform me my grandmother had expired.

Expired. As if she were a jar of mayonnaise or a vehicle registration. So very, very cold.

She told me she had tried to reach my parents but only got the answering machine and this wasn't a message she would leave in that fashion. I thanked her and told her I'd take care of reaching them.

I lived about thirty minutes away from their house. I drove as fast as the rainy highways would allow, still in shock but concerned about how my father–an only child–would react to the news. She had lived a long and seemingly happy life. Yet, she was Dad's only living parent, and he had cared for her as well as he could, though distanced by miles and a lifelong resentment of what, I'll never understand. Theirs had always been a difficult relationship, as were all but a select few of his relationships, but I had to believe he loved her. Didn't he?

By the time I reached their house, the rain had subsided. I parked and ran to the door, ringing the bell since the door was locked (and I didn't have a key). Dad answered and looked at me in surprise. "Well, hello there," he said, gesturing for me to come in. I couldn't wait–the tears and words flowed.

"She's gone, Daddy," I stammered. "They called and said Grandma has expired. Expired!" I was still standing on the front walk, unable to move as I watched him.

His face broke into a smile. "Thank God," he said.

That was his reaction to learning his mother had died? Happiness? Relief? A few decades later, I learned how exhausting and complicated it is to care for an aging parent, particularly one with dementia. Even so, while glad the suffering is over–theirs and yours–a decent person would have said something like, "I know how hard this is, but she really is in a better place," or something equally reassuring. "Thank God" wasn't reassuring; it was insulting and selfish.

I shook my head and said, "I can't believe you," before turning and walking to my car. Mom came out and called me, asked me to come in, said I didn't need to be driving right now. I don't remember responding, just jumping in my car and zooming away.

My father handled Grandma's arrangements; she wanted nothing beyond a graveside service since everyone she knew had died, besides us. Despite my plea, he did not invite Mom or me to go, even as we were both grieving her loss. I couldn't afford a plane ticket on my own, but it wouldn't have mattered since he made it clear he didn't want us there. He took from us the opportunity to pay our respects to the woman we loved more than he did.

I imagine he sought comfort with Van while he was there.

We imbue certain words with much more meaning, more gravitas than our experience tells us we should. Family. To me, it was a longing for security among people who loved you, no matter what, and who put your needs before their own. That's how I thought of family; clearly, the concept meant less to my father. For him, I suppose family was duty, much like his military service. You didn't have to like it, enjoy it, or appreciate it–you just had to do it without emotion.

I could not forgive his coldness, nor his utter disdain for how Mom and I were feeling. He didn't care, as he was busy putting his inheritance to work. He had gotten what he wanted. Though he didn't seem to notice, I began distancing myself, and I felt my own sense of relief. Mom tried to explain his behavior; I stopped trying to change her mind.

Good girl, growing.

Chapter Eighteen: Ascending

Nearly two years into my career, I was leaving the agency to run an errand at lunch when I got into a car accident right outside our building. It was raining, and I didn't see the silver sedan coming my way as her lights weren't on, so I started to turn left before realizing it was too late–I t-boned her car and crushed my front bumper. Yes, I got out of the car, and of course, I asked if she was okay. I noticed with concern her toddler in the backseat. Everyone was fine, and we exchanged information.

My car was barely drivable. I called Dad and asked him what I should do. He told me to call my insurance carrier and take it from there. He said he hoped I had enough to cover any deductible, still set at one thousand dollars because "you don't insure your own stupidity." Accidents, though, happen. The poor, bilious green Honda Accord that had been reliable throughout college and the early years of my career, now a slight embarrassment to drive, was totaled. All I could salvage were the seat covers my father had bought me for Christmas to hide the sadly shredded velour upholstery. At least I didn't have to worry about the deductible.

I told my father the news. Fortunately, they were in the process of buying Mom a new car. They had planned to trade in her sleek Nissan 300ZX, but I was welcome to it! It had a beautiful heliotrope exterior and was thoroughly decked out with T-tops and a wicked sound system. I was thrilled! I'd have to remember how to drive a stick shift, but I'd finally have a car that suited my new life in Dallas. I was beyond grateful.

But then, the catch. Always, always the catch.

He wasn't going to just give me the car. No, I'd have to make monthly car payments until what I paid equaled the Kelley Blue Book value, top end. I had never had a car payment and was living pretty much month to month, but I needed transportation, so I agreed to the deal.

He drew up a contract. My father loved drawing up contracts. There would be many more in the decades to follow. He enjoyed having the upper hand.

At the time, it was okay because that car was seriously fun, especially with the T-tops off. Guys were impressed I had a sports car and could drive a stick. I did get pulled over a few times for speeding but could talk my way out of the tickets. (The benefits of being young and wearing short skirts.)

In PR/advertising, like so many fields, the only way to get a bigger title and corresponding salary is by moving, and so I did. In the space of the next three years, I changed jobs three times: the first, a short stint with a national PR firm whose leadership changed my third month on the job. I knew the new regional president from the agency where I interned, and he was a weasel, both in behavior and appearance. I left for an account supervisor post at a local PR/advertising agency where I served as lead on several important accounts and managed two younger employees. One of my clients was a national healthcare company that soon needed a new manager of corporate communications. I adored the point person, so I threw my hat into the ring. He offered me the job at a lunch meeting, carefully writing my salary discreetly on a slip of paper, placing it face down, and pushing it across the table. It was like something from a movie! I told him I'd think about it and call the next day. (One of the tips my father had given me, so it must be right, yes?)

I called my parents that evening, ebullient that so early in my career, I'd gotten my first corporate offer! To think this was just three-plus years after my first job in retail. See? I didn't have to teach or marry well after all, Dad, to put my college degree to work. I must admit to feeling smug.

My mother was less than optimistic, having first-hand knowledge of the company through her work for the government prosecuting healthcare entities and individuals that tried to defraud the Medicare system. She said the company had some issues, clearly, and if I was to take the job, she'd have to recuse herself from any cases in which the company was involved. Seemed fair to me, though I later learned that recusal came at a marginal professional cost to her. My father, meanwhile, launched into another diatribe about decisions and how changing employers so many times would characterize me as a "job hopper." I countered that I'd be making more money, and this was a long-term opportunity. Not only did they have an employee stock ownership plan (employees were owners!), but I'd be eligible for an annual bonus. He asked how much money I had in savings and how many credit cards I was juggling. So much for any praise.

I changed the subject.

I took the job and stepped into the bastion of male executives nearly twice my age and thrice as slick. I started just two weeks after another break-up, this time with a man I had worked with at my first agency and dated, off and on, until he cheated on me. I was young, single, wide-eyed, and eager. In hindsight, I was raw meat.

This was in 1991; women were still expected to wear skirts or dresses–never pants–to work, and while some strides had been made for women's rights, tradition was still at play. Sexual innuendo, if not direct propositions, meant a new world to navigate, though I had had my share of touchy-feely clients. I was told once by the company's CEO that if I grew my hair longer (I wore it quite short), I'd be more attractive. I laughed and said it was a good thing being attractive wasn't a job criterion. He smirked. On another occasion, he asked if I had ever modeled. I told him I was on a teen board for a local women's shop in high school; he asked if bathing suits were involved. I laughed it off. Another executive once patted my hip as I walked by; I laughed it off. It all seemed a pathetic game I'd have to play for a place at the figurative table.

Dad called one afternoon saying he'd be in Dallas, and would I like to meet for drinks and dinner? I knew Mom was out of town, and while I probably wasn't his first choice as a dinner companion, I agreed to meet him at my favorite low-key spot near work. When I arrived, he already had a table outside and was sipping a cold beer. I ordered a glass of wine, watching him carefully for any clues as to the reason for this unusual invitation. He seemed in an unusually good mood. I lit a cigarette; he scowled. I sipped my wine, watching the patio fill up with professionals ready for happy hour. No one I knew, thankfully.

I asked how he was doing, and he launched into a lengthy story about finally being able to buy some stocks he had been following. He described his daily ritual of tracking stock prices on a spreadsheet and waiting for the exact moment to pounce; his full-time job now was growing the inheritance he had received from Grandma. He asked when I planned to open an equity account so I could make my money work for me. I told him I was still paying down debt. (Honestly, I was racking up debt, but I kept that to myself.) He told me Dallas was soon to get a hockey team, and he looked forward to attending a game or two; I shuddered and said hockey didn't really interest me–too violent. He laughed. I ordered another glass of wine as he eyed the young waitress lasciviously. I rolled my eyes, but I felt embarrassed. She was gracious.

He turned his attention back to me and asked about work. I shared a few stories of accomplishments I had achieved in a relatively short period, including launching a brand-new quarterly publication for which I would be solely responsible. He nodded half-heartedly. I so wanted his approval, yet I was trying so hard not to show it. He asked about my romantic life, and I stiffened; this was not something I wanted to discuss with him. I demurred and said I was seeing one or two people, off and on. Nothing serious, as I had burned through as many relationships as jobs in four years. He laughed. It wasn't funny.

Our burgers arrived, and I picked at mine, though I was salivating.

"So," he said between carefully chewed mouthfuls, "I'm worried about your health."

I took a gulp of wine. "Okay…"

"It seems you're not taking care of yourself," he said, wiping his mouth. This came out of nowhere–I was perfectly fine!

"I'm fine, Dad, just working," I said, taking a bite of my burger.

"We want you to quit smoking," he said. He had driven all the way to Dallas to deliver this news? "It's time."

I told him I didn't want to quit smoking, not right now. He said it was disgusting. I told him he and Mom smoked the first eight years of my life–hell, Mom smoked while pregnant with me! He said they didn't know better then, but now we know. I was making yet another bad life decision by continuing. I'd be sorry.

I put down my burger. "I don't want to gain weight," I said with a level gaze.

"That's ridiculous. You're too thin as it is."

I wasn't; I was just right, at least in my mind. Yet, after years of hearing that Mom's weight (among other things) was the reason my father cheated on her, it was a very sore spot for me, especially since I had been on the receiving end of an unfaithful boyfriend. Now, he was telling me I was too thin? Would I ever get it right?

I laughed.

"Appearances are important, Dad," I said. "Particularly in Dallas."

There are certain kinds of statements that you never forget; they become part of your emotional DNA forever.

"Suzanne, you're attractive enough," he said, pausing to sip his beer. "But you're never going to be drop-dead gorgeous–I'm sorry, but it's the truth."

I fought back tears while saying flatly, "That's your opinion." I excused myself for the restroom to break the moment I wanted to forget. I still haven't.

We finished our meal, and he reached for the check. I waved him off and said I'd get it. He didn't argue. I never sat at the same table again.

A month later, while still somewhat new to the organization, I faced a heartbreaking crisis: during a routine diagnostic procedure at one of our hospitals, a radiology technician gave a patient the wrong contrast medium and subsequently, the patient went into a coma. He was a young husband and father of three. His wife would have to make the difficult decision to take him off life support. I was called into a meeting with one of our attorneys, our risk management director, someone from HR, and the executive director of the hospital on a conference call to discuss how we should proceed. I was the youngest in the meeting by at least seventeen years, yet I took over. I asked questions and in real time began penning the official statement; everyone in the room agreed with me, and I calmly returned to my office to get it typed and ready for media inquiries. And oh, there were several. I served as spokesperson while the risk management director met with the family to avert litigation. I made it through the day calmly, methodically, much like Mom had taught us during our preparation for Hurricane Camille in Biloxi some twenty-plus years earlier.

Once I got home, I called my parents. Mom answered and, hearing my anguish, she told Dad to pick up the other phone. I told them what had transpired. Dad asked why I was crying.

"Because a young husband and father is going to die, and it's our fault!"

"You had nothing to do with it."

"But Dad," I wailed, "I feel terrible! This is a human being that didn't have to die!"

Mom tried to say that these things happen, that she sees these kinds of cases all the time.

"You don't understand," I said, wiping my nose. "There's something wrong with me."

My mom asked what I meant. "I made it through the entire day, all of it, with no emotion whatsoever. Like, I felt nothing until I got home. I got things taken care of, at least for today, and I didn't feel any of it. That's not right!"

Dad cleared his throat and said, "That makes you a professional. You're there to do a job, and you did it. That's why you get paid. Plain and simple. Case closed."

He always loved saying that. I could picture my mother glaring at him.

It's taken years for me to recognize what was really antagonizing my spirit, but here's the truth. In the heat of the crisis, I had subconsciously done what I had learned over my young life to survive my father: I had compartmentalized my emotions so I could function instead of fail. Did that make me less human? Less compassionate? Or was it a survival skill I had learned to protect myself? Only time would tell.

Daniel, the handsome in-house attorney who'd been in all the meetings, asked me to lunch, which turned into a series of lunches, which turned into dinners, which turned into a relationship. He was seventeen years my senior and had never been married. I was smitten, but we still worked together, so we had to keep things discreet. It was my first experience hiding a relationship, though I had been raised by an expert in the field. I now understood the thrill of secrecy.

We had been dating, secretly, for about four months when, the night of my birthday dinner, Daniel dropped to one knee and asked for my hand in marriage. He slipped a beautiful, one-carat diamond in a Tiffany setting on my finger, and in that moment, my future seemed perfect. I excused myself from the table to find a payphone so I could call my best friend. Let the planning begin!

The next day, I called my parents to share the news. Neither Mom nor Dad was happy about the news and the litany began. They hadn't met him. Wasn't I concerned about the age difference, wasn't I too young to settle down, and what about my career? Of course, they'd pay for the wedding, but wouldn't it be a good idea for everyone to meet first?

Sigh. Once again, I needed their approval to proceed with my life, though I thought I had been doing a pretty good job on my own. Kind of.

Daniel had been struggling with alcoholism even prior to our relationship, and as the wedding planning progressed, he drank even more. The bargains we make with ourselves, so we don't have to admit mistakes, never fail to amaze me. But there I was, thinking it perfectly fine to proceed with our plans, even as his erratic behavior concerned me. I compartmentalized my fears, thinking my love could "fix" him. Here I was, ever longing and hopeful I could override his demons.

Dad invited me to meet him for drinks and dinner at the same place he told me I'd never be drop-dead gorgeous. I agreed because they had the best burgers in town. Plus, he was paying for our wedding, so I couldn't really say no, could I?

Once we were on our second round of cocktails before ordering our burgers, he asked how things were going with Daniel. I'm sure I smiled and lied, saying everything was just wonderful and we were so happy together! "Good," he probably said.

Then, the conversation took a different turn.

"How are you all in the bedroom?"

It was bad enough I had knowledge of my parents' sex issues because they both shared their stories about what was wrong with the other and, in Dad's case, why he sought pleasure elsewhere. Asking about MY sex life crossed a boundary, though I didn't recognize it at the time. I still longed to have a relationship with my father, and if that meant betraying myself, as it would continue to mean for decades to come, so be it. I told my father everything was great in the bedroom.

"So, he pleases you, then?" he asked. I took a hearty gulp of my Chardonnay and just nodded before lighting a cigarette. He shook his head and grimaced.

"Well, just know that when men reach a certain age, they may have issues with, um, performance. You're a young woman, after all, so you need to be aware this might happen."

How on earth was I to respond? I nodded and changed the subject, asking how he thought the Dallas Stars would fare this season.

We had been engaged not quite two months when, after a weekend trip to meet Daniel's family–a truly eccentric bunch–he broke off our engagement in the parking garage at work. I was shell-shocked, but possibly a bit relieved, too.

I did my best to avoid him, to the degree my job allowed, and within a few days, he began calling me in desperation, asking if we could at least continue seeing each other. Again, I thought with time and (my) patience, we could make our relationship work. After engaging in this toxic tango of his drinking, my cajoling, our arguing, and periods of silence, I told him we were officially finished.

He said he understood, but could we at least be friends? No, no we couldn't.

It still broke my heart, though. In my mind, I had failed yet again, and I believed no man would ever make me a priority. Unless it suited their immediate needs.

Good girl, guarded.

Chapter Nineteen: Pivoting

A few years later, I left the healthcare company–which was then in the process of being acquired by a larger healthcare organization based in North Carolina–to join a publicly traded gaming corporation as director of corporate communications and investor relations. It seemed like the right move, given the uncertainty of what would happen once the acquisition was completed. By the first few weeks, I realized I had made another mistake. In other words, another bad decision on my part, made from the fear of the unknown rather than a deliberate and strategic career choice.

My mother, however, was pleased, since her father had worked for Bill Harrah in Reno for decades; she believed, in some ways, I was paying homage to Grandpa. All I knew was I was getting a much bigger title and corresponding paycheck, despite working with some unabashed misogynists. Dad was not so pleased because, as he put it, I really needed to grow up and quit being so impulsive. He couldn't understand why I would make a career move solely for money, though that was one of his two great loves.

I also began what would become a twenty-one-year relationship with a man with whom I had gone to junior high and high school and with whom I had triple-dated to prom some eleven years earlier. We became reacquainted prior to the marriage of two of our friends from the way back, one of whom was two years younger and had worked for me both as an intern and as an account coordinator during my agency days. After our first dinner get-together to catch up–I didn't go into it thinking it was a date–we got swept up in our shared high school histories and the ease of familiarity. By the time our friends got married, just a few weeks later, we were already in love and talking about our future. Three months later, we moved in together, and one month after that, he officially proposed.

My father was happy because Jack had asked my father's permission first, though Dad then asked him over drinks if he really knew what he was getting himself into; did he really know how difficult I could be? Yet, Dad liked Jack quite a lot and was more than happy to welcome him into our seriously messed up family. Jack assured him he knew exactly what he was doing. In hindsight, I'm not sure either of us really had a grasp of what marriage would entail, but we sure were ready to give it our best.

While making wedding plans, I traveled every week, as my job now involved grassroots lobbying. Several states were considering legislation to legalize casinos of varying types and of those, I represented our company's interests in five states. On some trips, all of which included flying first class and staying at the best hotels, as well as mind-numbing meetings with legislators and lobbyists, I had to look at my agenda to remember where I was going next. The flights and locations were blurred. I was happy, though, confident that this engagement would "take." And it did.

The hotel where we would host our reception was majestic. A historic old gem where I had joined my mother for lunch countless times over the years, I had always dreamed of the Adolphus as the site of the perfect reception after our very proper, very Episcopalian high-mass wedding. The night before the wedding, my bridesmaids and I checked in after a confusing rehearsal–we were assured the details would sort themselves out during the actual ceremony–and our mediocre rehearsal dinner, at which no one seemed capable of giving a particularly meaningful or heartfelt toast. (In his predictably inappropriate way, my father did refer in his toast to a "healthy sex life." Ugh.) It was my first slumber party in at least sixteen years, and we laughed and drank the night away. The morning came quickly and painfully.

Once I had begun to feel human, though, my wedding day proceeded in a flurry of hair and nail appointments for me and my five bridesmaids. There was Champagne, and laughter, and hairspray, and cigarette smoking…and nerves. And there was the anticipation that, despite a few viciously epic fights shortly before the wedding, we would get through the nuptials and be happy. Together.

Early evening and we all had begun to get ready. I immersed myself in the porcelain claw-foot tub with another glass of Champagne, at one point plunging my head underwater and holding my breath as I contemplated the next few hours. As a public relations professional, I had coordinated various important events over my career, so a fancy wedding really shouldn't have felt much different. Yet, of course, it did.

My wedding gown–an exquisite confection of creamy Alencon silk and lace–had been delivered to the bridal room at the church, so all I needed was to complete my hair (which I decided to cut short just three weeks before the wedding) and my make-up before climbing into the limo that would transport me to my future.

My bridesmaids already were at the church, along with my mother, and we sipped a bit more Champagne–completely against church rules–as we finished getting ready. Seems I was the only one dawdling, which has never been a personal characteristic of mine (ever), and I could feel Mom becoming impatient. A knock at the door reminded us the procession would begin in ten minutes, with or without the bride (which I thought seemed ridiculous). My mother and maid-of-honor hurriedly tried to get me into my dress, only to realize there were at least fifty extraordinarily small buttons up the back, requiring three sets of hands to fasten in time. There may have been expletives uttered–I hope not, since we were in the House of the Lord–and I know from pictures captured by my photographer that my mother was highly displeased, if not outright furious. But the dress got buttoned, my veil got pinned to my hair, and the bridesmaids and my mother went into the nave, preparing to walk the very proper walk to the altar.

They left me in the bridal room, alone. I took a deep breath. My father knocked on the door before entering, then stood primly for me to check out his fancy new tuxedo and the glasses he bought specifically for the occasion since they complimented his tie and cummerbund. Because, of course, everyone knows all eyes are on the father of the bride? I dutifully acknowledged his elegance and superb choices. He looked me over and said, as all fathers are so obligated, that I was a lovely bride. Briefly, I saw in his eyes a look of pride that, for as long as I could remember, was always held just slightly out of reach. I bowed my head for a moment to catch my breath as I heard the strains of the processional begin on the church's magnificent organ. I choked back tears of sentiment and, possibly, terror.

"Hey Dad. You know why it takes a couple hundred million sperm to fertilize an egg?"

He gave me a puzzled stare from behind his designer frames. "No." He wasn't amused.

"Because not one of them will stop to ask for directions!" I exploded into laughter. He handed me a breath mint. We stepped into the nave as the wedding attendants closed the doors so I could make a grand entrance.

"You know, Suz, you don't have to do this," he said, squeezing my hand.

Without missing a beat, I simply said, "Let's go."

The doors opened, our guests stood, and Jack audibly gasped as we walked down the aisle. I laughed nervously. I choked back tears. The ceremony was lovely, and the reception was even grander. My new husband and I retired to our suite and stayed up for hours, drinking Champagne and replaying the night's events. Eventually, I changed out of my gown, though reluctantly, because it made me feel like every cliché of the wedding princess. The dress would be wadded up the next morning and placed in a trash bag for my maid-of-honor to give to my mother, since we barely had time to pack and get to the airport for our honeymoon. We were on our way.

How many times I have replayed that moment with my father? I believe he really gave me the option to cut and run, though it would have cost him a fortune for a reception that would not have been. I think he already knew what awaited me down the road.

I believe he really said it. Or maybe I just hoped he had because maybe, just maybe, he finally cared about my happiness.

Good girl, no longer his problem.

Chapter Twenty: Emulating

Before we became engaged, the friends whose wedding brought us together warned us, though we didn't take it seriously, that Jack and I were like fire and gasoline. We thought they were trying to be funny. As it happens, they were right. It's taken several years, lots of therapy, and life experiences to recognize we are two big personalities–extroverts who are accustomed to owning the room. I don't know if we ever consciously sought to one-up each other, but we did. We loved passionately, and we fought passionately. It became difficult to separate the two.

Four months into our marriage, we already had outgrown our two-bedroom apartment in Las Colinas with all our furniture, plus his dog, my cat, and our new greyhound adopted from the rescue center in Alabama. Given how much we were paying in rent each month, we decided it would be a good idea to buy our first house. While I had sworn vehemently from the moment I left for Austin years earlier, I would never, ever, ever live in Arlington again, we had to think about practicalities. And the truth was, I worked in far North Dallas, and Jack's sales territory was Fort Worth and beyond. We needed some place equidistant. Plus, as he calculated, we would likely have a family one day, and wouldn't it be nice to be close to my parents and his mother?

That was a loaded question.

We hadn't really talked about children, as we hadn't really talked about so many critical life decisions prior to taking our vows, but his argument seemed logical. He called a well-known realtor in Arlington, and he immediately told us about a house in North

Arlington where we both had gone to school. We arranged to see it the next night after work.

Here we were, a young married couple, each of us professionally successful and not even thirty-years old, sauntering into this process as if we had been there before. Meaning, we didn't ask my father for his counsel or advice. It was, after all, our decision and our money. Mostly Jack's if I'm being honest. That next evening, we met our realtor at the house–nine streets south of my parents' home–and toured the recently renovated property. It was lovely, though it had its quirks, and it was affordable. Mostly, though, it was the ginormous big-screen television that turned Jack's head. He offered the full asking price if the owners would throw in the monster. The next day, our bid was accepted. How we celebrated! We were going to be homeowners. Imagine!

We called my parents to share the good news.

Dad asked how many homes we had toured. Just one? Did you bother to check the comps in the neighborhood? Why would you offer the full asking price? Was a television set honestly worth jumping into the first house you saw? You didn't bother to ask my advice, unfortunately, but I really think you're making a mistake (for unspecified reasons). Remember, this is a man whose favorite pastime was comparison shopping on anything and everything; he'd drive ten miles to save three dollars. We thought the price was fair, and Jack, to his credit, didn't tell Dad to "piss off."

Once the owners had moved out and prior to closing, we invited our parents for a tour. My mother-in-law was thrilled for us and offered nothing but support. Mom was eager to teach me how to quilt, her new obsession, once we got settled since clearly, we had the room. Dad just walked quietly from room to room, making note of all the things we should have asked about before putting down our earnest money. "This house will need work." Don't all houses eventually need work?

We closed, we moved, and I began juggling decorating and house-wife-ing with my extensive travel schedule. I unpacked and arranged everything except, clearly, my lifelong baggage related to relationships and how they were supposed to work. I mean, who teaches us how to be married except the parents who raised us? Neither Jack nor I had been privy to happy unions.

We were at odds. I assumed the same habits with which I had been raised would naturally become part of our lives: nightly discussions over a cocktail or three about our days, followed by dinner and, hopefully, no arguments. Jack didn't like to talk about his workdays because, as he would say, "I've already lived through it once. Why do I need to re-hash it?" Well, I needed to re-hash mine, and when he seemed disinterested, my temper would flare. Didn't he understand how much bigger my job was than his? Yes, that was my attitude. I was a corporate badass, and he was a sales rep. An exceptionally successful one, but still. I was such a bitch.

Five months later, I found myself pregnant (very much unplanned) and quite depressed. We were still too new in our marriage, and we were struggling to figure out what we were supposed to be doing. Though unhappy at work, my career was what I knew. And honestly, if I was bad at being a wife (which I was), imagine how I'd be as a mother? Jack was thrilled; he loved children and wanted several. All I could see was the effect motherhood would have on my career, especially now that I had started to ascend. I told my parents; they were lukewarm. Are you really ready for this? (No.) Why are you all in such a hurry? (We're not.) You realize we will not be the standby babysitters while you're traipsing all over the country? (Wouldn't have considered it, for so many reasons.) We hope you know what you're doing. (Not a fucking clue.)

One Saturday, early in my pregnancy, we had friends over to watch football. Something felt wrong, and before I knew it, I was miscarrying. I remained quiet as I didn't want to ruin the fun, but it was happening, and there was nothing I could do to stop it. I wasn't upset, just in pain. By the time everyone had left, I was fully hemorrhaging, though I didn't know it. That night, we went through three changes of sheets; by morning, Jack knew he needed to get me to my doctor. Fortunately, I was fine. Just anemic. I went back to work the following Tuesday.

When I called to tell Mom what had happened, all she said was, "Something must have been wrong with the fetus. Good that you lost it." Not quite the warmth I had hoped for, but honestly, she was right. She asked if I wanted to speak to my father. I declined. Somehow, it would have devolved into a discussion about life decisions, and frankly, I didn't want to hear it.

I continued fumbling through our first then second year of marriage, unwittingly imposing on our lives the habits of my parents, and when Jack wouldn't engage, or when he challenged what I believed was the "right" way to do this thing, I'd start a fight. We never fought fairly. We crossed so many lines early in our marriage, both of us; we had not fortified our foundation enough.

So, when we faced the unexpected, but not surprising, death of Jack's grandmother two years later, all that was wrong in our marriage exploded for all to see. And it was ugly.

Jack had moved his paternal grandmother, Maureen, from her home in Alabama to an assisted living facility in Dallas shortly before our wedding. While cordial to Maureen, my mother-in-law deeply disliked her. Eventually, Jack moved Maureen to a nursing home just a few miles from our house, and soon after, he visited her every few days to ensure she was getting the proper care.

By this time, I had begun another corporate job in Dallas–director (and within a few months, vice president) of corporate communications and investor relations for a real estate investment trust. The company was gobbling up as many hotel properties as we could metabolize. The job was intense, my boss demanding, the schedule relentless, and the pressure extreme. I was surrounded by investment bankers in Brioni suits and Hermes ties and Gucci loafers–it was a brand-new world for me. I was making substantial money, so I dabbled in the world of Hermes myself–to the degree I could so afford. Jack was still Jack–down to earth, unpretentious, working to live versus living to work. How different we had become–I more than he.

My job came with perks, though, including the ability to stay at any of the properties we owned (and there were some swell resorts) for free. We planned a trip to one of our resorts in Arizona a few months into my position; it would be good for us to get away. The night before we were to leave, Jack got a call letting him know his grandmother had passed.

His emotions were complex, and honestly, I didn't know how to help him. We canceled the trip, notified family, and began making arrangements. We contacted the priest who had married us, now in Houston, because of a church transfer, and asked if he would conduct the service. He agreed and made travel arrangements for the coming Saturday. Jack let his mom, brother, and sister know about the details. They would ride to the funeral together; we would arrive early to meet Father P.

The mausoleum where Maureen wanted to be interred was in an area unfamiliar to all of us–she and her husband had lived in Dallas for years, and when he died, she returned to Alabama–but I believe this was where he had been interred. Saturday morning, we made the drive and, though we got turned around quite a bit and only had our MapQuest printout to guide us, we eventually arrived. My father was there–for some reason, he seemed to like funerals–and Father P was there. Mom didn't attend–she had recently been appointed to an administrative law judge position and was required to be in Washington D.C. at "judge school," but she sent her well wishes. Jack's family was nowhere to be found. Dad was impatient and judgmental. How on earth could they be so irresponsible as to be late? Father P grew antsier by the minute; he had a flight out of Love Field, and we needed to get this show on the road. Jack and I had our Blackberry phones; his family did not. We waited until we couldn't wait any longer, so Father P began the service.

My dad was fuming. I was fuming. Jack was calm. What else could he have done?

Just as Father P was concluding the service with a prayer, the doors opened and in walked Jack's family. Seems they had gotten lost. VERY lost. But instead of apologizing to Father P, and to us, for missing Maureen's service, they just dithered as if it were nothing.

I couldn't even speak to them and instead, walked my father to his car, then leaned against our SUV to smoke. Fortunately, Jack had packed a bottle of bourbon, so on the way home, we each had a sip or two. I didn't realize how flammable the situation was about to become.

We got back in the early afternoon. I poured a stiff drink while he went to lie down. Admittedly, I was less concerned with his grief–if that's what it was–than my indignation about his family arriving late. Yes, I was being just as judgmental as my father, though I didn't see it as such. That night, we got into a hellacious fight that centered on what had become a common theme: Jack believed I thought my family to be superior; I had always looked down my nose at his family, and just who in the hell did I think I was? I fought back. Of course, I did. And in the next few minutes, I was able to re-create a familiar, if not toxic, dynamic: he packed a bag and left with his cocker spaniel. I went to bed.

Sunday morning, he wasn't back, and I wasn't sure where he was; he wouldn't take my calls. I called his mother; no, he wasn't there. I called my father, crying, telling him Jack had left. He responded, "I don't know what to tell you." Seriously? You're the pro at this! A few hours later, his mother showed up, crying and wringing her hands. I invited her in. She told me she felt responsible for this situation. I told her she was. (She wasn't.) God, I was a bitch. But I had to be right–just like my father, unfortunately. I had to stay perched on my high horse.

That high horse kicked me in the gut. Hard. But two days later.

On Monday morning, Jack and I spoke by phone and agreed to meet that evening and "talk things out." I had taken the day off, so I drove to Dallas to do some shopping, then went to a girlfriend's house that afternoon to drink wine and process. Well, drinking cheap wine on an empty stomach wasn't the best idea. I called Dad from the car and told him I was heading home to meet Jack at our house. He wished me luck, though not sincerely. Unbeknownst to me, he had someone else occupying his thoughts, and it wasn't my mother or my marriage.

Jack was waiting for me, and the minute I walked in, he could tell I had had a few too many. He stood up, told me this wasn't what he had had in mind and clearly, I was in no condition to have a serious discussion about how we could fix what was broken. I argued. He went to the bedroom and began gathering more clothes. I followed him through the house, crying and begging. He ignored me, proceeded to his car, and drove away.

I took the next few days off from work, not sure when Jack would be home or how I could save this marriage, but I promised myself I would try. On my second night alone, I called my father, crying, and told him I was shaking and couldn't eat, and I wasn't sure what to do. He said he wished he could help, but he had to take Helen a salad because she was exhausted after moving all day.

Helen was his latest mistress, whom he was sure he loved and for whom he might leave my mother. She had had a rough day moving. Rough day?

Not only had my father ignored me when I needed his advice, but he was now abandoning me when I needed support. Never mind my mother, whom he had betrayed for decades.

Good girl, alone.

Chapter Twenty-One: Expanding

Once the storm had receded, Jack and I found our way back to our version of normal with little more than a backwards glance at the damage we had done to one another. Mom returned from D.C., and after a few explosive arguments with my father, during which she told him to just pack his shit and leave, they, too, returned to their version of normal. Everything was swept under the metaphorical rug, as they say. Sworn in as an administrative law judge, her career had reached a new apex, and like me, she was enthralled with her professional responsibilities. Neither of us could talk about much more than our daily dramas; our husbands weren't particularly interested or impressed, but we could share our days with each other (until she had to hang up and make my father dinner).

Admittedly, I no longer loved my job as much as I loved the idea of my job and its corresponding perks. Flying in the company jet, staying in $600 per night hotels, eating at Manhattan's finest restaurants, and interacting with bankers and financiers was sexy, to be sure. The sexual harassment, condescension, late hours, and at times, verbal abuse absolutely were not. One mistake (mine) and one acquisition too many (the company's), and I knew things were about to change–that change came in the form of a management re-org and a healthy severance package for me. I was glad to be gone, but I didn't know where I was going.

My mother had a series of favorite adages she'd trot out at appropriate times, none better than this: "We plan, God laughs." And so, when I learned a few weeks later I was pregnant, I could only imagine a celestial aria of giggling angels. I wasn't amused. I mean, I was thirty-four years old, so the clock was ticking away, yet I had never heard it over the din of my swanky job.

My husband was thrilled. After a few miscarriages, perhaps a more relaxed lifestyle would enable me to see this one through. To me, it felt like a consolation prize in a game that seemed rigged. I couldn't see it then, but that "consolation prize" turned out to be my life's greatest reward.

Mom and Dad seemed happy enough for us, though my mother would cautiously ask if I planned to go back to work. She knew I wasn't meant to be "just a housewife" though she, herself, had so served for many years. I didn't like the idea of being dependent on my husband, but damn–pregnancy is exhausting! So exhausting, in fact, that it seemed perfectly logical that we should put our starter home on the market and buy a bigger house...yes, with stairs and a swimming pool! (Clearly, I hadn't thought through life with a baby.)

To get the house we selected, we had to agree to purchase with no contingency, which we thought was fine since our current home was one block away from the best elementary school in Arlington. My parents asked, once again, if we had any idea what we were doing. (No fucking clue.) We forged ahead, closing on the new house and moving in the blistering July heat. Our nerves were frayed, both from the unforgiving weather and the fact that after two months on the market, our old house hadn't sold. We were two months from the end of my severance and one month from having to pay two mortgages. My pregnancy was not relaxing. By demanding we buy a new house, I had successfully complicated our lives unnecessarily, yet I was sure it would somehow work out.

We had been in the house just a few weeks when I got a call from a recruiter about a contract position. It was with a global hospitality company in the process of a major acquisition. She said they needed someone with considerable mergers and acquisitions communications experience (check) and they needed that person immediately (check). I interviewed the next day, and by week's end,

I had landed a long-term contract that would extend off and on for the next four years.

My father marveled at my continued good luck, which was a backhanded way of ignoring my hard work over the years. Mom was concerned about my driving to far North Dallas every day, in the heat, in my condition, yet I assured her going to work was more palatable than obsessing about impending motherhood.

From day one, I loved the job, my boss, the executive team, and the paycheck. Shortly thereafter, we sold our first house and finally, things were falling into place–five months before we would welcome our new daughter into the world. We felt like grownups! Yet, we still weren't really connecting in the way I had hoped we would. I assumed parenthood would fix that, though it clearly hadn't worked for my parents. Arguably, it only made things worse. For them, I mean. Kind of.

Remember Mom's adage? Well, I had always sworn that if I were to have a child, it would not be a holiday baby; the poor things just get the fuzzy end of the lollipop, don't they? Yet here we were awaiting the birth of our daughter in early December. Fall crept up on us, and before we knew it, we were planning Thanksgiving dinner at our house, as we had taken on that family responsibility (for both sides) the first year we were married. I was now in my third trimester, meaning I was exhausted, uncomfortable, cranky, and FAT. Though I had gone back to therapy to help me sort out my issues related to family dynamics and my fear of gaining weight, I still couldn't look in the mirror and see the beauty of my pregnant self. And I certainly didn't hear it from my father. He said little except that the prospect of a granddaughter had given him a reason to live.

What a burden to put on a baby not yet born, but not unlike the burden placed on me some thirty-four years earlier. We all were here to serve him.

Thanksgiving went well enough, and the following week, I went to the office for the last time until my due date. I couldn't afford to be that far away if our daughter decided to make an early debut. Fortunately, she didn't and, in fact, was a day late.

Every mother has her own birth story. My mom told hers every year on my birthday: it was a Saturday morning in Germany when she began going into labor. My father put her in the Mercedes ("Brunhilda") and sped to the base hospital, where not a doctor could be found–seems Saturday was the day to golf in Wiesbaden. He ran the halls frantically and found one white coat in the facility, belonging to Dr. Lucey, a neurosurgeon. Dad grabbed him and said, "Come quick! My wife's about to give birth!" They barely made it before I joined the world with what my mother called "a bullet head" and a very loud wail. I always cringed at the next part, while my parents always laughed. "When your father came into the room to see us," Mom would say, "he took one look at you and said, 'She's not much to look at…we'll just to have to hope she's sweet.'"

My story was different. I began going into active labor around 12:30 a.m., and by one in the morning, my husband said we needed to get to the hospital. Once there, we called our families to let them know it was "show time," though it really wasn't, not yet. Around four in the morning, family and friends showed up just as I was getting my epidural. Mom almost fainted. Dad just seemed irritated that there were other people there. My best friend made a breakfast run; everyone else camped in my room. Four hours later, nothing was happening, so my doctor gave me a Pitocin drip. The drip and the epidural were at odds; my labor wasn't progressing. The epidural wore off, so a new anesthesiologist injected more juice into the IV, but I think it may have been a total nerve block. I became numb from the neck down; shortly thereafter, both I and my baby were in distress. The nurse shooed everyone from the room as the delivery team began to prepare me for an emergency C-section. They put me on oxygen while the doctor worked to correct the baby's position– she was sideways and needed to be turned. I was crying and alone with the doctor and nurses. Miraculously, everything calmed down– C-section averted. We would wait another two hours before our courageous daughter greeted the world at one-thirty in the afternoon, looking just like my husband's late grandmother.

Once she was swaddled and in my arms, and once my husband and I had shed our tears of happiness that we did it...we had a healthy, perfect daughter who looked like his grandmother but hopefully, would outgrow it..., the parade of visitors began. First, our parents and then our friends. Everyone was exhausted, but happy. A new chapter had begun.

It was the same book, though.

My parents met us at our house when we brought our baby home, largely to ensure our three eager dogs and one recalcitrant cat were in check as we got settled. Mom said she'd come over every day to take care of newborn G so I could sleep, and my husband could get back to work in his home office. That first day, we were sitting in the living room and G began to cry, so with no modesty, I brought her to my breast and began feeding her. The look on my father's face was a mixture of wonder and disgust — mostly disgust. Mom suggested I drape a blanket over the baby's head "for privacy." Heaven forbid my father had to witness the uncomfortable sight of his daughter feeding his granddaughter naturally. Clearly, boobs were meant for other things. I knew my father had "strongly encouraged" my mother to get first-generation breast implants in the late 1960s. I would later find, amidst his personal stash of photos, that he was breast-obsessed...objects of desire, nothing more.

Fortunately, my husband had witnessed my excruciating delivery, the epidural having worn off, and he told everyone who would listen what a rock star I was. How courageous I had been, soldiering my way through the pain (and corresponding forty-three stitches). He was one proud father and an outstanding one at that.

Now that we were parents, we naturally assumed we'd be taken a bit more seriously by my father.

You know what they say about what happens when we assume?

Good girl, mothering.

Chapter Twenty-Two: Rule-Breaking

I have to take a pause in this narrative to offer a mini epilogue before I can write the next part. I grieve for my father, but not in standard ways. I still long for him, even knowing all the salacious things he did. This book isn't a betrayal, I hope. I just must tell my story for all he put me through and all I somehow survived without turning into a complete lunatic. And I love and miss him, anyway. How fucked up is that? You'll see.

Chapter Twenty-Three: Schooled

Before our daughter was born, my father told us they would start a fund for her college tuition. That seemed perfectly logical given that his parents had paid for his college, and my grandmother had contributed to both my mother's and my college tuition. I was doing contract work, which I would continue off and on for various entities until my daughter turned four; my husband was doing well, but we understood children are expensive. We welcomed this show of family support.

Admittedly, it didn't take me long after she was born to conclude that while I was in love with my daughter, I wasn't cut out to be a full-time, stay-at-home mom. My first Mother's Day, just six months after I gave birth, my father gave me a custom-made t-shirt he had ordered that read, "Every mother is a working woman." I suppose his intention was to reinforce my choice not to put her in daycare, as many of my friends had done with their babies, but to give her the best start I could with a fully engaged, fully attentive, fully at-home mother.

By the time she was around nineteen months, I was ready to get back to work. After much discussion about the pros and cons of private school, which my husband thought to be elitist, he finally relented, and we enrolled her in a Montessori school just a few miles from home. She was resistant at first, then grew to love her teacher and her fellow toddler classmates. I don't recall my parents having any real opinion about it other than to question why we would pay thousands of dollars each year for school for a child not even of kindergarten age. She was flourishing, though, and I could get to

Dallas a few times a week to work in person for the global hospitality corporation that took a chance on me when I was pregnant. They kept offering me a full-time staff position, but I wasn't quite ready for that level of commitment.

One Tuesday morning, I was driving my toddler to school, listening to NPR as I always did. Jack was traveling, and I wasn't scheduled to go to the office, so I was looking forward to a quiet day working from home. An announcer cut into the feature story with news that a plane had hit the World Trade Center; it was shortly after eight o'clock in the morning, and they were still trying to piece together the story. Like everyone, I assumed it was a freak accident. I walked my daughter to her classroom, stopping to say our daily "Good morning" to the turtles sunning themselves on the side of the pond. I gave her a kiss and told her I would see her soon.

I walked into my house to the phone ringing; it was my friend, Hank–a former newsman–urging me to turn on my television. I watched, as did the world, the second tower being hit and soon, both towers collapsing. Jack was scheduled to fly home that day; I couldn't reach him. Then, news of a third plane in Pennsylvania crashing, and I started to shake. Were we under attack? What was happening?

I called my father, and when he answered, I burst into tears. "Why are you crying?" he asked cooly. I told him I was afraid. "Of what?"

I said there might be other attacks. I told him I knew people who worked in the World Trade Center. I didn't know where my husband was, nor how to reach him, since he wasn't answering his phone. No response, other than a deep sigh. "What are we supposed to do?"

Another deep sigh, then he cleared his throat before speaking in the tone he only reserved for people he believed to be morons. Slowly, with a sharp note of disdain. "Well, Suzanne, what have we taught you?"

Geez…that was a loaded question. To my knowledge, the only time we had believed ourselves in genuine danger was during Hurricane Camille in 1969. I couldn't see how scrubbing bathtubs, filling them with water, and securing our windows with plywood would help in this situation.

I said nothing. In his supercilious tone, he asked if I had plenty of staples in the kitchen. I thanked him, told him I loved him, and hung up. My next call was to the school: were we supposed to get our children? They assured me the students were safe, and while I was welcome to pick up my child, school would continue as usual. That was a relief, as I wasn't ready to be okay. I called my best friend, Margot, who arrived at my door just minutes later. We watched CNN for a few hours before hitting the grocery and liquor stores. Once we picked up my daughter from school, we sat outside while she played until dinner time. By this point, I had heard from my husband; because flights had been grounded, he and his colleagues had rented a car and would drive home the next day. My daughter went to bed, and Margot and I curled up on the oversized red chair, grateful for companionship as the world we had known seemingly died.

Two months later, I joined a cause-marketing firm based in New York City, working from my home office unless I needed to travel for strategy meetings. I enjoyed having time to focus on my clients, all of whom were major, national, non-profit organizations. The work felt important, particularly after 9/11. Finally, I was emerging from the fog of new motherhood and re-connecting with my former professional self, though the world certainly had changed.

Nearly a year into my position, the agency president and other executives flew to Dallas to meet with one of our biggest clients. They invited me to join them at a prestigious restaurant for dinner the night following the strategy session–it was an important opportunity to expand the account. My husband was scheduled to be out of town, so I planned for my daughter to spend the night with Jack's mother, who said she'd handle school pickup that afternoon so I could properly prepare.

That same afternoon, I had just wrapped up a conference call on my work phone when my home phone rang. I didn't recognize the number on caller I.D., so I let it go to voicemail. A few minutes later, I retrieved the message, which was from my father…chatty, upbeat, just wanted to see how I was doing…strange. He didn't yet have a mobile phone, and it clearly wasn't their home line, so I called the number back.

The number was for a motel in South Dallas, a good forty-five minutes away with traffic, and known to be quite seedy.

I asked the man who answered for my father's room by name. He responded that he had just checked out. Moments ago, in fact.

My father had called me from a motel room in South Dallas. My mother was at a conference, out of town.

I needed to get ready to meet my boss and clients for dinner, but my head was pounding, my blood coursing like ice through my veins…so cold it burned. I poured myself a glass of wine, which I drank urgently while changing clothes and freshening my makeup. I was feeling a lot of things in that moment, none of which made the idea of sparkling small talk remotely appealing. Yet, I was a professional, so I drove to Dallas, all the while seething. I made it through dinner, offering appropriate comments and doing my best to be charming, while my mind fixated on the ugly question: why on earth had my father driven to South Dallas for an afternoon…what? I just couldn't imagine it. I didn't want to. I shouldn't have had to. Yet, he clearly wanted me to know–he was too smart, or so I thought, to risk being outed by Caller I.D. Wasn't he?

I got home, admittedly a little tipsy from the evening, but the top shelf margaritas had done nothing to numb my anger. If anything, the tequila intensified it. I picked up the phone to call him. It was on the late side, but I knew he'd be awake. He answered, and I launched into my interrogation. "Why in the ever-loving hell did you call me from a motel in South Dallas?" At first, he tried to deny it until I shouted, "Caller I.D., Dad! You left me a fucking message. I called the number. I found out where you were–you can't lie your way out of this one." Silence, then the sound of ice clinking in his Waterford glass as he took a sip of what only could have been Scotch. "I asked for your room, Dad, and the operator said you had just checked out. You had just fucking checked out. Why the fuck were you there?"

In his steely tone, he told me to stay out of his personal life. Then he hung up.

I wasn't finished.

In four minutes, I was at my parents' door. I rang the bell. He answered with a drink in hand. He didn't invite me inside. We glared at one other for a moment, then I began to cry. "What were you doing there?" He grinned, then shrugged. I repeated my question.

He just shook his head, still slightly grinning, and said, "It was just sex, Suzanne."

My father was sixty-seven years old; he and my mother had been married for thirty-nine years. While my mother was traveling on a case as a federal fucking judge–respected, educated, and accomplished–my father was hooking up for an afternoon romp with a prostitute in a sleazy South Dallas motel. I nearly threw up on his shoes.

Instead, I wiped my eyes and, while pointing at him with a shaking hand, told him if he ever, ever involved me again in his illicit double life, I would not keep it to myself. I told him he was putting me in a position of being complicit in his activities, betraying my mother, or telling her and thereby betraying him. I told him no daughter–no one, actually–should have to make such a choice. He simply smiled, lifted his glass in a toast, told me to have a nice evening, and shut the door.

I can't remember if I told my husband what had happened, though surely, I must have. What I do remember is that at our next holiday meal, which my husband and I prepared, my father asked us how we were doing with our daughter's college savings account. Had we opened the fund he recommended?

Jack and I looked at each other, confused. "Um, Dad, you said when G was born that you all were starting a college account for her." My husband watched, quietly.

My father cleared his throat. "I never said that, Suzanne." He took a sip of wine. I looked at Mom; she gave me a look that telegraphed, "Not now." I ignored her.

"Dad, yes you did! That's why we haven't set up an account...you said you were going to!" I was fighting back tears.

"It isn't our responsibility to put your daughter through college. We've already done that, twice, with you and your mother." I stared at him, speechless.

"Honestly, instead of paying for private school, you could put that money in savings, and you wouldn't have to worry about her future tuition." I raised my eyebrows at my husband, who just shook his head.

"It's all about decisions, Suzanne. It's time you start making better ones."

I didn't realize it then, but in hindsight, he had just shown his hand. If I challenged him, there would be consequences. Painful ones. And how I would see that play out over the duration of his life still sickens me.

Good girl, schooled.

Chapter Twenty-Four: The Line

While still relatively young–that is, when she was in her mid-sixties–Mom developed osteoarthritis, which eventually required hip replacement surgery in 2003. She failed to continue her physical therapy at home (despite my father's badgering, or perhaps, because of it) and had never particularly enjoyed exercise, so the osteoarthritis took over, and soon, her knees also became compromised. When she walked, she did so slowly, looking like a much older version of herself. My father prided himself on his physical fitness, sure as he was that he would never grow old, so his contempt for Mom's physical limitations became yet another justification for seeking other sources of companionship. If she would not take care of herself, why should he care for her? He wore his self-righteousness like a buttery leather jacket, flaunting his virility in sharp contrast to her increased weakness.

I pretended not to notice, as we had other priorities. Our daughter was flourishing in kindergarten. I had just taken a new full-time job with a local advertising agency, and my husband had received a promotion; our world, for the moment, felt stable. Until the following spring.

My father loved college basketball. Each year, he made it a point to attend one or more of the NCAA March Madness regional matchups. Of course, he never took Mom because she didn't really share his passion and he didn't have the patience to watch her navigating arena stairs. There were many local college teams he enjoyed watching, so he often attended their games, too. She didn't seem to mind his attending these events alone, as it gave her time to eat what she wanted for dinner and work on her beloved quilts.

One Saturday morning, he told me he was planning to drive to Waco to see Baylor play. I don't remember who the opponent was, but it was supposed to be a critical game prior to March Madness. That afternoon, my husband had the game on in the den while I was puttering in my office. The home phone rang. I didn't recognize the number, so I didn't answer. Shortly thereafter, I retrieved the message–it was my father, euphoric that Baylor had managed to come from behind to win the game. Did I see the game? It was unbelievable. And so on.

By this point, he had gotten a cell phone, but that wasn't the number from which he called. I sat down and pressed "redial," holding my breath. A woman answered. "I'm calling for Frank. Who is this?" She disconnected. I called back, and this time, my father answered. "You've got to be fucking kidding me, Dad," I said. "Who are you with?"

He said his phone had died, so he borrowed one from a woman sitting next to him. Not really the truth and not really a lie. How stupid did he think I was? I said as much. He sighed and said we could discuss it when he returned home. The next day. Whoever he was with would stay with him overnight. I hung up on him. And then, I lost it. I told my husband what had happened, and he just shook his head before telling me the parable about the scorpion and the frog. In short, the scorpion wants to ride atop the frog to cross the pond. The frog is reluctant because the scorpion packs a lethal sting. The scorpion promises to do no such thing. The frog agrees, and the scorpion climbs aboard. They reach the other side of the pond and before the scorpion dismounts, it stings the frog who, before dying, asks why the scorpion would go back on its word? "It's just my nature," the scorpion responds. And so it was with my father; he just couldn't help himself? I wasn't sure I believed that.

There I was, swinging from the horns of dilemma as my daughter asked about dinner. Do I betray myself, and my mother, by keeping this information secret? Do I risk hurting her by informing her he had traveled overnight with another woman and, worse, that he called me from her cell phone? Do I gamble with incurring his wrath, and God only knew how that would be manifest, by protecting my articulated boundaries and "outing" him? Would any of my choices really change anything?

The next morning, I drove to my parents' house. My father had not yet returned. Mom offered me a cup of coffee, which I gladly accepted, and I joined her at the kitchen table. She started making small talk about what she had had for dinner and what movie she had watched before I interrupted her. She looked annoyed.

"I told him the last time something like this happened that I wouldn't keep his secrets anymore," I began.

She raised her eyebrows. "Something like what?"

Great. Poor start on my end. I tried to back into it by telling her about his calling me from the basketball game using a woman's cell phone. "He told me his phone was dead, and he had to borrow hers, but I don't buy it. Not for a second."

She took a measured sip of her coffee. I waited for a reaction…something. She stared out the window. "He'll probably be home any minute," she said. "Why don't I come over later?" I nodded, gave her a kiss on the forehead, and drove home.

It's amazing what the internet can do, even back then. For reasons I couldn't explain, I had to know who this woman was. All it took was a reverse phone look-up, and bingo, I found her name. And with her name, I could find out she was a widow, a volunteer, and a mere high school graduate. I found her picture, and she was attractive enough for her age; at least she was on the thin side, which my father preferred, and she sported a hairdo that looked as though she had it "done" weekly at the beauty parlor. She was blond-ish, and her name was Judy. I'm not sure what I expected, but clearly, she was nowhere near as accomplished, educated, or talented as Mom. That made me feel worse.

Later that afternoon, my husband took G to the park so Mom and I could talk without interruption. She joined me on our patio; I opened a bottle of Pinot Grigio and began pouring into the two glasses I had set on the table. She shook her head, but I left her glass in front of her.

"All right, so let's hear it," she said. I repeated the story about Dad calling from the arena and how I didn't answer because I didn't recognize the number and then calling back and a woman answering, hanging up, and Dad calling me back. I started to cry. Her eyes blazed.

"You said this morning that you told him if anything like this ever happened again, you wouldn't keep it a secret," she said. She was in litigator mode. "What, exactly, did you mean?" She took a sip of her wine and then a second.

"It's been a while," I said, buying time. Her eyes were Gamma knives, slicing their way to the truth, but she remained silent.

"He called me on my home line. You were out of town. I didn't recognize the number, so I let it go to voicemail. He left a chirpy message, and I thought it was weird. It wasn't like him, not really. So, I called the number back, and it was a South Dallas motel. In the middle of the day," I spewed, watching for a reaction. She took another sip of wine; I followed suit.

"And?" Her stoicism scared me. Mom was never at a loss for words, nor reactions.

"And…when I confronted him, he told me it was just sex and to mind my own business," I said slowly. She shook her head, then sipped her wine before refilling the glass.

"I told him I wouldn't again betray you by keeping his secrets, Mom. I'm so, so sorry," I stammered, wiping the shame springing from my eyes. "It had to be a prostitute, Mom. South Dallas…I'm just…I'm just sorry."

A few moments passed before she looked back at me. "I appreciate you telling me now. But why didn't you tell me then?"

I didn't have an answer then, and I don't have an answer now beyond my fundamental, lifelong wish to be Daddy's girl. To be the daughter whose father would protect her, support her, praise her, nurture her, guide her. I thought by not making him angry, I was pleasing him. It was a Devil's bargain. I could see in my mother's eyes that I had gotten it all wrong.

Moreover, I couldn't bring myself to articulate the truth: that while my mother was earning the salary from which their bills were paid, my father was sneaking to seedy motels to buy sexual gratification. Who wants to know that about their parents? Worse, what kind of parent feels the need to involve their children in such depravity? As if, truly, he was proud–as if he wanted to be sure I knew!

"I'm in a no-win situation, Mom," I whispered as the tears rolled down my face.

She was ready to leave. "All I can say is, life is about making choices, Suzanne. Thank you for letting me know. I need to get home to start dinner. I think we're having meatloaf tonight."

Choices? What were mine, really? What were hers? I gave her a quick hug before walking her to the door.

Over the next few days, I kept thinking I'd hear from one of them–I didn't. I was too afraid to call and have my father answer. I wanted to know what was going on with them, yet I didn't. While my husband had his own fair share of family issues, he couldn't relate to the position I was in. Thankfully. I had to navigate the situation alone, while still doing my best to honor my parents because, you know, that's what you're supposed to do. Right?

It only took a few weeks for the dam to break. What apparently started out as an argument about Mom's reluctance to explore knee replacement surgery erupted into a scorched-earth assault–hers–about his character and continued infidelity. Why had he taken up with Judy–a woman who didn't even have a college degree? Why had he felt the need to involve his daughter? If he was so miserable in the marriage, why didn't he just leave already? He volleyed back, matching each accusation with a searing barb about why she was sexually repellant and had been for years. The toxic battle ended, predictably, with him packing a bag and speeding off. Mom assumed he was on his way to Judy's.

I know all this because she called me just after he fled, her anger fueled by wine (or so she sounded). I listened to her rant, then assured her he would be back. She said she didn't care, but I knew that wasn't true. How many times had we had similar conversations? I told her she was more than capable of filing for divorce; she didn't need this constant emotional abuse, and really, was it ever going to change? She countered that she didn't want to be a "two-time loser," referring to her first divorce. I reminded her we weren't living in the 1950s and wouldn't she rather be happy and alone than married and miserable? She said she was afraid she wouldn't make it financially. I replied that she was paying the bills for both, so why would it be any different if she were on her own? She had never lived alone, she said, and was too old to try it now. But wouldn't you be alone if he died? She scolded me for suggesting I wished him dead. I didn't say that. No, but you implied it. I told her I needed to take my daughter to soccer practice and would talk to her later.

It was a late Sunday afternoon, and my daughter didn't have practice, but Mom was too preoccupied to know that. I simply needed to distance myself from their situation, though I hadn't been successful thus far. Why did it seem I was more invested in their marriage than my own?

An hour later, my doorbell rang. I looked out the kitchen window and saw my father's car. Shit. My husband and daughter were at the park with the dogs. I could opt not to answer the door, right? No, better to address things now. I opened the door hesitantly; my father simply handed me an envelope before turning on his heel and heading to his car. "Dad? Do you want to talk?" He ignored me, got in the car, and sped away.

Another of his infamous "poison pen letters." While he prided himself on his communication skills, he preferred pouring his accusations and criticisms onto paper (and later, via email); this way, the recipient could not immediately respond but rather, had to sit in the awfulness of his scathing words. This letter was no different. In a nutshell, I had put my nose in his business, his personal life was off limits, I had no right to tattle on him to Mom, he was tired of my blatant disrespect and ingratitude, and he was done with me. He signed it, as he only signed letters to me when righteously indignant, "Your Father."

When my husband and daughter returned, I showed him the letter. "That's fucked up," he said, and I agreed.

"Here's the thing," I said. "If he's done with me, he's done with us. Period. And that means he doesn't get to be around G."

He looked at me, cocking his head. "Do you really want to involve her in the way they involved you?"

Don't get me wrong—my husband tolerated my father but had seen firsthand the head games he played. He wasn't defending my father but rather, trying to help me break a cycle, of sorts. I guess. Yet, while I kind of understood his logic, I didn't agree with it.

"I don't want him to do to her what he's done, and keeps doing, to me," I said. Were we saying the same thing?

My mother called me the next evening. She had taken a sick day to contemplate life. My father had returned and was out on a bike ride. She was making pork chops for dinner. Did I have a good day?

I felt like I was losing my mind. I poured a glass of Merlot and told her, simply, that I couldn't keep doing this. That I couldn't tolerate my father's abuse any longer; I told her about his letter. But, as she reminded me, "He is your father."

"So?"

"So, you're supposed to honor and respect him."

"He isn't honorable or respectable, Mom!"

"Well, he's the only father you'll ever have."

"Whatever. If he doesn't want to have anything to do with me, he won't have anything to do with his granddaughter."

Heavy sigh.

"Now, you're just being vindictive."

Wow. I told her I had to go.

I elected not to respond to my father's letter. Instead, I went into avoidance mode. For the next few months, I spoke infrequently to Mom and only when I knew he wasn't around. I didn't see or speak to him; frankly, I had nothing left to say. When my birthday came around that August, I took the day off so I could meet Mom for lunch. She gave me a pair of her jade earrings I had coveted. I steered the conversation to work and one client who was giving me fits. We went shopping, and she bought me a tiled art piece I was eyeing. I could tell she was trying to compensate for my fractured relationship with my father. I let her.

When I got home, I retrieved the mail and saw a card from my father. The message was clear: I don't want to see you, but you can't fault me for ignoring your birthday. Classic. He spent an inordinate amount of time selecting greeting cards with the perfect sentiments for the moment. This particular card was of the flowery, overwrought variety, with all the right words about the special bond between dads and daughters, blah blah blah. He signed it "DoD," which was code for "Dear Old Dad." Which was code for, "Let's just sweep everything under the rug and pretend all is fine between us."

I never took ballroom dancing classes, though I wished I had because I felt like I was trying to do the foxtrot in double time to an album that kept skipping. And I felt guilty that I couldn't understand the footwork.

I called and thanked him for the card. He was cordial and wished me a happy birthday. He hoped I had a nice afternoon with Mom. That line I held so dearly was erased in a one-minute conversation.

Good girl, stuck.

Chapter Twenty-Five: Stretching

Three months into my newly appointed position as the director of global internal communications for a technology company, one of my undergrad professors, who remained my mentor and dear friend, died after a thirteen-month fight with ALS. During my sophomore year at Texas, I had the opportunity to work as Hal's research assistant while he was completing and refining his dissertation. He was the professor who believed I had a future in academia, even as I chose another direction. Years after I graduated, we worked together on a few projects, and he continued urging me to consider a bigger world than marketing communications.

Wanting to honor his legacy, I decided to pursue my master's degree at the University of Texas at Arlington. I had no idea how steep that challenge would prove to be, particularly given my promotion at work and my daughter's busier schedule, yet I leaned on Mom for moral support. Interestingly, my daughter was the same age as I was when Mom went back to school; I knew Mom would understand all the complexities. Initially, I had planned to study sociology, but after further discussion with her, I decided to focus on history. Did it have anything directly to do with what I did for a living? Not directly, as I would tell people later. It did, however, have everything to do with dissecting critical elements of leadership and the power of public opinion to foment social change.

Once again, my father didn't understand why I was wasting my time on something that wouldn't further my career, but I didn't care. I was committed to challenging myself and doing something–just one thing–that was only for me. Given my schedule, I could only manage one graduate class per semester, meaning my degree would take several years to complete. Mom advised me to take one semester at a time and not to get ahead of myself. She reminded me of this often when I wrestled with self-doubt, which happened frequently during my first two semesters. One thing I loved most about my graduate classes was how much more I had to discuss with Mom. She read nearly all my papers and was as proud as I was when I received an A in my first class and, actually, every class through the mind-numbing program. We talked every night on the phone. My father, as she told me, glowered in the wings, eavesdropping, and then growing impatient because I wasn't talking to him. Why would I, though? He didn't share my interest and couldn't be bothered acknowledging my achievements.

My academic workload was intense, so I had to learn to compartmentalize to meet all my obligations as a wife, mother, employee, and student. Fortunately, Jack was supportive and gave me time over the weekends to sequester myself in my office and finish the mountain of reading and writing assignments I had to complete. I don't know that he believed I would stick to the program through completion; I don't know that I believed it, either, but I was going to give it my best.

As it turns out, my best was better than I thought. I submitted the first original research paper I wrote — a lengthy analysis of music as propaganda to build public support for the Mexican American War — to be considered for a history conference at the University of Southern Mississippi. Mom had read the paper and thought, as did my professor, that it was exceptional. I was in my first semester of grad school, but I rolled the dice to see what happened.

Two weeks later, I was notified the paper had been accepted, and they invited me to sit on a panel with two other presenters. I was gobsmacked. That same evening, we were hosting a sleepover for my daughter's birthday, so I could only revel in the moment briefly before shifting my focus to her, but it was intoxicating. Never, other than in my creative writing class in college, had I received such confirmation that my abilities were far greater than I realized.

I called Mom and squealed the news. She, too, was thrilled. "Will you go with me?" I asked. She said she would be honored. My heart was racing. She asked if I wanted to share the news with my father. I didn't, really. But she put him on the line, anyway.

"So, what do you get for that?" he asked.

"Well, my paper will be published," I said slowly.

"And?"

"And, if I decide I want to go on to a doctorate, getting published would be enormously helpful."

"Why would you want to do that?"

And just like that, my bubble burst. I told him our guests were about to arrive and that I needed to go.

The conference was scheduled for February–just over two months away–yet I began to panic. What if I really wasn't good enough? I wasn't an academic, not yet anyway, and the other two panelists were fully tenured professors. I didn't even have a master's degree. Everyone attending the conference would be highly educated instructors, authors, researchers...I would be outclassed. Would I embarrass myself? I hadn't been to a history conference, so I didn't even know how to go about preparing. What if I got a question I couldn't answer?

I started my second semester of grad school that January. During that same time, I learned I was to be in London for eleven days the following month to embed in our regional office there. Work was competing mightily for my attention, as was my daughter. Who did I think I was to believe I could manage all of it? I emailed the conference coordinators just three weeks before I was due to present and told them I was unable to participate due to a work conflict.

I lied. I could have done both, yet my confidence had evaporated. When I told Mom, she was disappointed. Why did I do that? I couldn't tell her the real reason, but here it was in a nutshell:

if it didn't matter to my father, it wasn't important. I wish I had believed otherwise. I would learn.

My graduate program required the completion of eight courses plus a thesis–no less than one hundred and twenty pages, not counting footnotes or bibliography–based on original research. This meant, based on taking only one class per semester, it would take me at least two and a half years to complete my coursework before I could begin researching and writing my thesis. I encountered a crisis of faith in my second year. That semester's professor denigrated every version of my research paper-in-progress, and, on top of that, I contracted the H1N1 version of the flu, which nearly hospitalized me. I went to my graduate advisor and told him I was seriously considering dropping out of the program. He asked why, and I explained I just couldn't handle my professor's abuse: I would make suggested changes in the approach I was taking with my research, only to be re-directed yet again on the subsequent draft. My advisor suggested I turn my frustration to anger and "prove your professor wrong." Still recovering from the virus, I took his advice, completed my final paper, and received an A in the class. Honestly, it was the most hard-fought A I've ever received.

A few semesters later, I received word from the university's Office of the President that I had been named "University Scholar," an honor given only to the top one percent of the institution's undergrad and graduate students. The criteria were two-fold: grades combined with professor recommendations. I would join just over two hundred fellow students at the President's Convocation for Academic Excellence, with a reception to follow. Once again, I had a hard time believing I had earned such an honor. I could still hear my mother's words reverberating from my sophomore year in college. ("By God, we'll make a scholar out of you yet.")

Predictably, I called my parents to share the news. Mom answered, and I excitedly told her about the honor and corresponding event later that spring. She was congratulatory, of course, and told me she had said all along, if I could just take things one semester at a time, I would do well. She put my father on the phone. I repeated my news, intoxicated with happiness. Finally, I had found the purest causal relationship that I had ever experienced: you do the work required, and you get the results you desired. Family didn't offer that, marriage didn't offer that, parenthood didn't offer that, and work certainly didn't offer that–each had too many variables. But school? School offered that. I was overcome with pride by what I had accomplished.

"Congratulations," he offered curtly. "What does that mean?"

"Well, it means I'm in the top one percent of all students at UTA," I said.

"Whoopee."

"And I get to take part in a special convocation, where I'll receive my honor cords and a certificate," I continued.

"What else do you get?" he asked, meaning was there a financial prize?

"It's an enormous honor, Dad," I said, feeling a too-familiar hurt spreading through my body.

"Well, if you say so. But do you think this somehow proves you're intelligent?"

I didn't know how to respond.

"Your mother is intelligent," he said. "You...you're smart, but you're not intelligent. Not like your mother," he said. "Don't confuse the two."

What the fuck?

I took a deep breath and told him, perhaps for the first time in my life, he had really hurt my feelings; this achievement meant a lot to me.

"Fine, then it shouldn't matter what I think." With that, he said he needed to go and asked if I'd like to be returned to my mother. I declined, hung up, and bawled. Later, he denied having said what he did, claiming he hadn't said those exact words, and I was just too sensitive. My hurt feelings weren't his fault, but mine.

My husband, daughter, and mother-in-law attended the President's Convocation and clapped loudly as I crossed the stage. My parents elected not to attend. Insult, as they say, on top of injury. Yet, I did my best to keep my disappointment from diluting the excitement of the day and, once home, proudly displayed my honors cords in my office as encouragement to make it to graduation.

The next semester, I wrote another original research paper that resulted in rave reviews from my professor. It was an analysis of two female Civil War spies, and honestly, it was one of the best pieces I had produced. I now was a member of Phi Alpha Theta, an honor society for students and professors of history. Our chapter hosted an annual competition for the best undergraduate and graduate research papers, and my professor encouraged me to enter this particular work. I did, and a month later was advised that my paper was selected in the graduate division. This honor felt like more than just an award, though; it felt like validation that in competition with my fellow graduate students, many of whom were on their doctoral track, my work was deemed superior.

This time when I called my parents to share the news, I could tell my father that besides a certificate, I also would receive two hundred and fifty dollars.

"Congratulations," he said. "That's not much of a prize. But good for you."

Mom tried to excuse his obvious contempt for my academic achievements by saying he just didn't understand, as he had never been much of a student, and I shouldn't let him diminish the moment.

It had. At a cognitive level, I knew better than to keep dropping my achievements at his feet and expecting at least a pat on the head. At an emotional level, I still believed I'd do something worthy of his praise and favor. The textbook definition of insanity, right? Doing the same things over and over and expecting different results…yup. Guilty as charged.

I chose not to tell him when, just one month later, I was nominated for and accepted into the Honor Society of Phi Kappa Phi, the nation's oldest society of academic scholars. It was another prized accomplishment, and I was determined not to have it minimized.

In fact, I elected not to discuss school with my father at all, which only provoked him further because I still spoke with Mom almost daily. Once I completed my course work and delved into the research for my thesis, we talked even more frequently.

I took a one-year break when I began a new job at an executive level. Along with my parental responsibilities, it left time for little else. It was a welcome break, though I wondered when I could finish my master's program. The answer came as my involuntary separation from the corporation, though it was coupled with a generous nine-month severance. While initially crushing, I found the silver lining: essentially, they would pay me to write my thesis.

I opted to expound upon a paper I had written much earlier in my graduate program–an analysis of Adina De Zavala. She played a seminal role not only in elevating Texas history but in saving the Alamo immediately prior to its planned demolition. My research took me to San Antonio and to Austin, where I immersed myself in her original papers — thousands of them. As I began piecing together my theories, I'd call Mom–now retired–and we'd talk for hours (until my father would give her a look that forced her to get off the phone) discussing what I was finding. She became as invested as I in my subject and would ask pertinent questions that frequently helped redirect my thinking. I spent four months on my original research, besides reading at least fifty different journal articles and over twenty books about Texas history, Tejano struggles, historic preservation in the early twentieth century, and beyond. It was a dizzying amount of research, and by the end of November, doubt overwhelmed and crippled me. I had no idea how to turn all this work into a coherent thesis.

Since it was the holiday season with plenty of distractions, I took advantage of all of them! Almost daily, Mom would ask how the thesis was coming. My first complete draft was due to my committee on February 11. Shouldn't I get to work? I told her I was thinking about it. And so it continued, until finally, I asked her firmly not to mention the "T" word until the new year. She reluctantly agreed but said I really didn't want to compromise all that I had achieved by letting myself down before the finish line. Mom was a tough coach.

Beginning January 2, I got to work and wrote every day, all day, to meet my first deadline. I spent a fortune copying four thesis copies for my committee members and one for Mom, but I finally had time to relax. Mom read the first draft and, as always, provided salient commentary with a few critical questions. Her mantra throughout the process was "causation versus correlation." Interestingly, that would become my mantra for so many other things in the future.

Next to Mom, my thesis chair, Stephanie, was my strongest advocate, while the remaining committee members picked apart every draft, directing me to re-think my analysis, find additional research to support my theories, and even consider taking one more semester to ensure I had left no stones unturned. For the next two months, I alternated between crying jags and temper tantrums. I was receiving conflicting input and began to think this entire process was an exercise in futility. Stephanie held her ground with the rest of the committee, and they deemed my final draft "acceptable" such that I could move to my thesis defense. I dropped by my parents' that afternoon and gave Mom my final draft to read.

A week later, and one week before my defense, Mom invited me over. They had recently bought a new house, so she always enjoyed having a reason for a visit. When I got there, she offered me a glass of Merlot and invited me to sit down. Dad was upstairs in his office, as per usual. I saw my thesis sitting on the coffee table.

"Well?"

"I am truly amazed, Suzanne. Beyond amazed," she said as she snuggled into her wingback. I waited.

"This work is phenomenal. You should be so proud." I beamed, embarrassed and elated at the same time. I still wasn't accustomed to this level of praise.

"I never could have done this," she said wistfully, taking a sip of her ginger ale. She had stopped consuming alcohol a year earlier when she was diagnosed with congestive heart failure. Alcohol was contraindicated for her medications, and her condition was more serious than she had shared with me. But more of that later.

"What do you mean?"

"The discipline it took for you to have done this much research and to knuckle down and write your first draft in forty-one days...well, that's extraordinary."

"But, Mom, you went to law school and passed the bar!"

"Not the same, Suz. I couldn't have produced something like this. You should be so proud of what you've accomplished because I certainly am."

I could have died on the spot. It took forty-seven years, but I felt I had finally impressed my mom. And it felt...strange. Good, but strange. I stood up with tears in my eyes and went to give her a hug as my father came downstairs. He said hello, poured a glass of Scotch, and turned on the news, clearly aware he was interrupting something but not interested in what that something was.

The moment with Mom was over, yet it remains in my heart to this day. He never looked at my final thesis, which I had bound and presented to them just before my graduation ceremony. In fact, I'm not sure he even knew what it was about. I didn't care. This accomplishment was mine.

They attended my hooding and commencement ceremonies, then joined me, my husband, my daughter, and my mother-in-law for dinner that night at one of our favorite restaurants. Incidentally, my graduation was on Mother's Day, so I was sharing my celebration, anyway. Disregarding both events, my father complained indignantly to the manager because they were out of his first and second entrée choices. Again, he had taken center stage; he wasn't getting what he wanted.

Good girl, overshadowed.

Chapter Twenty-Six: Plot Twist

Two days after I walked the stage to receive my master's, I turned the page to my next professional adventure, beginning my position with a local college. Interestingly, a few months prior, I had considered teaching history at this institution. Fortunately, God had other plans, and I began what would become the best job I ever had leading the public relations and marketing division and directly supporting the college's chancellor. I was surrounded by people with doctorate degrees, many of whom quizzed me about the relevance of my master's degree. By now, I was accustomed to this question, so I ceased letting it bother me. I was a corporate type navigating the world of academia, complete with its unique brand of politics that would take a few years to understand, but I loved my job, anyway.

Our chancellor was as demanding as she was friendly. I believe I got the job because, during our interview, she asked if she intimidated me. (She was a genuine force of nature, much like Mom.) I laughed and asked if she was trying to? She chuckled in return, and our bond was sealed. In just a matter of weeks, she was calling me after hours and on the weekends with ideas, questions, requests, and more ideas. I stepped fully into my expected role and immersed myself in the work, to the chagrin of both my husband and my daughter, both of whom had shared with me just months earlier with the demands of my thesis committee. I guess I didn't realize just how much they resented my focus. I was too busy enjoying being needed. I failed to recognize they needed me, too.

Three months into my new job, we had planned a family vacation to the Gulf Coast. My boss was more than happy to allow me the week off, even though I hadn't accrued vacation time yet. The only twist was my parents' fiftieth wedding anniversary coincided with the start of our trip. I would have done the appropriate, daughterly thing and planned a big celebration, yet they didn't really have many shared friends, and those they had lived in different states. So, I told them I'd take them to a nice dinner instead. The next day, I would catch a flight and join Jack and G in Corpus Christi. They were fine with that; my parents were fine with that. Everything would be fine.

I made reservations at the finest restaurant in Arlington and put together what I thought was a nice gift bag for my parents. They picked me up, and we headed to the rooftop restaurant where we were seated at one of the best tables with a view overlooking the city. Dad and I ordered cocktails; Mom ordered a sparkling water then, as our meals arrived, a single glass of wine. The evening was off to a good start. Until the restaurant was out of what my father wanted to order. "Here we go again," I thought, hoping he wouldn't make a scene. He didn't, though he was dour for the rest of the evening. I did my best to make it as nice a celebration as I could.

The next morning, I caught my flight to Corpus Christi, where I was met by my husband and daughter. We thoroughly enjoyed our time in Port Aransas (visits there had become one of our traditions) and spent time in Austin before returning home. G would head back to school in a few weeks, beginning her last year of junior high, and I went back to my still-new job, thrilled to have work I loved doing even though it occupied much more of my free time than I had expected.

By the holiday season, our marriage had become strained–much more than usual–and by Christmas, my husband and I were barely speaking. The fault for that rift lay solely at my feet, and while it's not relevant to this story, it was informed by my parental role models. I could not admit my mistakes. Seems like I came by that naturally, in hindsight, but at the moment, I was hell-bent on defending myself rather than listening to my husband. I would not bend to his wishes, though I sure bent to the wishes of others. Namely, my boss.

That spring, she was under fire from the faculty, many of whom wanted to call for a vote of no confidence that would have put her position in peril. During the next few months, she relied solely on me to help develop her talking points, to read each room in which she was called upon to address faculty questions, and to keep my ear to the ground so we knew what the faculty was saying. We frequently talked late into the night, but she needed me, and I would do my very best to help her...even advising her what colors she should and shouldn't wear. I felt as though I was protecting my mother; that's how much she meant to me. In the end, she prevailed–we prevailed–and I was gratified to know I had earned a special place with her. My ego plumped more than it should have, which didn't play well at home.

Of course, there were other issues as well, but I was too enamored of myself and my career to notice the deepening divide between Jack and me. His spending less and less time interacting with me didn't seem like any kind of red flag. After nearly twenty years of marriage, I just assumed we each were doing our own things.

Until one early Monday morning in June. I was in the garage drinking a cup of coffee and smoking a cigarette before getting ready for work. Our daughter was at summer camp. My husband came out and told me I should hold up on driving to work since storms were coming. He didn't want me to get stuck in the downpour while on the highway. I appreciated that, so I took my time getting ready. About twenty minutes later, he came into the bathroom and told me I had a delivery. I told him I had ordered nothing, and he shrugged. I went to the door where I was met by a young woman asking me to confirm my name. Once I did, she handed me an envelope. I asked what it was as my husband stood a few feet from me. She said it was divorce papers. I took the envelope and shut the door, shaking.

After we shared a few choice words, I finished getting ready and, with the envelope in my tote bag, left for work. My first call was to my parents. Mom answered, though it was a bit early for them, and I told her what had happened. She said I should come over after work and told me I'd be okay. I had no choice but to believe her. My next call was to my immediate boss, whom I asked to see shortly in his office before heading to mine. He told me he'd be waiting. Adrenalin coursed through me like neon. As with so many of my life's events, I was propelled into action before contemplation.

I had already taken off my wedding ring and put it in my wallet by the time I reached his office. I still had shed no tears and didn't when I met with him. After calmly telling him my husband was divorcing me and that I would have to move out in the next month (as per the terms of the suit he filed), my boss assured me I could take all the time I needed. I appreciated that, as I would need it. "Grateful" seems too banal a word to describe my feelings. I had only been there a year, and here I was, needing. I wasn't sure what quite yet.

Once I got to my office, I shared the news with my small team, and they rallied around, pledging whatever support I needed and offering words of encouragement. After making a few calls, I scheduled an appointment with a divorce attorney for five o'clock that evening. A long day, to be sure, but I somehow compartmentalized enough that I could be productive before leaving early to head to his law office.

After polite introductions, he reviewed the documents and told me he'd be happy to represent me for a five-thousand-dollar retainer. I had money in savings, but I wasn't sure–based on verbiage in the divorce documents–if I could spend it until the divorce was final. I told him I'd consider it and be in contact the following day.

I didn't even bother ringing the bell when I arrived at my parents' house around six that same evening. They had their nightly routine, and I knew I would interrupt it. But honestly, I had never gone through a divorce (they both had), and Mom invited me, after all. She met me as I walked into the foyer and engulfed me in a hug. Mom wasn't a demonstrative woman, but she knew, in that moment, I was doing what I could to hold myself together. I breathed in her perfume and felt the tears begin to fall. She motioned me to the couch and brought me a glass of wine. Dad was in his chair, sipping his nightly Scotch and nibbling on his nightly peanuts.

After showing Mom the documents, Dad asked if I knew what had precipitated my husband's decision. I did, of course, but I didn't want to go into detail. The truth was, our marriage always had been turbulent, and my parents knew it. Frequently over our twenty-year relationship, I had spoken to Mom about my thoughts on filing for divorce. Each time, she advised me to consider the financial ramifications and what it meant to be a single mother. She had done it, so I never understood why she discouraged me from taking the same path, especially since I had a college degree and had achieved a fair amount of professional success. Yet, I let her fears become my own. Not just in this regard, but in so many other areas. My fear of what might happen obscured any thoughts of what could be.

This wasn't the time for reflection, though. I had several decisions to make and to make quickly, given the deadlines imposed by the petition for divorce. Simply put, I felt scared before I felt anything else.

Dad asked about my divorce attorney, so I told him who I had hired, what we had discussed, and how much it would cost. He went to the dining table, which had become his improvised desk, and wrote a check for the entire retainer. I could only nod, wiping tears from my face, and thank him. I poured another glass of wine.

"You want to go easy on that," Mom admonished.

Next, Dad asked where I planned to live. I told them I really hadn't gotten that far since I just received the papers that morning. He looked at Mom, who nodded, and told me their old house–the one they first bought when we moved there from San Antonio–was mine. Though they had been in their new house for almost two years, they had never cleared out the old one and put it on the market. I would later learn, from my new next-door neighbor, that he told her once on his bi-weekly visit to water and check for any errant mail that they would not sell the house because "my daughter and her daughter will need it someday." He knew before I did that this day was inevitable.

Again, all I could do was thank them for their generosity. This kind act would keep me from having to rent an apartment and, though the house was smaller than my current house and in dire need of work, I would have a familiar place to make into a new home. I knew I needed to get to my house and face the situation, so I thanked them profusely, hugged them both, and prepared to leave. Mom asked if I'd like to meet at the old house on Friday to see what needed doing, and I told her I could be there around ten in the morning. I knew we'd talk before then.

The next few days were heart-wrenching. My daughter arrived home from camp that Wednesday, and we had to break the news, doing what we could to help her accept this would be best for everyone. She was only fourteen and about to start high school, so this wasn't an ideal time–if it ever is–to dismantle most of what had been familiar to her. Yet here we were.

As agreed, I met Mom at their old house that Friday morning. I hadn't been there since helping them pack to move two years earlier. As I pulled around back to enter the garage, I was stunned. The backyard was small but had been left untended; imagine an Amazonian rain forest in a suburban neighborhood. I didn't dare explore because God only knew what might live in there. The garage was chock-full of my father's old power tools, cans of paint that likely hadn't been opened in more than a decade, shelves stacked with garden treatments, and so much more. I took a deep breath before entering the house.

Mom was inside with bottled water, which I took gratefully. The den, which had been their shared office, still had the wall-length desk my father had built and was piled high with junk they opted not to move. The galley kitchen still sported the thirty-year-old linoleum, oak-stained cabinets, and a Formica countertop; everything was greasy to the touch. The dining room looked mostly untouched, though all Mom's China had been moved. Otherwise, the dated dining room set (which I never really liked) remained. The ivory carpet in the dining and living rooms was heavily soiled from years of neglect. I was speechless.

Next, I walked through the guest bedrooms, both of which Mom had commandeered as sewing rooms. The dog-shit brown shag carpet, original to the house, ran through all the bedrooms. In the sewing rooms, the floors were littered with pins and fabric scraps. Her sewing cabinet—a monstrosity—remained. But it was the sheer volume of quilting fabric and books that brought me to a halt. For years, she purchased fabric by the bolts, having thought she'd open a quilt shop after she retired (she didn't), and while she moved a huge amount of fabric to their new home, what remained could have stocked a large store. She had set up banquet-type tables in both rooms. The tables were buckling under stacks that probably would have measured four feet in height. And that's not counting what already had been cut, folded, and stored in various closets. Quilting books and magazines crowded the remaining bookcases, also struggling under the weight. It was nearly impossible to walk through the two rooms. I panicked; I had to move in three weeks.

I proceeded down the hall to the primary bedroom, which was the only room that had mostly been emptied, then peered into the primary bath, which still had the 1970s wallpaper (hideous), as did the wet bar and the powder room at the front of the house. There was no way I could envision living here. I just kept shaking my head and finally fell to my knees, beginning to sob. Mom had no patience.

"Are you just going to sit there and fall apart or are you going to figure out what we need to do next?" she asked, towering over me with her hands on her hips.

"I'm going to fall apart," I said, hiccupping as I cried my first tears that week.

"Well then, you've got five minutes." And with that, she turned on her heel to return to one of her sewing rooms. I curled into a fetal position and sobbed, angry tears, scared tears, sad tears. Then I stood up and got to work.

I had taken my boss at his word and took the next few weeks off from work, spending every day at the "new" house to purge it enough that I could bring in a handyman for some much-needed updates. First, I wanted tile installed in the kitchen and primary bathroom, as well as having the kitchen cabinets and walls painted (once the wallpaper was removed) and a granite countertop installed. Spencer, my handyman, was kind if not slow, and because he lived forty-five minutes away, his hours were inconsistent. Once I had the local mission dispatch an army of teenaged volunteers to remove everything I didn't want from the house, except Mom's excess quilt fabric that I boxed and moved to the garage, Spencer's work began. A cousin of my daughter's soccer coach was a painter, so he agreed to tackle every room in the house, including the oak paneling in the living room. His fee was reasonable, and his work was swift. Things were taking shape. Each night, after a full day of manual labor at that house, I'd return to what had been my home to continue packing, a daunting task since we had lived there for fifteen years. I was exhausted, and over the course of the next month, I think I lost around fifteen pounds.

Before moving in, Dad hired a landscape crew to raze the backyard jungle. He bought me a new refrigerator and a dishwasher. Mom bought me a washer and dryer and brought me homemade banana bread every few days, since she was sure I wasn't eating (I wasn't). After seeking guidance from my attorney, I began using my limited savings for the repairs and upgrades. While I could have waited on some projects, I was keen on making the house as nice as possible, since my daughter would be here every other week. I was staggered by, and deeply grateful for, my parents' generosity and support during that vulnerable period.

One afternoon, while repairs were still underway, and I was doing some heavy cleaning in each room, Mom stopped by to check on progress. Spencer had taken a lunch break, so I was there by myself. I showed her what I already had done, and she remarked that it already felt like a different house. (That was my intent.) As I walked her to her car, she turned and stared at me. "I'm really proud of you, Suz. I never, ever could have done this."

"What do you mean?" I was standing barefoot on the curb in the hundred-plus degree heat, wearing an old t-shirt and denim shorts that had become baggy. I wanted to get back indoors before the temperature and my fatigue converged to stall my progress.

"This. Taking on this kind of job. Getting ready to be on your own. I could never have done it." Though she had, hadn't she, when she left her first husband?

"It's not that I had much of a choice, Mom," I said, wiping the sweat from my forehead. "But I think you could have handled it if you had wanted to."

"Well, too late for that," she said breezily, getting into her car. I waved as she drove off in her metallic blue Lexus. In that moment, I believe she was jealous of what felt like the greatest tragedy I'd experienced.

Dad dropped by a few times but withheld any comments about the work I was doing. I should have known that was a dangerous sign.

Moving day coincided with my parents' anniversary, so even if they had wanted to help, they had other plans. I was secretly pleased I wouldn't have to manage them along with everything else. Waiting for the movers to arrive, I moved from room to room to ensure I had overlooked nothing I wanted to take while packing.

Steeling against any feelings of sadness, anger or regret, I had asked my husband to make sure our daughter wasn't there when the movers arrived. She was already visibly upset at seeing so many things boxed and ready to go. I didn't think she needed to watch the house being emptied of most of its furniture, too. My request wasn't heeded, and when the movers arrived, she was there to witness it all. I'll never forget her look of abject despair as she stood in the empty living room, crying. I hugged her tightly and assured her that as soon as I set the house up, I would be ready for her to spend the night. (I still needed to buy a bed and nightstand for her room.)

Unfortunately, I only had been in the house for a week or two when Spencer (who still was finishing a few projects, though I had returned to work) let me know my old dog, Macy, a Swiss mountain dog with the biggest heart and kindest brown eyes, seemed to be ill. I had moved her to my house right after I had my furniture set. She was deaf, partially blind, and did not make the transition well–she was away from her pack and in a strange home she couldn't navigate. My vet confirmed she was suffering from heart failure, but I wondered if it was simply a broken heart at being separated from the rest of her family. Two days later, I had to say goodbye.

My relatively peaceful transition was quickly met with the type of vitriol exclusive to divorce. His attorney was ferocious; mine was far too mild. I just wanted to get it over with as quickly as possible and without my daughter having to go before the judge. So I left a lot on the table. Periodically, my father would ask where things were in terms of negotiations; I chose not to tell either him or my mother.

Once the divorce was final, my father asked, again, about the settlement we had reached. When I didn't tell him, he threw a bit of a fit saying that dammit, he had paid for the attorney, so honestly, he had every right to ask. I gave him a rather disingenuous overview. The next time I saw him, he handed me a notice from the tax appraiser's office regarding estimated property taxes on the house. While he said he would pro-rate my share since I would only have been in the house for five months by the time the bill was due, he expected me to pay him by December 31. I had all but depleted my savings account to make the house livable (not to mention, hundreds of gallons of sweat equity), so couldn't my upgrades apply, and we call it a wash?

"That was your decision, Suzanne. Life is all about decisions. I'm sure you'll figure out a way," he said, getting back into his midnight blue SUV.

Shit. I was still re-learning how to pay bills since my now ex-husband had always managed our money, and I was expected (rightfully) to cover half of my daughter's expenses while also paying off furniture and electronics I had purchased on credit. I was on an emotional rollercoaster, hanging on for dear life, and soon realizing my spending and wine consumption had gotten a bit out of hand.

But, I had a house for which I didn't have to pay rent. And with a rather lavish purchase of several pieces of abstract art painted by a new friend I had made, my home became a place of refuge...for me, anyway. My daughter struggled with the adjustment of living with me for a week, then with her father for a week. Thankfully, during the weeks she was with me, my parents stepped in and picked her up from high school, bringing her to their home for snacks until I could pick her up after work. Actually, it was mostly my father, who was also interested in her transition from soccer to basketball. He joined me at her games, kept the team's statistics that he shared (unsolicited) with the coach, and tried repeatedly to coach her post-game. She hadn't asked for his help, nor did she want it, but she was too young to put her feelings into words. I tried to intervene, which threw him into a rage. "If she has something to say, she can say it to me directly!" he bellowed. No, she really couldn't. I knew all too well that wouldn't be a safe move for her; it never was for me, anyway. Such began what would become a permanent rift in their relationship.

Amid my divorce, the chancellor gave me a promotion, which involved a bigger title and moving two additional departments under me, but I didn't receive a pay increase. Her rationale was that I was hired (one year earlier) at the top of the salary band because I came from private industry. At the time, I wasn't concerned because I had greater responsibility when I truly needed a "win." Any kind of win. When I shared the news with my parents, Mom was predictably pleased. My father was predictably disgusted.

"When will you ever learn?" he asked. "When will you stop letting people take advantage of you?" Interesting question, as I didn't feel I had been duped. Not by my boss, anyway.

Two months later, on the night of what would have been my twentieth wedding anniversary, I joined twenty-two other women being honored as "Great Women of Texas" by the Fort Worth Business Press. A professional associate had nominated me, and I was chosen from among over 250 nominations–another win when I felt broken. What did I get for this? Yes, I received that question yet again. Well, I got a crystal award with my name on it, a write-up in the magazine, a makeover at Neiman Marcus, and a pretty swell swag bag. That was more than enough. Wasn't it?

Thanksgiving would be the first post-divorce holiday, the rules for which already were established in the divorce decree, and I was dreading it. Since we had gotten married, we had hosted every Thanksgiving dinner. This year, our daughter would be with my ex, his girlfriend, and his family; I would have her the following day. Mom agreed to postpone Thanksgiving until then, much to the chagrin of my father, so G and I could dine with them. While a friend invited me to her family luncheon, which felt awkward at best, I spent most of the day alone with my German Shepherd (whom my ex allowed me to bring to my house after Macy died) and my two cats. I felt grateful for my home and pets, but not much else.

We went to my parents' the next afternoon, and already, I could see Dad spoiling for a fight. Mom was tense, the turkey was overcooked, my father railed, and my daughter and I just stayed quiet and ate what we could of the meal. It was not a festive day, and we couldn't wait to leave.

G's birthday was just two short weeks later. Again, I would have to share the event uncomfortably with my ex, who stayed upstairs while she opened her gifts in the living room. I know I overcompensated with the presents I gave her, but isn't this what newly divorced parents do?

Next came Christmas. As per the divorce agreement, my daughter would be with her dad and his family until nine o'clock on Christmas Eve. I was a nervous wreck the entire day, wondering if I had bought enough, decorated enough, and baked enough to make this holiday special enough. Our plan was to watch movies, sleep in, then open our gifts Christmas morning before joining my parents at their home for dinner that evening. Just two weeks prior, my father issued another of his special edicts: we were only to give one another three gifts. Period.

I followed his direction, mostly, except that I had purchased two items for them both, in addition to the other presents. G and I laughed as I wrapped the Shark vacuum cleaner in some of the 1970s-era metallic bathroom wallpaper I had saved from renovation. I packed up my Nissan Pathfinder with our presents and the chocolate torte I had made, and off we went. As I began unloading the car, with a few of the presents being quite large, my father opened the door wearing his favorite Santa hat. I had given it to him many years earlier, and while he continued to despise the holiday, he would always wear the hat while shopping two or three days before Christmas. I took his sporting the hat as a good sign of festivity.

That hope evaporated once we got into the house and began placing the presents around the small, flocked tree near the gas fireplace. I already felt anxious, not knowing how to "do Christmas" in this new chapter, but I had vowed I would make the very best of it. All that changed in a heartbeat. As Mom put the appetizer tray on the coffee table, my father began yelling over Christmas carols in the background. "Dammit, Suzanne, I said only three fucking presents each! Don't you EVER listen?" I watched as my daughter shrunk into the couch.

Something snapped. I used to have a therapist who said that emotions unexpressed become a capped tube of toothpaste, of sorts—when enough pressure is applied, the toothpaste will come out sideways. Yes, my seams ripped wide open, and I yelled back.

"If this is the way it's going to be, we'll just leave right now," I said, fighting through angry tears. "How dare you speak to me that way, on this of all days!" Mom tried to calm me down with a touch to my shoulder; I waved her off.

"Why don't you sit down and eat something," she said. I wasn't hungry. My father stormed into the other room while the three of us sat awkwardly. Mom prattled about the unseasonably warm weather while I considered my options.

He finally came into the living room and poured himself a Scotch; the rest of us were sipping ginger ale. The plan was to eat a few appetizers before our traditional meal of prime rib, then open presents after. Because we always had to follow his plan.

After we noshed on her signature cheese spread with celery, Mom got up and took the roast out to rest while I made my signature green beans. Once they were ready, I dished up the beans while she took her homemade croissants from the oven. G helped put all the side dishes on the table, which Mom had decorated beautifully with her Lenox Christmas China, Waterford crystal, and her treasured sterling flatware. We took our seats while my father carved the roast. We heard a heavy sigh.

"How you managed to ruin an eighty-dollar roast is beyond me," he said to Mom. She got up to see what he meant.

"Look at this! Dammit, you overcooked it!"

I looked at G and shook my head, then took her hand. We would find a way to get through the next two hours. I could see she was miserable, and why wouldn't she be? She had not grown up with this, but I had.

My parents sat down, and my father asked who would say the blessing. That seemed rich, given the tension heavy in the air. I took it for the team and offered as sincere a prayer as I could muster, mostly thanking God for his son Jesus and the gift of family and friends. We said, "Amen," and ate our meal. I couldn't resist telling Mom I thought the roast was delicious (it was) and that her croissants were as good as ever (they were slightly burned). She raved about my green beans. My father chewed in silence.

Once we were finished, we took our assigned places in the living room so my father could do his thing. Yes, we all got calendars (present number one). I don't remember any other gifts, though Mom thought the wrapping paper on the vacuum cleaner (which my father said he couldn't understand why I bought) was lovely. She didn't recognize it as the old wallpaper from the powder room and missed the irony altogether. I gave G a wink. After all the presents had been opened, I served my chocolate-orange torte, eager to leave as soon as we could. I could sense my daughter's disappointment in the entire evening, though at least she knew better than to say anything.

As we were leaving, my father pulled me aside and said I had done too much in the way of presents. I shrugged, thanked him for our dinner and gifts, and gave him a half-hearted hug. My daughter already was in the car, ready to get back to my house.

"Don't forget–I need a check for $3,850 by New Year's Eve. I hope you managed to keep your spending from getting ahead of you."

Good girl, not merry.

Chapter Twenty-Seven: Half-Time

After a few months of unsuccessfully trying to meet men who were gainfully employed, well-educated, addiction-free, and kind–yes, all were prerequisites–I concluded I was better off alone. At least, for the moment. My ex was now in a seriously committed relationship, which amplified my feelings of loss and loneliness, and my daughter was fully immersed in her freshman year of high school, with friends now eclipsing family as preferred company. My fiftieth birthday was just seven months away, and my life had never felt so uncertain. Weren't things supposed to be easier with age?

Mom urged me to lose myself in my work, yet that wasn't enough. The shine of my promotion had lost its luster and trying to manage a few male direct reports who resented my being their boss only intensified my angst toward men. I was brittle and angry at the world. Not a good look, and very much not a good mindset. Shortly after my divorce was final, I sat on my patio drinking Pinot Grigio and writing in my journal. I had made a list of all the things I was looking for, not just in a partner, but in myself. Now months later, I could see my list was failing me, across the board.

One evening, I met a friend and potential financial advisor for dinner. When we were finished, she recommended we go to a dive bar off Camp Bowie Boulevard in Fort Worth. I enjoyed her company and the brooding vibe of the place. The next morning, I realized I had left my leather jacket there, so I called to confirm they would hold on to it. That afternoon, after mindlessly wandering through a nearby antique mall, I went back to the bar to retrieve my jacket. While there, I received a text from a man I had been seeing, off and on, canceling our plans for that evening.

I sat down at the bar and ordered a vodka soda with lime. The bartender couldn't have been more than twenty-four and was very, very pregnant. After she served my drink, I turned into a cliché: the bitter divorcee who had just been dumped by a man she thought she liked. After being dumped by a husband of nearly twenty years. What's wrong with me?

The bartender nodded. She said that's the way it goes sometimes. I began to cry (further to being a cliché) and told her about my list. "He was almost everything I said I wanted," I told her. That wasn't quite the truth, though he was handsome and quite wealthy. She put down the beer mug she was drying and peered at me as if I was having an "episode." (I was.)

"Did you ever consider," she said carefully, "that maybe you shouldn't focus on what you want but, instead, what you need?"

From the mouths of babes, as they say. For the first time in my life, someone actually was giving me permission to put MY needs before expectations–my own, my parents', my daughter's, my friends'–hell, society's in general. I felt a stranger had just given me a clue to the meaning of life! I drove home feeling more resolute than I had in some time. Maybe I really could get to own my space, as I had counseled others, and make my needs a priority. Never doubt there are angels among us.

At least I had finally gotten my finances under control. After writing my father a check for the property taxes I owed (and that I couldn't claim on my taxes because the house was still in his name), I was feeling strapped, but I was making it work. I had to since I was facing my future alone.

Valentine's Day fell on a Saturday that year. As usual, my parents sent me cards. I sent myself flowers. My daughter was staying with friends; my ex and his girlfriend were on a romantic ski trip (or so it appeared on Facebook). A friend came over the next day, and we drank a lot of wine as I shared the wealth of my self-pity. After she left, I sat on my living room floor with my sable German shepherd and a fire roaring in the fireplace. I wasn't looking forward to work the next day, but I perused my email accounts anyway, just to give myself something reasonably adult-is to do.

And there it was, in my personal email: notification from eHarmony they had found me a match.

Once I had moved into my house, I signed up for the various online dating services, including eHarmony, the only one requiring a monthly fee. I took their lengthy questionnaire seriously and answered everything with brutal honesty and surprising self-awareness. What did I have to lose? Months went by, thirty-plus dollars per, and nothing. Until February 15.

I looked at his profile. He was handsome, worked in education, and lived in Arlington. He had a master's degree (check), a son in college (check), and while his screen name was strange ("Ateve"), I was intrigued. I poured another glass of wine and responded to the nudge from eHarmony, communicating with my "match" I was interested in learning more. Within a few minutes, he had apparently accepted the nudge, and the platform did its thing: we each were given another set of questions about life priorities, pet peeves, what we could and could not tolerate, etc. From there, we were invited to chat via the platform. We did, for a while...breezy banter, nothing more. About thirty minutes later, he asked if I'd like to text. I gave him my number, and we texted back and forth for another thirty minutes or so. He asked if I'd like to talk. Eek. I stoked the fire, poured another glass of wine, and then replied, "Sure."

He called and introduced himself by his lifelong nickname, Butch, though his given name was Noble. After talking for what seemed like hours, he asked if I'd like to meet on Monday. I had a hair appointment after work, but I told him I could meet after. He asked if I had a preferred location, so I suggested a local pub where I could smoke (and where people knew me). I told him I smoked. Might as well get it out there, right? He said that would be great. How was seven?

I woke up giddy, and after perusing my wardrobe, I selected a red jersey dress and black suede pumps. While it was difficult to focus on work, I got through the day and made it to my hair appointment. My stylist gave me a glass of wine to settle my nerves and listened while I told her everything I knew about him thus far. She asked me to text her with a report and gave me an encouraging hug before I left. I was running late–one of my greatest pet peeves–so I texted him to let him know I'd be there in ten minutes. "No problem," he responded.

The pub, which has subsequently closed, very much emulated what you would find in London: a long bank of booths to the left, tables in the middle, and the bar to the right of the entrance. I took a deep breath and walked in, quickly surveying the place. Two men in different booths stood up as I entered; the man closest to me was short, bald, and pudgy. He smiled. The man toward the back waved. He was tall and slender. Okay…here we go!

For the next three hours, we talked and laughed nonstop like old familiar friends, except with that special spark. His eyes were the bluest blue I've seen anywhere except the Caribbean, and they twinkled as he grinned at my stories and my over-gesticulating, which sent at least two full wine glasses flying. I don't remember feeling embarrassed because he was such easy company and, more importantly, he didn't shame or ridicule me. By the end of the evening, we both knew we had clicked, so we made plans for dinner at his place the next day. We saw each other every night that week and into the weekend. By Saturday night, we had declared our love for one another.

I cautiously told Mom about Noble. She told me to take things slowly. (We didn't.) I told Dad he worked as the head of the upper school at a college preparatory academy; he didn't offer any commentary, surprisingly. I knew Mom would love Noble because he radiated kindness and compassion, and I figured Dad would judge him because he had a strong Oklahoman accent and came from a farming background. I didn't much care.

My only concern was how to tell G. Many of her friends attended the school where Noble worked, and because he had invited me our first Friday together to attend the school's annual musical, several of those friends saw me with him. Clearly on a date. Under any other circumstances, I would have waited until we were more established to broach the subject, but I didn't want her to hear from anyone else that I was involved with the head of the upper school her friends attended. She was still embarrassed enough by our divorce.

That Sunday evening, her dad dropped her off at the usual time, and she immediately asked me to take her to Ultra–the ultimate beauty amusement park favored by teenaged girls and mature women alike–for a haircut. On the way, I casually told her about Noble. She didn't seem bothered in the least. At least, not then.

Her first post-divorce Spring Break would be with her father, so Noble and I decided to go to Austin for a few days — our first trip together and just over a month since we first met. It was a blissful getaway, though I broke two fingers throwing a football back and forth with him at Zilker Park. (He played college football and coached for more than twenty years after that. I should have known better than to think my tomboy ways would stand a chance.) I showed him all my favorite places. As an Oklahoma Sooners fan, he even allowed me to buy him a Texas Longhorns shirt at the university co-op. We took country roads from Austin back to Arlington, and when we drove through the Hamilton town square and he asked if I would mind if we perused the local antique mall, I knew he was the one.

Before being surprised with divorce papers the prior summer, I had been one of ten staff members selected to participate in the Salzburg Global Seminar that July–a weeklong event specific, in this case, for those working in higher education. It thrilled me to have been selected, and while my passport was current and I was ready to see Austria, I asked to defer for a year. The optics simply would not have been good leaving amidst a divorce and all.

Once the dates were set for the next year's seminar, I asked Noble if he might consider a vacation in Germany the week following the seminar. Having never been to Europe, the invitation delighted him, and we made plans to meet in Frankfurt once the seminar concluded. This trip would mean, of course, that I'd be gone for two full weeks, throwing my custody schedule out of whack. Thankfully, my ex-husband was amenable.

I was five hours late meeting Noble in Frankfurt because of oversleeping and missing my early train. By then, we had only been together six months, but it seemed much longer. Though newly in love, we experienced a mutual comfort and familiarity neither of us had known before. It was just so easy. I had not yet introduced Noble to my parents, though they were aware of our trip. Dad even agreed to check on the cats each day (my dog was staying with my former neighbors). They didn't say it directly, but I think they thought we were moving fast. (We were.)

Our trip was magnificent. We spent the first few days in Cologne, then headed to Munich, our home base for three day trips, including a boat cruise along the Danube and a trip to Bavaria to see a few of the exquisite castles there. Before heading south to Hohenschwangau Castle, the childhood home of King Ludwig II of Bavaria, we stopped at the neighborhood Aldi to put together our picnic basket, complete with wine, bread, cheeses, salami, olives, grapes, and raspberries. Once we arrived at the castle, we found a place to sit by the neighboring lake and enjoy our feast while watching the beautiful, iconic swans for which the castle had been named. The day couldn't get any better–it was postcard perfect.

After buying our tickets for a tour, we meandered around the castle grounds, enchanted by the architecture and expert landscaping. I found a corner spot away from the public to sit and have a cigarette before getting in line for our time slot. After I finished, we walked through a stone alcove on our way to the line, and upon seeing several large stones–boulders, almost–along the wall, Noble asked if we could sit down. I was confused; hadn't we just been sitting? He was, after all, eight years older than I–was he feeling all right? I sat down, hoping we wouldn't be late for the tour. In a heartbeat, he dropped to one knee and with tears in his eyes told me he had loved no one as he loved me, and would I be his wife? I, too, started to cry and stammered, "Yes!" as onlookers passed, clapping. A kind gentleman asked if he could take our picture. We were more than happy to let him!

Just before we stood to make the upstairs trek for the tour, he took my hand and said, "Right now, I can't buy you much, but I can give you everything." I've never forgotten those words and the sheer impact of what they meant. But I would come to understand.

Though we were engaged, I asked that we not yet tell anyone since I didn't want the barrage of commentary sure to follow. Isn't this too soon? How can you possibly know he's the one? You've only been divorced for a year–isn't this a bit, um, fast? Noble agreed to my request, though we called to tell his mom that night but asked that she, too, keep things quiet for a while. She was thrilled and, yes, promised not to say a word. We would join his family the weekend we got back to the States for a family reunion in Oklahoma City, so, as she said, we could decide if we wanted to say anything then. But we put it off.

A few weeks after our vacation, I invited my parents for a late afternoon visit to meet Noble. I still hadn't shared our news; what if they didn't like him? I couldn't imagine it, but it was possible, especially with my hyper-critical father. We told them about our trip and shared our pictures. Dad couldn't understand why I hadn't bothered consulting him about what we should have seen and where we should have gone, particularly as they had lived there, for

God's sake, for over three years! I explained that we only had so many days and enjoyed each one thoroughly, giving Noble a knowing smile. True to his character, he let my parents do most of the talking and answered each of Mom's questions with his unique combination of humor and humility. As they rose to leave, Noble shook my dad's hand and asked if he might be up for a drink the following week. Dad agreed, so they scheduled the place and time before my parents left.

Noble met my father, as planned, and after a beer or two, Noble began telling him how much I had changed his life. He then respectfully requested my father's blessing for us to get married. As he shared with me later, my father put down his drink and looked at him quizzically.

"Why do you want to marry her?"

I loved that Noble was honoring tradition and showing respect for my father though, really, I had been married before, so was this really necessary? Yet, I shouldn't have been surprised that my father would counter Noble's question with a question.

"Well, what did you say?"

"I have to admit, I was a little caught off guard. That really wasn't what I was expecting," he said, shaking his head.

Oh, just wait, honey. You're not just marrying me. You're marrying them too.

"So, I told him you're the most amazing person I've ever met, that you're wickedly smart and funny, that you've got the biggest heart, and that we're just easy together," he said with a smile.

I asked if he told my father he already proposed and if so, was he irritated?

"He didn't seem to be," Noble said. "But when he wished me luck and told me you're a handful, it didn't feel like something a father would say about his daughter. It seemed...strange."

Oh, you have no idea.

Several years later, as I was perusing my father's emails after his death, I found a message he had written recounting the event. It was to his ex-wife, whom he had divorced sixty years earlier, yet still maintained contact. He said he thought Noble would be a steadying influence on me as I had always let my highs get too high and my lows get too low. While that wasn't and isn't true, I found it interesting that he actually was describing himself.

Good girl, engaged!

Chapter Twenty-Eight: Recalibrating

Having been engaged since July, Mom urged me to consider marrying Noble as soon as Christmas that same year, but I still felt the need to wait. On the weeks G was in my care, Noble joined us for dinner periodically, but never spent the night. She was slow to warm up to him, which I understood–she wasn't accustomed to having to share me with anyone. Noble understood and gave her the space she needed to come to terms with our engagement. But by this time, my ex's girlfriend had already moved in with him, and I was racked by jealousy that she would have greater exposure to–and possibly influence over–my daughter than I did. My jealousy was a bad look, and the more I expressed my feelings on the matter, the farther G pulled away from me.

The following January, Noble had knee-replacement surgery, which meant he would need to stay at my house for several weeks through recovery and physical therapy. I didn't want to plan our wedding until he had fully recovered. I joked at the time that I needed to know what kind of patient he was before officially tying the knot. The truth was, I was still reluctant to proceed until things had calmed down with my daughter. My parents didn't understand why I was letting her dictate our plans. I couldn't explain that I still felt guilty about the divorce and didn't want to further alienate her.

After Noble's surgery, I was able to work from home for a few days to care for him. Once I returned to the office, Dad stepped in and shuttled him to and from doctor's appointments and physical therapy sessions. One thing about my dad: he loved being needed, especially if it meant he held the power. It was the feeling of superiority, I believe, that he valued more than giving assistance, no matter what kind. I would later see he extended the same white knight gallantry to the many women in his orbit. I imagine that's what kept them around.

Once Noble recovered and returned to work, we began discussing potential wedding scenarios. The idea of a blended family event, with friends, was simply too overwhelming–and expensive–to consider, especially since we were paying for this ourselves. He officially moved in a few months before we planned to marry, and together, we began re-landscaping the backyard to suit our preferences. We were making this our "together" home while making plans for our future.

Considering all angles, we elected an elopement of sorts, just the two of us. Dad said he'd pay for a reception once we returned. When I started putting together some ideas with associated costs, he all but recanted his offer and said we could discuss it later. I wasn't surprised, really...perhaps more relieved. I didn't want this to turn into a repeat, albeit less grand, event like my first wedding reception, which he continued to call "the best party (he) ever threw." No, we wanted this to be about us and us alone.

I knew I didn't want a beach wedding; I always thought those were trite. We considered Paris–way too expensive for our budget, and G never would have forgiven me. We contemplated a few more options before I suggested we select our wedding venue by thinking where we'd like to honeymoon. Wine country? I checked rental properties in Sonoma, California, and found a picturesque guest house associated with a local vineyard. Perfect. Our plans really took shape when I learned San Francisco's stately, museum-quality city hall had been the site of Marilyn Monroe's wedding to Joe DiMaggio. The architecture was exquisite, the décor impeccable, and I knew it would make for a perfect occasion and even better photography. Noble agreed, so I began orchestrating the details of our June wedding. We would be married by a Justice of the Peace. Easy!

After a few days of sight-seeing in San Fran, we arrived at city hall, completed our paperwork, and waited amidst several much larger and predominantly Asian wedding parties, all younger and more nervous than we were. Our female JP called our names, and our photographer was our witness. We were officially married in the exquisite rotunda, then spent the next hour getting our photos taken in various areas of the famous building. It could not have been better. Neither of us missed having people in attendance, and without guests, we could focus solely on one another.

The next day, we picked up our red Mustang convertible and drove up to Sonoma, where we were greeted by the owner of the vineyard and served a delicious wine made from his grapes. The next four days were idyllic: sightseeing and wine tasting by day, quiet evenings on their shared patio before we retired to our guest house. We remember that part of the trip fondly, as I learned I could add "emu whisperer" to my resume. Yes, I was able to hand feed–and pet–their eight-year-old emu, Ishi, whom neither the owner nor his wife had ever touched. They watched from the deck above in wonder. Each following day, Ishi came looking for me and my loaf of white bread. I was sad to say goodbye to her.

Returning home, I realized I truly was living a fairy tale. I basked in my happiness. Finally.

Except that fairy tales aren't real. Doesn't everyone know that?

I had taken the day after our return as another vacation day so we could ease back into reality. And reality punched me in the gut. Hard. Retrieving my mail, I found a letter from my ex-husband's lawyer–seemed my daughter wanted to live exclusively with her father. I would be required to pay child support in addition to what I already paid each month toward her school expenses, college fund, and medical care. I sat down on the couch and cried as Noble watched helplessly. Why was I being rejected by my child? I picked up my iPhone and hurled it across the room where it crashed into my antique curio cabinet, shattering two panels of its beautiful, beveled glass. I didn't care.

I would be forced to either contest this new custody agreement or accept it for what would be two more years before she graduated high school. I also had to agree to work with the same attorney (and pay him) for legal filings. I couldn't breathe.

Mom had quite a bit to say about this, but she understood my heartache. My father simply said, "It is what it is." He had already decided his granddaughter wasn't worth his time, and at least now (though he didn't say it directly), he'd be off the hook for carpool duties.

I negotiated child support and within a few weeks reached a compromise I could accept as much as any mother in my position could. The only bright side I could see was Noble and I would have the space to enjoy newlywed life. I felt guilty, though. Every single day. I also felt I had lost a significant part of my identity, which I hadn't necessarily prioritized until it was taken: "Mom." I knew I would always be her mother, but how much of the next few years would I miss? As it happened, quite a lot. Yet, I had to keep going.

So, we threw ourselves into our jobs and, on the weekends, home improvement projects. We decided to paint our natural brick fireplace in a nice, creamy white, which did wonders to give the illusion of more cohesive space in our favorite room. I emailed Dad a picture of our work. His response was an unexpected, vitriolic rant asking why we would put up faux brick–it looked tacky and he couldn't believe we would do such a thing without asking. Why? "Because it's STILL MY HOUSE."

I called, and Mom answered. I was in tears. "What's wrong with him?" I asked. "Why is he so mad?" She said I'd have to ask him. She put him on the line, and he answered curtly.

I told Dad we primed and painted the fireplace to blend with the rest of the living room. Why, did I ask, would he think we'd install some kind of vinyl faux whatever? He relented slightly, then reminded me he still owned the house in which we had been living RENT-FREE, and until we opted to buy it, we needed to ask his permission before making any other substantive changes.

I hung up, furiously shaking, and told Noble what my father had said. He looked at me in disbelief.

Welcome to my family, I thought. Over the next several years, Noble would get to see, up close and personally, how my father played. The house was just the beginning.

In the space of a few months, I'd lost custody of my daughter and learned the house Dad had told me was mine…really wasn't. Yet, I had a wonderful new husband whose last name I had taken and a job I loved. That would have to suffice.

Good girl, recalibrating.

Chapter Twenty-Nine: Storms Brewing

A few months into my new marriage and while still grieving the absence of my daughter, Dad called from his cell and asked if he could come over. Noble was working at a school function, so I said he was welcome anytime. I didn't really feel that way, but he sounded upset. I hoped it would not be a rant-fest about Mom and how she continued to ignore her health. He arrived at my door within five minutes and came in, breathless and shaky.

He sat on my couch while I brought him a glass of water. Spencer, my cat, jumped in his lap; Greta, my German Shepherd, laid down at my feet. I waited for him to catch his breath. He reached into his pocket and pulled out a prescription bottle, popping a Xanax into his mouth and swallowing it with a gulp of water.

"This is the third one I've taken today," he said, coughing. And then he began to cry. I was frozen with fear of what he was going to tell me. Greta began nuzzling my hand nervously with her mighty snout. She sensed my apprehension.

"She broke it off," he said. I looked at him quizzically.

"What?" He couldn't be talking about Mom, or could he? In our conversations, she kept threatening to leave and move away, maybe back to Reno. I constantly reminded her by doing so, she'd be leaving me behind. Did she really want to do that?

"After all this time, I guess she's had enough," he said cryptically. I was confused.

"Who, Dad?"

"JUDY!" he yelled. Spencer jumped; Greta cowered. I got up to get a glass of wine.

When I returned, my father's head was in his hands, and he was sobbing. What on earth did he expect from me at this moment? To comfort him that his mistress had dumped him? Hadn't he learned not to involve me in his sordid double life?

All I could do was wait. Finally, I asked why.

He said she was a good Presbyterian and could no longer carry on with a married man, that unless he was willing to leave Mom, they were over. So, this so-called, God-fearing Christian church lady, after more than ten years canoodling with my father, finally realized what she was doing was wrong? Or, was she really throwing down the "ole-tomato," as my friend Heidi used to call it, and forcing him to choose? Why would he when he had been able to have his proverbial cake and eat it too?

I couldn't think of anything to say, other than, "I'm sorry you're hurting." I wasn't. But he was carrying on like a sixteen-year-old who caught his first girlfriend making out with his best friend. It was, in a word, ridiculous. And honestly, I had not seen him this upset too many times–if ever–in my lifetime with him.

"I need to find a shrink," he said, wiping his eyes and motioning for more water. I brought him a fresh glass. I didn't dare offer him a beer on top of his third Xanax of the day.

"That's probably a good idea," I said. I wasn't about to refer him to my therapist, and besides, I'm sure she wouldn't have taken him as a client. Conflict of interest and all. (I would later find out my therapist lived down the street from Ann, but I don't want to get ahead of my story.) "You might ask your PCP for a referral."

He nodded. I heard Noble's car pull into the driveway. He walked into the living room and gave me a questioning look. I subtly shook my head. He subtly nodded.

"Well, hello!" he said to my father in his typically jovial fashion.

"Hey," my father said, finishing his water.

"Mind if I join you?" Noble asking, loosening his tie.

"I was just leaving," my father said, standing up. I walked him to his car and asked him to stay in touch. He raised his hand in a half-wave and then zoomed away. He hadn't seemed to want a hug, which I would've offered, if not with mixed feelings.

As I was walking back inside, my landline began to ring. It was my parents' number. Of course, it was Mom. I poured myself another glass of Merlot.

I answered, and she launched into questions. My father should have been home from his errands hours ago. Had I heard from him? He'd been acting strangely and had thrown three temper-tantrums in the last two days, rocking and crying himself to sleep each night, clinging to her and then pushing her away. She wondered if he was having some sort of nervous breakdown. Did I have any ideas? Had I talked to him?

Shit.

Once again, I was trapped in a no-win situation. So, I opted for the safe, not-the-truth but not-a-lie response.

"I'm not sure what to say, Mom. You don't deserve this."

I could feel her litigator-turned-judge senses kicking in, even though she had been retired for years.

"Why do I think there's something you're not telling me?" she asked. Um, because there is?

"I don't know," I said, trying to find a way out of the conversation. "I'm sure he'll be home soon."

"Ah, speak of the devil," she said. "He's pulling into the garage now. Gotta let you go." She hung up; I exhaled loudly. And then I became angry.

Noble refilled my glass and sat down. "What's new?" He took a sip of his beer.

I began to cry. Seems I had been doing too much of that as a newlywed, and not because of my marriage. I told him about my father and then having to play dumb with my mother.

"You know, I'm fucking sick of this! They don't seem to give a rat's ass that I have my own issues right now. No! They just keep going through the same toxic dance, year after year after year, and I'm the one who gets trampled. I'm not their fucking therapist!"

Greta pawed at my leg, staring intensely into my eyes with her protective canine love. I stroked her silken ears and calmed down.

"I mean, I think he's out of control," I said wearily. "I'm worried about how this will affect Mom."

Noble nodded patiently.

"Given what you've already told me, I'm amazed you turned out to be the way you are. I don't know how you did it," he said, coming over to give me a hug. I've never been comfortable receiving hugs when upset; it feels claustrophobic. I don't know why. I pulled away, then gave him a quick kiss.

"I'm sorry you're having to deal with all this," I said, holding his hand.

"We're in this together," he said, rubbing the back of my neck.

Neither of us had any idea how much more we'd weather with my parents. But we would learn.

Good girl, bracing.

Chapter Thirty: S(mothering)

When my daughter was a newborn, Mom used to tell me that in a blink, she'd be grown and to cherish each moment. At the time, I couldn't fathom what she meant; eighteen years seemed like an eternity. Yet, after my baby turned sixteen, time sped up. And once she passed her driver's test and was armed with her license, she became even more remote.

She always had loved Dad's Toyota Highlander and its metallic emerald paint. He was making plans to trade it in for a new Mazda SUV, so I asked if he would gift it to G. He looked at me as if I was a stranger.

"My hair stylist needs a new vehicle, and she's willing to buy it," he said sternly.

I couldn't believe his selfishness. It's not as if he needed the money. We were talking about his one and only grandchild! He already had written her off.

"How much, then?" I asked. I was still working on savings and debt-reduction.

"Thirty-five hundred," he said flatly.

I knew if G's dad were to buy her a car, I'd be on the hook for half, and it would likely be much more expensive than what my father proposed. A few days later, I called Mom and protested my father's stinginess.

"He is who he is, Suzanne." She didn't seem surprised, nor should she have been. He was still lording over us the fact that we were living in HIS house rent-free; she would correct him by saying it was community property, so it was THEIR house. The marital hamster wheel from hell.

I told her I wasn't about to ask Noble to contribute, and my ex already had said he wouldn't give my father a penny (I understood that), so I wasn't sure what to do.

Mom being Mom, she said she'd write me a check for three thousand dollars, if I'd kick in the remaining five hundred, and to not tell my father what she had done. I thanked her profusely, and two weeks before my daughter's birthday, I wrote my father a check. He handed me the title and keys. I asked if I could move the SUV to my house so G could practice driving it before she got her license. He said I could keep the SUV at my house, but she was not allowed to drive it until he had "checked her out on everything." This was the same man who wouldn't let me drive my first car until I knew how to change a flat, change the oil, and change the spark plugs…none of which I ever needed to do. I simply nodded and thanked him. Given the tenuous nature of our relationship, I desperately needed a "win" with my child.

The night of her sixteenth birthday, Noble and I took her to dinner at her favorite taco spot. I had wrapped the Highlander keys in a deceptively large box; Noble had bought a bronze keychain engraved with a brief prayer of protection. When she opened the shirt box with the keys nestled inside a smaller box, her expression was priceless: pure joy! She couldn't wait to drive it. I cautioned her we'd have to wait until my father had gone through everything with her. She rolled her eyes. I laughed.

The week after her birthday, her father scheduled her driver's test. She would test in the Highlander, so Noble and I believed she needed to practice in it–logical, right? One evening that week, we drove to Ultra for yet more hair supplies (one of my daughter's many obsessions), and on the way home, I let her drive. We pulled into the main street leading to my neighborhood, and of course, there was my father, driving in the opposite direction. He slowed down. Shit. I told G to keep driving.

I could feel it coming, and boy, was I blasted via email. I simply responded with an apology and explained she needed to be test-ready in the vehicle. Not to mention the fact that it's not like we were talking about a Mercedes or a Porsche or hell, even a Prius, each with their complex computer systems. This was an eleven-year-old SUV that had been beautifully maintained. I didn't think it was a big deal.

Yet, he did. It was further proof that I had no respect for him and, further, that my daughter didn't either. He added this latest transgression to his list of grievances about me and how much I had disappointed him.

G passed her driver's test on the first attempt. Her father and I had found a driving "contract" online that outlined parental expectations for their teen drivers, which she dutifully signed. Yet, I still worried about her safety driving by highway to and from school each day and who-knows-where at night and on the weekends when she wasn't with me. Having worked among teenagers for nearly thirty years and having himself taught driver's education as a side gig, Noble agreed we needed to monitor her driving.

After some research, we found a monitor to install in the fuse box that connected to an app we both could access. We did this surreptitiously, as neither of us wanted to give the impression we didn't trust her. (We didn't!) Everyone remembers that first taste of freedom–and sense of invincibility–that a first car delivered, right? I was following my maternal instincts. I only wanted to know where my daughter was and to be assured she was driving safely. The app showed us how many times she exceeded the speed limit, hit her brakes suddenly, and accelerated too quickly. It also provided her real-time location.

I felt guilty keeping this information to myself, so I told Jack what we had done so he could install the app, too. He seemed appreciative enough.

That app quickly became Pandora's box. I was obsessed, checking it throughout each day and night, particularly focusing on the weekends. Because G now lived full time with her dad and his fiancée, I assumed their eyes weren't as watchful as mine. Big mistake.

Every time I saw she was out late on a Saturday, thirty minutes from home, driving well past the speed limit on highways after curfew, I'd send angry texts–mostly to her father but some to her, too. Through my fog of maternal good intentions stained with gallons of jealousy and resentment, I was unwittingly alienating her. I didn't know how to manage my emotions, and I paid the price. We became even more estranged.

The following year, she had a freak accident on the highway while driving home from school. Her now stepmother rushed to the scene and followed her home; G called to let me know she was fine. Her beloved freedom mobile, however, was totaled. And my heart sunk even further, not only because she was upset, but because I wasn't the first person she contacted.

I called my parents to tell them what had happened.

"Too bad," my father said gruffly. "You shouldn't have bought her the car. You wasted your money."

I wasn't sure what that was supposed to mean, nor did I care.

Mom was more sympathetic, especially when I told her the details: a tire from a truck traveling in the opposite direction somehow flew off, sailing over the median into the lane G was in. She swerved to miss it and hit the concrete barricade. She could have been seriously injured, or worse. At least Mom recognized that.

While waiting for her dad to get a replacement car, G asked me carefully if she might borrow Mom's newish midnight blue Lexus for a while. After all, she suggested, Grandma didn't really drive that much. I approached Mom cautiously, already sensing her answer, which was, of course, "No." Years later, after my father's death, I would find this story shared with one of his girlfriends. His post-script was a salty epithet about his one and only grandchild, not to be repeated but shocking in its ugliness. He had written her off because he couldn't manipulate her as he could me, my mother, and his other women.

At just seventeen, my daughter was proving herself stronger than I. Good girl, bypassed.

Chapter Thirty-One: Bending

My daughter's senior year was a whirlwind, and sadly, I rarely saw her. One Saturday afternoon in January, G came over for lunch and a visit, which was very much welcomed. In a matter of months, she'd be heading off to college in Nebraska, and I treasured every moment I could spend with her, even with the heartaches and hurt feelings. Mid-visit, my father called, and I explained I couldn't talk because G was there. Not ten minutes later, my doorbell rang. We were standing in the foyer, so I opened the door. He handed her a Kroger plastic bag with something in it, turned on his heel, and marched stiffly back to his car. I took the bag and opened it. Inside was a decorative plaque she had bought them several years earlier that read, "Grandparents are a blessing."

We stood there in shock. She then let a few expletives fly, while I kept apologizing profusely. Didn't he understand that his behavior only made my relationship with her more difficult? She said it wasn't my fault–I knew that, but I still felt ashamed and profoundly sad that her only grandfather was so mean-spirited. Once she left, doing her best to hide her feelings, I went to my computer and sent my parents a heated email. Neither of them responded, though Mom called the next day when he was "running errands" and said nothing he did surprised her anymore, which helped me not in the least.

My birthday falls in late August, just a few weeks after we took my daughter to dinner and said our goodbyes before she left for college. My team at work threw me a delightful party. Noble joined us, and afterward, we went to an exhibit at the Kimbell Art Museum before going to a French restaurant for a birthday dinner. It was a wonderful day, followed by a horrible one.

The next morning, I woke up feeling a bit off, but I made it to work. All morning, I felt shaky and light-headed, so at noon, I went down to our cafeteria for a baked potato, which is all I thought I could stomach. I ate half of it and continued feeling stranger still. After struggling to walk normally to the ladies' room, I returned to my office area. My assistant said I didn't look right, and I told her I didn't feel right but wasn't sure what was wrong. She and another of my employees walked me down to the campus nurse, who took my blood pressure and said it was sky high: 180 over 100. I told her I'd call my husband to come and get me, but she said she already had called the campus police and that an ambulance was on the way. I argued, my two employees just folded their arms and glowered at me, the campus police officers assured me I needed to go to the emergency room, the Fort Worth Fire officers reiterated the assessment, and the MedStar team (all women, thankfully) said at minimum, they needed to get me to the ambulance so they could run a few more tests. After being wheeled out of my office on a gurney, a humiliating journey, they put me in the ambulance. The EMTs ran an EKG and a few other quick assessments; my blood pressure had not come down. Off to the hospital, we went. They spared the lights and siren, fortunately.

My assistant had called Noble, who likely drove like a demon from his office in Arlington because he was waiting in the emergency room as they wheeled me in. Honestly, I don't think I had ever been so scared. Something was wrong. I only hoped it wasn't a cardiac event. I was one day into my fifty-third year.

After the triage team ran a few tests and concluded I had not had a heart attack, I was momentarily relieved, yet my blood pressure wasn't moving. I told the nurse I needed to go to the bathroom. She helped me, letting me lean on her because my left side wasn't working. I must have looked like a drunk toddler, trying to not fall. I felt my body betraying me for the first time in my life.

A few hours later, a neurologist came to run a few more diagnostic tests, and in short, I failed them. I could not control my left leg. In that moment, I looked at Noble and feared the worst: would he be saddled with a now disabled wife for the rest of our days? He held my hand as I tried not to cry. An administrator came in to get my credit card, and I asked why. She said they were admitting me. I didn't remember agreeing to that.

Next, I had an MRI and a CT scan to determine if permanent neurological damage had occurred. None had. They admitted me anyway for observation. I still didn't have a diagnosis, but they wheeled me to a small room in the overflow wing, just across from the nurses' station. It was bright, loud, and disorienting. I was scared and starving, both for food and for information. Neither was available. Around nine, I urged Noble to go home and get some rest. Shortly after, one nurse brought me a boxed "meal" with a soggy sandwich and a carton of juice. I couldn't sleep, so I finally asked for a sedative. My blood pressure still wasn't even close to normal. I had asked Noble to notify my parents and my daughter that I was in the hospital, but I didn't hear from anyone, though my cell phone was at my side.

Eventually, a physician's assistant came to my room to evaluate my vitals. She said while the neurologist would see me early the next afternoon and sign off on my discharge, she recognized I was likely terrified (yes), so she told me they were ruling my "episode" as a transient ischemic attack, otherwise known as a "mini stroke." Just like my father experienced while I was in college. I wasn't sure what this diagnosis meant for my future, but I sure didn't want to be like my father. For so many reasons.

After a fitful night and an excruciatingly long morning of waiting, I was finally released at two that afternoon. Noble took me home and got me settled before returning to work. I called my parents to tell them what happened (having still not heard from them), and my father argued that I couldn't possibly have had a TIA. I assured him that was what was noted in my discharge papers. He didn't ask how I was feeling, so I didn't offer any further information other than that I was due to see my primary care doctor the next day. I took the rest of the week off to recover and get situated with new medications. Not exactly how I pictured beginning my fifty-third year on the planet.

Dad was an avid collector of very expensive brass model trains and, over the years, had amassed a staggeringly extensive collection. A member of several collectors' and enthusiasts' associations, he attended the organizations' annual conferences and eventually was asked to speak on various panels. Mom no longer accompanied him; neither of us really shared his interest. Before my divorce, Jack routinely helped my father put together his PowerPoint presentations; after our divorce, that "privilege" fell to me. For someone who prided himself on his vast computer savvy, Dad's inability to navigate the presentation software both surprised and amused me. Yet, I helped anyway. A week after my TIA, he informed me he was due to present at a conference in Seattle in just three weeks but would need to send his PowerPoint in the next two weeks. He invited himself over to begin refining a prior version.

Here's the thing: I still didn't feel particularly well and was having a hard time adjusting to new medication while obsessively monitoring my still-unsteady blood pressure. Yet, I agreed to help him, and over the next two weeks, he came over at least every other night to oversee the changes he wanted me to make. When the software froze, or a transition didn't work on his computer at home (though it worked on my laptop), he became irrationally agitated and started barking. On at least two occasions, he left in a huff. He may have asked how I was feeling once or twice; I'm sure I didn't tell him that after each of our sessions, my blood pressure was significantly elevated. All he cared about was a perfect presentation, no matter the expense to my health. He certainly didn't pay me for my time.

A few days before he was due to depart, he finally deemed the presentation "ready" and thanked me for my help. He also asked if

I would be able to pick him up from the airport upon his return. Again, I agreed to be of assistance. He called after his presentation to let me know it had gone "perfectly" (of course) and to thank me again for my work. When I picked him up from the airport, he was ebullient and very proud of himself. He failed to notice my newly acquired glasses. I elected not to point them out.

That conference was his swan song in the model train conference world, and I believe he knew it at the time. What I wouldn't find out until after his death was just why that conference was so damned important to him. He had invited Van, his on-again, off-again mistress of five decades, to attend with him. Afterwards, he stayed at her condo. The pictures I found on his computer painted the full story, though I wasn't quite ready to see what the elderly "Princess" looked like in the buff.

Good girl, used.

Chapter Thirty-Two: Shapeshifting

Sometimes, life presents sudden changes that are impossible to ignore or deny. Other times, changes are so gradual you miss their progression until they stun with their permanence. As children seem to grow to adulthood overnight, so our older parents begin fading before we know what's happening. Such was the case with Mom and Dad, though I didn't string the single episodes — physical, cognitive, and emotional — into a recognizable pattern until the latter part of 2019.

Mom eschewed doctors of any kind, finding last-minute reasons to cancel appointments with her primary care doctor, cardiologist, orthopedist, and neurologist, much to the dismay (read: fury) of my father. In fact, she was dismissed from her long-time primary care practice for her continued no-shows, which furthered her distrust of the medical community (and enraged my father even more). Her physical health was deteriorating rapidly, some of which she blamed on her difficulty sleeping or my father's meteoric tantrums. While I cajoled her to make her appointments and stay on top of her self-care, I only regret not taking a more forceful position when I had the chance. Mom wasn't one to be led to anything she didn't want to do. Attempts to persuade her only cemented her stubbornness. I had long learned to "leave it alone." Her words, not my wishes.

On the other hand, my father was a certifiable hypochondriac and had been as long as I could remember, though it intensified with age. In trying to understand this behavior after his death, I read in Psychology Today that narcissism and hypochondria often go hand-in-hand because narcissists are seeking to "transform their psychological frailty into physical fragility." It makes sense now, but then, I viewed my father's constant doctors' visits–during which he wanted cures for all the ailments associated with aging–as his belief that he could somehow avoid the inevitable: death. He had a psychiatrist for his anxiety and depression, a cardiologist for his erratic heart rhythms, a urologist for his prostate issues, a neurologist for his hand tremors, and probably another few specialists about whom I didn't know. He took great pride in cycling up to fourteen miles a day (always without a helmet, because he believed himself invincible), ingesting a full array of vitamins and supplements, keeping almost hourly records of his blood pressure and mood swings, and weighing himself obsessively like an anorexic teen. (I should know.) He truly seemed convinced that a magic prescription, or a handful of them, could prevent his reaching the eternal finish line. He even augmented all the medicines and vitamins with home remedies he discovered on the People's Pharmacy, gin-soaked raisins (for arthritis, I think) among his favorites. As in so many other areas, my parents truly were a study in self-care extremes.

It surprised me as much as it likely surprised Dad that in the spring of 2019, his heart problems had worsened, and he recognized, with the help of their very patient cardiologist, that surgical intervention would become necessary. Dad had only had one surgery over the course of his eighty-three years, and that was a tonsillectomy as a youngster. While he knew intervention was necessary, I believe it terrified him, though he was too stalwart to say. Instead, he just got angrier with the world, including his doctors. Over the next few years, I would try to soften his blows with all of them. Ever the good girl, the fixer, the peacemaker. To a fault.

In late May, Dad told me he and Mom were putting their affairs in order. He asked if I could commit my Fridays off to a series of appointments with their family attorney so I would have full visibility into the responsibilities they were handing me. While that wasn't my choice of ways to enjoy my precious days off, I agreed.

On one hand, I was honored to be involved in the process, recognizing this meant, in some strange way, that they trusted me and, in fact, knew they needed me. Flip side: I was deeply aware this meant they saw their ends in sight. And though wishing to pretend they had several more years, they knew what had to be done. I was terrified and deeply saddened by all of it. Despite a lifetime of turmoil, I honestly couldn't imagine my world without them. For possibly the first time, we all had to confront life's realities together. Or so I thought.

Both of my parents selected me to be the executor of their wills and gave me their medical and financial powers of attorney, which felt like a tremendous responsibility, but I readily accepted it…with questions. Dad also wanted to establish a pour-over trust to make probate somewhat less complicated; as he repeatedly said, he didn't want to leave me with a financial "mess." During the sessions with their attorneys, and subsequently with their banker, I watched my father soften toward me–a version of him I had never experienced. On one occasion, while waiting for the banker to draw up some paperwork, my father reached over and took my hand, saying that while we had always had a complicated relationship, he was glad we were finally "here" …meaning, in a good place. I think his gentleness toward me was more alarming than it was comforting. It was unfamiliar, though I had wanted THIS Dad my whole life, but it also felt like his acknowledgement that his end was near.

Mom, meanwhile, was concerned that by giving me her power of attorney, she somehow was losing agency over her own affairs. I assured her she still was responsible for her own decisions, and these measures protected her when and if necessary. She wasn't ready to relinquish control, and she wasn't ready to need help, though I think she knew she needed it. She had become as fragile emotionally as she was physically. In just a few months, it seemed, both of my parents had morphed from stubborn giants to frightened geriatrics, while I was called to emerge as their custodian. It was, quite simply, overwhelming. Yet, inevitable.

Thankfully, while Noble hadn't yet walked this path with his own family, he recognized the weight this transition had placed on my shoulders and, more significantly, on my heart. His support and compassion would continue to carry me through the heart-wrenching years to follow.

That August, Dad was scheduled for a cardiac procedure that would require an overnight stay in the hospital. We assured him we would take him, as he didn't need to be driving, and I promised I would be there before and after the surgery. Seeing him in the color-coded hospital gown–marigold for cardiac patients–was unsettling; he just seemed so frail. He was in good spirits going into the procedure, which took a few hours, so I parked myself in his room to watch CNN and get a bit of work done. Mom kept calling. I assured her as soon as he was out of surgery, I'd let her know. Trying to ensure she didn't go into stress-induced A-fib while Dad was in the operating room was no small feat, honestly. I managed to keep her calm while waiting for my father to be wheeled back to the room.

When he returned, he was out of anesthesia but still groggy. I moved my chair closer to his bedside so we could talk. I told him the doctor said everything had gone well. He nodded with his eyes closed. Though he refused to remove his wedding ring prior to surgery, he had given me his Rolex and dental bridges for safekeeping, so I asked if he was ready to have them back. He nodded, reached out his hand, and put the partials back in his mouth. I put his watch on his wrist, and he gave my hand a squeeze.

"Suz, I owe you an apology," he said slowly. I sat back in my chair, nervous.

"That text wasn't meant for you." I nodded. A week earlier, while my daughter and I were chatting, he sent an odd message along the lines of, "I thought we were getting together. Communication, please." I responded that I didn't remember making any plans, and that G was at my house. He didn't answer, so I had thought he was in a snit because I chose to spend my time with my daughter instead of him.

I wish it had been as simple as his predictable passive-aggression.

Instead, he told me about his massage therapist, Linda. I didn't know he had a massage therapist. Linda had a silly little dog named Darryl, who amused him. He waxed on about how talented an artist she was, how they had a lot in common, how they couldn't be more different, yet he was drawn to her, how she had put the spring back into his step, and how she was married yet she and her husband didn't have sex anymore. I had become really uncomfortable at this point.

"And the crazy thing is," he said with a smile, "we're twenty years apart, but I'm in love with her, and she loves me too." My stomach began to churn.

"Does Mom know?" I asked. "That you have a massage therapist?"

He shook his head, brought his finger to his lips, and said, "Shh."

Shit. Here we fucking go again. I changed the subject before kissing him goodbye and asking him to call when he was discharged the next day.

Noble was waiting outside to pick me up. He could see something was wrong. I had gone from a concerned center-stage daughter to an enraged stage-prop daughter in a nanosecond. Noble listened patiently, shaking his head while saying, as he had before, that my father was a "genuine piece of work." That was putting it nicely. Why, I kept asking, why does my father always have to include me in his salacious, secret life?

Despite my having earned a master's degree and having invested over twenty years in genealogical research, my father underestimated my ability to find information. Yet, with just a few Google entries, I was able to track down Linda. I found her last name, her address, her phone number, and then, with a search using her phone number alone, "the rest of the story."

Seems that Linda had quite the loyal fan base, as indicated on several escort- and sex-worker websites where she advertised her "services." Seems that Linda worked out of her home and provided a wide variety of "happy endings" to her male clients. Strangely transfixed, I learned through these sites a whole new vocabulary of acronyms for the types of massages she gave and their corresponding "benefits." Interestingly, I found her husband was a licensed therapist! Putting everything together, the picture was beyond anything I ever thought my father capable of: he was in love with a sixty-something sex worker married to a psychologist with whom she wasn't intimate, working out of her home while her dog, Darryl, watched (but hopefully, didn't take part).

When we got home, I poured a glass of pinot noir, lit a cigarette, and called Mom.

"So, how's the patient?" she asked anxiously.

"No surprises," I said. "Same old Dad."

Good girl, disgusted.

Chapter Thirty-Three: Falling

Every day following my father's return home, I called to check on both parents and to inquire if they needed anything. Now that he had mostly recovered, Dad had defaulted to his old behavior. So, depending on his mood and what real or perceived slight or inconvenience he had experienced that day, he was chatty or sullen. Mostly sullen. Though he always had been mercurial, it seemed his emotions were swinging more dramatically. I never knew what to expect when he picked up the phone. Yet, I called anyway.

As Mom would tell me, Dad spent most of each day upstairs in his office "doing God knows what," as she would say. She didn't know because her painful arthritis and physical unsteadiness prevented her from traversing the staircase. I had learned many years prior that if I spoke to her but didn't ask to speak with him, we both incurred his fury. So, one evening, after talking to Mom, she hollered upstairs for him to pick up the line. She hung up so she could continue making his dinner.

I asked, as I always did, "How are you?" He grunted, then said I needed to stop asking that question because he didn't owe me a daily report card chronicling his well-being. I flinched at the sting of his tone.

"What's new?" I thought perhaps this would be a safer question. It wasn't. He launched into a diatribe about his energy level and why it hadn't returned after undergoing the procedure that was supposed to fix him and his erratic heart. I suggested he should make a follow-up appointment with his cardiologist. He said he knew what he was doing and didn't need my advice. Fine then.

Because I hadn't been able to shake what I had learned about Linda, I asked about her last name and wasn't this the woman he had described while in the hospital?

"God dammit, Suzanne, leave it alone. Stay out of my fucking business."

Again, I recoiled.

"Dad, you were the one who told me about her," I said calmly.

"Leave. It. Alone. This has nothing to do with you."

Well, apparently it did because once again, he had put me in the position of complicity and betrayal of my mother to keep his dirty secret. Yet, he knew I wouldn't tell her–not now, as her health had begun to fail. "Rage" doesn't describe my emotions in that moment.

I continued anyway. "I know who she is, and I know what she does, Dad. And it's disgusting. I don't understand you."

"And I don't understand you, Suzanne. Goodbye." With that, he hung up on me.

We had established a new tradition of having them over for dinner every Sunday night, which meant spending a full day cooking, cleaning, and preparing for their arrival. Most Sundays, Mom kept up her usual chatter about nothing in particular while Dad chewed his food and occasionally complimented the meal. Some Sundays, if he was feeling upbeat, he and Noble would talk sports, sometimes politics, and whatever was on my father's mind. Occasionally, I'd offer stories about work or something I had read, but mostly, I just served the food and cleared the plates. Once again, the stage prop.

The Sunday following my phone call with Dad, they came to dinner, as usual, yet something was sticking in his craw, and honestly, he challenged every damned thing I said, just to be argumentative. I knew he was baiting me–I had walked this road most of my life–yet with what I had discovered but couldn't voice, I wasn't in the mood to take it, so I argued back. That I challenged him so incited his rage that he stood up after his last bite, threw down his napkin, and barked at Mom that it was time to go home.

We followed them to the car, mostly to ensure Mom was okay. Walking had become difficult for her, and she followed my father slowly as he stormed to his car door without opening hers. I gave her a hug goodbye. She whispered her apologies and slowly sat down in the SUV. Before she had even closed her door and fastened her seatbelt, my father hit the gas and sped down our street. She could've fallen out of the car and been seriously injured, or worse. Yet again, he had behaved in a way I'd not seen, and it terrified me.

"Did you see that?" I asked Noble, whose Caribbean blue eyes had darkened.

"Yup. He's out of his fucking mind."

I knew that.

I waited for about fifteen minutes, then called to check on Mom. She laughed it off, saying he was just in one of his moods, and she again thanked me for dinner. I heard him bellowing in the background, so I said goodbye and hung up.

"I don't want to do this again," I said to Noble. "I think Sunday dinner is tabled for a while." Yes, pun intended.

"Whatever you need, baby," he answered, enveloping me in one of his fierce bear hugs. I burrowed my head into his chest and cried.

"I'm scared he's going to hurt her," I whispered. At the moment, I did not believe her well-being was a priority for him. Yet, his girlfriends were.

Two months later, on a Wednesday in early October, I had just walked in from work when my phone rang. Noticing it was my parents' number, I rushed to answer. It was my father, nearly breathless and his voice quavering. He explained he had returned from his standing Wednesday lunch with his model train bunch and subsequent shopping excursion to find my mother on the floor in front of the staircase. My blood turned to ice.

"What happened? Is she okay?"

He said she had apparently taken a fall in the bathroom, could not get up on her own, so had scooted herself on her bottom from the bathroom, through the bedroom, through the hall, and through the living room to reach the staircase railing. She thought she could pull herself up but didn't have the physical strength. Nor could she get to the phone. I asked to speak with her.

Predictably, she laughed it off, saying she was trying to do some exercises in her bedroom closet (which really was room-sized) and slipped on the floor rug. I knew this wasn't true since Mom never exercised, but I let her have her story. I asked how long she had been on the floor, and she guessed it had been around two hours or so.

"Did you hit your head? Is anything hurt?"

She couldn't remember hitting her head, but she said she had slightly bruised her arms. I asked if we should take her to the emergency room. She declined (of course). I told her I loved her and asked her to call if she needed anything, and she promised she would.

Noble and I ate a light dinner, drank some wine, and were in the process of watching a movie when around nine fifteen, the phone rang…again, from my parents' line. I answered, a little woozy from the wine, to hear my father in a panic.

"Your mother had an episode in the bathroom. I've called for an ambulance," he said shakily.

"We're on our way," I said quickly, hanging up, and running to grab a jacket and my purse. Noble already had gotten to my car and started the ignition as I flew out of the house and closed the garage. We sped to their house, just a mile or two away, and arrived to find Mom in bed with Dad at her side. She had a ghostly pallor and seemed confused. As the paramedics were arriving, I asked what happened, and she said she felt faint on the toilet, then sick to her stomach before falling, once again. She yelled for Dad, and he came running to find her on the floor a second time in one day.

After checking her vitals, the EMT team said she was in A-fib and her blood pressure was through the roof; she needed to be taken to the emergency room straightaway. I removed her watch, though she insisted on keeping her wedding ring before they loaded her onto the stretcher and deposited her in the back of the ambulance. I grabbed her purse, then we raced to our car. With Dad behind us, convoyed to the nearest emergency room just a few miles away. She was spared the lights and sirens, so I took that as a positive. As we were driving, I considered what must have happened, and I realized my father likely railed at her for her fall earlier in the day, probably blaming it on her refusal to take care of herself and all the other things she was doing to him. I said a quiet prayer that she would make it through the night.

Because the emergency room was full, the nurses installed Mom in a temporary room while we awaited a series of tests and her inevitable admission. Under the harsh fluorescent lights, she looked fragile; her eyes resembled those of a spooked horse. She clutched Dad's arm as we waited for her to be seen by the attending physician. I sat and watched helplessly while Noble waited in the lobby. With each passing hour, I grew more irate and, finally, marched to the nurses' station to ask when the hell someone would check on my mother. They all but yawned and said she would be seen when it was her turn. I explained loudly that while they had many patients, I only had one mother, and they needed to take our situation seriously. Their contempt was palpable, but now, I didn't care. I found her some apple juice, and as she sipped it carefully, I peered at the monitor. Her blood pressure was still dangerously elevated, her pulse was unsteady, and her oxygen rate was low. By two o'clock in the morning, she had grown agitated and asked to go home. Dad and I explained she needed to be evaluated first.

Finally, the on-call cardiologist came in to review her vitals and immediately said she would need to be admitted to the Intensive Care Unit. My heart nearly stopped. Mom was terrified of hospitals, and the thought of her in the ICU, well, it didn't sound good. I stepped outside as the doctor was leaving and cautiously asked about her prognosis.

"It's too soon to tell," he said before moving at a fast clip to see his next patient.

I returned to her makeshift room and gave her a protective hug, telling her everything was going to be okay. Looking to my father for some sort of reassurance, I just saw a flat expression.

Around three o'clock in the morning, they informed us her ICU room was ready and that Dad and I could move to the ICU waiting room, where we would remain until they settled her. A few hours earlier, I had sent Noble home as only two family members could be in the ER. I was alone with my father, sitting awkwardly in the waiting room in silence. Shortly before the ICU nurse came to take us to Mom's room, Dad sighed loudly, then launched into a tirade.

"Suz, I am just so fucking pissed," he said. I looked at him incredulously. This was not the expression of concern I would have imagined.

"I know, Dad. I'm worried, too," I said, reaching over to squeeze his hand.

"No, I'm not worried, Suzanne. I'm furious that she would let this happen," he barked, his face and eyes growing red. Truly, I didn't need BOTH parents in the ICU simultaneously, though that would come later.

"She did this on purpose," he continued. What? Fall? Remain on the floor for two hours, alone? Have a cardiac event?

I remained quiet–frozen, actually.

"She's punishing me. She's been punishing me for years by not going to the doctor. By letting herself go. By refusing to do what I told her to do and get her god-damned health under control. She's doing this to hurt me. She's trying to get even for the other women in my life. She's so fucking vindictive. I can't take this!" he said, running his hands through his sparse silver hair.

All I could do was stare at the grayish-green wall ahead as I fought back tears of fury. Here we were, at nearly four in the morning, waiting to hear if the medical team could stabilize Mom, and all he could think about was himself. He wasn't offering any comfort to me as I sat wondering if my mother was about to die. All he could feel was anger at how this was affecting him and how it might affect his future.

Shortly after four, a nurse came to the waiting room and asked us to follow her to Mom's ICU room. When we got there, she seemed smaller than normal–her five-foot ten frame shrunken in the antiseptic hospital bed. Her skin was a pale grey, and her eyes gleamed with fear. I kissed her and told her I'd see her later. My father did the same, and we walked to the parking lot together, wordlessly.

I arrived home by four-thirty in the morning. Noble was waiting for me, arms wide open and face softened with concern. Too wired to sleep, I poured a glass of wine and recounted the last several hours. He was as astounded as I was by my father's unvarnished narcissism, but he encouraged me to let it focus on Mom.

Mom. She was in the ICU, alone, attached to a constellation of monitors and likely wide awake and frightened. I quickly changed clothes, grabbed one of her smaller quilts and the stuffed fox my father had given her when they were dating (which, for some reason, was still in the primary closet at my house), and headed back to the ICU. I got there shortly after five-thirty in the morning and found her awake, staring glassily at the ceiling.

"Mom?" I said, coming into the room and pulling up a chair. She started to cry.

"Oh, Suz, I'm so happy to see you," she said, wiping her eyes. I handed her a tissue, then showed her Reddy Fox, which made her smile, before placing him where she could see him. Then I opened the quilt and laid it carefully over her blanket. She clutched it by the ends and brought it to her eyes. I pulled up a chair so I could hold her hand. Despite her fragility, she held on with a death grip. Maybe, I thought at the time, that's why they call it that.

"Please try to sleep," I said as I stroked her hair with my free hand. Soon, she closed her eyes. I found an extra pillow and put it by her side so I could rest my head near her heart. Within a few minutes, I fell into a fitful sleep. I had no idea how loud ICUs could be.

Around seven-thirty that same morning, my father strolled in and raised his eyebrows when he found me in the room. The nurse had awoken us a few minutes before he arrived, so we were up, but neither of us was alert. I desperately needed coffee and sleep, but I wanted information about Mom's prognosis before heading home.

She, of course, was delighted to see him–as giddy as a teenage girl being asked to dance by her first crush. He came to her side, gave her a chaste kiss on the forehead, and pulled up a chair across from me. At that moment, I felt invisible, as I so often had with them, yet I stayed put.

"How long have you been here?" he asked, his first words since his meltdown just hours before.

"Since around five-thirty, I think," I said, rubbing my eyes. "I didn't want her to be alone," I said pointedly. He tried to smile, but it looked like a grimace. He told me to go home and get some sleep. I nodded, put my chair back in the corner, and hugged Mom before leaving.

"Suz," she called as I opened the sliding door, "thank you for bringing me Reddy Fox and the quilt," she whispered. "You're the best daughter in the world."

I blew her a kiss and left, wiping away my tears.

Having already alerted my boss that Mom was in the ICU, I checked my email anyway before sliding under the covers for a few hours of sleep. By two that afternoon, after struggling to rest, I took a shower and returned to the ICU, stopping first at a florist to pick up a bouquet. When I arrived, she was awake and alert and smiled as I appeared with the colorful blooms. Quickly, her nurse grabbed the vase and told me flowers weren't allowed in ICU rooms, but she'd put them on the nursing station where Mom could see them.

Clearly, Mom hadn't rested much either and was anxious about what was happening. Unfortunately, the only answer I got from the nurse was that her cardiologist was scheduled to see her later that afternoon.

One benefit of living across the street from your pastor is knowing she's at the ready for moments like this. I called her before coming back to the hospital and asked if she would come and see Mom. She told me she'd get there as soon as she could. Within thirty minutes of my arrival, she appeared at the door with her Bible and a smile. I introduced her to Mom. Pastor Leslie asked if she'd like to visit for a while, and Mom nodded. Intent on giving her privacy, I said I'd be back that evening to see how she was doing.

Though my father's mother was a very devout Christian and my mother had been raised as a Catholic, church membership wasn't part of my family's life. We attended a few, here and there, but my father eschewed organized religion. In fact, he had chosen never to be baptized. As with so many things, the family ceded to his wishes, so God had seemed a distant concept in our daily lives. By the radiant expression on her face, though, I could tell she was receptive to my pastor's ear and counsel. I whispered a "thank you" before giving them their time.

That evening, I would learn that Mom had unburdened herself to Pastor Leslie, telling her about the decades of betrayal by my father and how that must look in the eyes of God. She confessed she had wanted to divorce him so many times but didn't want to disappoint God, nor did she want to be a "two-time loser." Pastor Leslie explained from his first indiscretion, my father had broken the marital covenant. God would not judge her for any choices she made. I believe that gave her great relief, if not validation, that she would be eternally free. Yet she would never let him go.

After visiting Mom that evening, then leaving when my father arrived, I spoke with my pastor and thanked her for comforting Mom. I also felt the need to apologize for her having to hear about my family's ugly secrets. She took my hand and said she understood, more than I would know, and that my father's choices had nothing to do with me.

Yet, he always involved me, I told her. And then, the epiphany: over my lifetime, he had made me his conscience so I would carry the burden and he would be free to continue as he pleased. Mom and I deserved better.

Mom stayed in the ICU for four more days as the medical team tried everything to get her A-fib under control. On the fifth day, they moved her to the telemetry unit for continued monitoring of life-threatening dysrhythmias or even sudden death (as they explained to me). I visited daily, taking her books and crossword puzzles and snacks I thought she might enjoy, since she wasn't eating much of her meals.

"Since I was a little girl," she explained to everyone, "I've never been able to eat when I'm upset." I could see she was losing weight.

After another week in telemetry, her cardiologist told us she needed to be moved to a rehabilitation hospital to regain some of what strength she had had. I gathered her things, and we met her at the new facility. By now, she was using a walker and unsteady at best. But she was still alive. I continued my daily visits and brought her anything I could to cheer her up.

Predictably, my father had assumed the posture of the concerned and loving husband, playing to the sympathies of the junior nurses attending Mom. It disgusted me. He was all but flirting while I ran interference, trying to get information about Mom's progress and what would happen next. After several difficult discussions about how to care for Mom when and if she got released, my father said we needed to find her an assisted living facility. I argued they had the means to bring in a home health nurse. Dad rejected any suggestions I offered that did not involve institutionalizing her, so I took the job of finding a place to move her. I was sick with guilt, knowing she would never understand our choice.

Had I known amidst the crisis what I learned the following year, I don't know that I could have contained my rage. I definitely would have made a different choice.

Perusing my father's emails while he was hospitalized the following year, I found a message he had sent Linda the evening he found my mother by the staircase. He had so enjoyed their time together that afternoon, it was "as good as always," but it was "ruined" the minute he found my mother incapacitated.

While Mom lay in pain, alone and afraid for two hours, my father had been canoodling with his girlfriend. Had he been where he was supposed to be, instead of fucking around with Linda, Mom's current situation may have been prevented. That his email to his married mistress focused more on his gratitude to her than concern about his wife sickened me beyond words. His wants and needs ruled the day, no matter what.

I'm glad I was spared that knowledge at the time, though it still burns like acid when I think about it.

Good girl, gasping.

Chapter Thirty-Four: Managing

Having grown up as an Air Force brat, I knew how to prepare for a move. Mom was an expert at getting us packed, unpacked, and settled into our next home. Once I graduated from college, I learned how to find the best apartment I could afford and, once married, houses that met our family's needs. I had no idea how to find the right facility for Mom, especially while working full time. My father said he was confident I would figure it out. Already, he had happily turned my mother's care over to me since I had the power of attorney and all. I wasn't ready. I had to do it, anyway. She was on schedule to leave the rehabilitation hospital in two short weeks.

The world of eldercare is fraught with manipulation, deception, and greed. I scoured the internet for places offering the best care, were reasonably close to our homes, and would provide scaled services depending on how Mom's condition progressed. I learned quickly that if pricing information depended upon my providing my email address and phone number, I was setting myself up for a litany of unwanted calls and emails. As a professional marketer, this shouldn't have surprised or bothered me, but it did. Several places I identified on my own required a full presentation of my parents' assets, which would be held in Escrow through the duration of her stay. I also read that in so many cases, families who fell prey to this requirement spent years in court upon the death of their loved one, seeking to recoup their unused assets. We would not fall for that.

Again, I tried to convince Dad that bringing her back to her own home, with daily home health support, would be the best option.

Again, he said he could not care for her when a nurse wasn't there and that she needed to be in a facility with twenty-four-hour care.

Fortunately for me, her stay at the rehab hospital was extended by a few more days. The clock was ticking, and I panicked. While I would have done anything to bring her to our house, the layout and my two enormous German shepherds would have been dangerous for her to navigate. By this point in my life, I had navigated a few situations–namely, my divorce, that were frightening. But those situations only had to do with me finding my way. Here, I was deciding for my mother. The responsibilities of her care, comfort, and security rested heavily on my shoulders. Yet, I was her daughter, which meant I would face the challenge with courage.

Ten days before she was to be discharged, I contacted the assisted living facility within two miles of their home and mine and was encouraged to hear they did, in fact, have one or two apartments available. I arranged to meet with their sales director and tour the facility with my father that same evening after work. As a marketer, I knew to read reviews on each of the places I considered. While they were somewhat mixed for this place, I was running out of options.

After touring the facility, which looked pretty nice, and looking at two apartment options, we reviewed the paperwork and told the sales director we would discuss it. As every good salesperson will do, she said she had another family looking at the same apartment we had chosen, and we probably should decide quickly. Of course. In the parking lot, my father asked what I thought. Yes, he was putting the decision in my hands, conveniently. I said it was the best option at this point and that we should take it. He nodded and said he didn't have his checkbook, but we would return tomorrow and secure the space. As he drove off, I went back inside and told Cassie we would be there by nine the next morning to sign the contract and pay the deposit.

And so, we did. I co-signed all the forms with a shaking hand. Dad gave her the deposit with a cool demeanor. We told the team while we weren't precisely sure what day she would be transported, it would be within the next ten days.

No pressure.

From there, I went to work and did my best to stay focused, all the while wondering how we were going to explain to Mom that after a month away from her home, her quilt room, her favorite chair, her kitchen, and the bed she shared with her husband, she wouldn't be going there after all. She had never lived alone, not once, and the last month had taken a toll on her. She only wanted to return to what was familiar and safe. And despite my best efforts, I couldn't give her that. I hated myself, but I had to do the best I could under the circumstances.

Once home from work and with a glass cabernet in hand, I called Mom to see how she was doing; I didn't have the emotional energy to visit her that day. She sounded the same as she had the last few calls: a bit confused, a lot lonely, and ready to get out of there. Next, I called Dad to check on him. He was in the middle of watching the news and drinking his Scotch, but he could talk for a minute. Had I begun thinking about how to furnish her apartment?

No, I really hadn't.

"Well, I'll leave the outfitting of her apartment to you," he said. I suggested I could come by the next evening, and we could make a list of what she would need and review what we could move from their house to make her feel comfortable. He said that would be okay.

Her apartment had a living area with a small kitchenette, which meant a small refrigerator, microwave, abbreviated counter with a sink, and minimal cabinets for storage. She would have an area for a table, a spacious bedroom, and two bathrooms. I wanted to keep the décor somewhat minimal so it would feel larger than it actually was, which meant handpicking items that would be both beautiful and functional. We agreed the queen bed and the corresponding antique nightstand in the guest room would work. I selected a few lamps, also from the guest room. I evaluated some of the artwork she loved in her quilt room and office and put Post-it notes on the items I thought would be most appreciated. I pulled pictures and various objects, including her courtroom gavel and other personal effects, which would remind her who she was. Dad followed me, agreeing to my choices, until it came time to discuss occasional chairs and other items for her living room. He wanted nothing else removed from his house.

Having inherited my love of antiquing from my mother and grandmother, I decided I would spend the next few days sourcing additional furniture she would need, including a dresser for her bedroom and chairs for her living room. Dad told me he would reimburse me for what I spent, so I went to my neighborhood antique mall and found a lovely carved bookcase, a side table, and an occasional table that doubled as a magazine rack. He joined me the next day and agreed the pieces were nice, so I bought them and loaded them into my SUV. Next, I found two cordovan leather recliners in beautiful condition on our Next-Door website. After taking that Saturday afternoon to make the drive and see them, I wrote a check on the spot, and my husband picked them up the next day. Dad had found an unclaimed freight store in Arlington that sold new furniture, so I met him the following Monday after work to look at the dressers; we selected one, I paid, and we arranged for Noble to pick it up later in the week. While there, I found a sturdy oak rocking chair that I also purchased, thinking that would be comforting for her to have in her bedroom. At Target I bought new bathmats, towels, wastebaskets, and shower curtains. All that was left, besides schlepping everything to the apartment and getting it decorated and ready for her arrival, was packing up clothes. I left that one small task for my father.

The last week in October, the rehab facility called to let me know Mom would be ready to be transported on November 1 but that I would need to come sign her do-not-resuscitate paperwork specific to transport. (I already had signed that same document twice before.) We hadn't yet told her she would not be coming home. I dreaded the conversation but didn't trust my father to handle it on his own. So, we agreed to meet at the hospital and begin packing the things she had accumulated, as I signed the paperwork. Then we sat down for our chat.

The month she had spent in the hospital had accelerated her confusion, as I later learned was common for elderly patients hospitalized for long periods. She wrung her hands and chewed her lips as Dad and I explained she would get out of the facility in a few days. Her face lit up, and she exclaimed how ready she was to be back in her quilt room. I anxiously stole a glance at my father. He gave me an encouraging nod.

Shit. He was making me do this. I took a deep breath. Where were my professional communicators' skills when I needed them? There was no way I could be totally honest; there was no way I could lie. One of my mantras as a publicist and strategic marketer always had been, "Use the available truth." And so, I would have to do that here.

"Mom," I said, taking her hand. She looked frightened. I was frightened.

"The last month has really been hard on you, and while they're releasing you from here, you still will require additional care and support to get your health and strength back," I began slowly. She just blinked and nodded.

"We've found a place that will feel more like home than this, but you'll still have access to care when you need it...care that we're not qualified or capable of giving you ourselves," I continued, hating every word I was saying. Hating having been put in this position by my father. I looked at him, and he just nodded. Again.

"So, what does that mean?" she asked quietly.

"Well, it means you will have an apartment at the place we've chosen, where you'll have lots of company and can make new friends, and you'll be there until you're strong enough to come home." My voice caught, and I clenched my fists in my lap to keep from crying.

"How long will that be?" I looked at my father. He was expressionless.

"I guess that depends on you!" I said brightly, attempting to sound as encouraging as I had when urging my daughter to eat pureed peas.

"You're such a fucking liar," said the voice in my head.

"Honestly, Mom, this place is prettier than anywhere I've ever lived. I promise you'll be comfortable there, and we'll see you every day!"

The room fell quiet. I was trying to keep from digging my fingernails into my palms. I bit the inside of my lip instead.

"But I want to come home," she said, her mouth quivering as if she were a toddler. "I want to be with you," she said, reaching for Dad's hand. I had to excuse myself to the hall to pull it together. At minimum, my father deserved to own part of this, so I gave them some time together before returning.

When I came back to the room, she was crying on his shoulder, and for a moment, it looked like tenderness. For a moment. I told her I needed to get home to Noble. She looked up, and with a slight smile, she told me she loved me and looked forward to my next visit. I sobbed the entire way home.

The next day, Noble and a family friend drove to Dad's house to get the bed, mattress and box springs, and all the other items I had earmarked for her apartment. I packed the items I had purchased, along with nails, a hammer, and other tools I knew we would need to get her apartment ready. Once Noble moved the items from Dad's house into the apartment, he went to pick up the items I had purchased from the antique store and the recliners I had purchased a few miles away, as well as the dresser and the rocking chair from the unclaimed freight store. Once everything was moved into the apartment, I spent the next full day (with my father's oversight) arranging the furniture–including a card table I bought at Target and two of my grandmother's antique occasional chairs–hanging artwork, making her bed, putting her clothes away, and whatever else I could conceive to make the apartment feel like home. That evening, I purchased a beautiful wreath for her door and bought fresh flowers that would await her arrival the next day.

I was exhausted, but the apartment looked just as I had hoped: elegant, beautiful, and every bit my mother. As we left for the evening, my father agreed I had done a nice job, yet forgot he said he would reimburse me for my purchases. I reminded him of our discussion. He said that never happened, and I had made the choice to buy what I bought. I didn't feel like arguing the point. I had to be in the right emotional space to welcome Mom to her new home the following afternoon.

Good girl, guilty.

Chapter Thirty-Five: Free-falling

As I had learned, the medical community operates on a completely different time standard than everyone else (besides, perhaps, airlines), so it didn't really surprise me that Mom's transport to the assisted living facility was delayed by several hours. After going through her apartment one last time, arranging her flowers and putting some juices, sodas, and water in her mini-refrigerator, I returned home to await the call she was underway. I had spoken to her earlier, and while she wasn't exactly chipper, I knew she was ready to be out of the hospital.

Finally, the call came, so I alerted my father, and we all met at the facility to await the transport van. Joined by the facility's executive director and Cassie, the sales director, we stood like royal servants awaiting the queen's carriage. At least, that's how I wanted to see it. My father's face was inscrutable as he stood to the side, and Noble held my hand as my stomach churned. When the van drove into the circle near where we were waiting, we all stepped forward to greet her as the driver helped her from the wheelchair and steadied her on her walker. Dad immediately approached her with a hug. She looked at the building's exterior and garden, then at us, and her trepidation was palpable.

"Hey, Mom!" I said, moving toward her with my arms outstretched. She hugged me with one arm, then accepted Noble's kiss on her cheek. The executive director introduced herself and said, as I cringed, "Welcome home!" I'm not sure that registered with Mom; I hoped it hadn't, anyway.

We escorted her inside and showed her around the dining room, the sitting room, the beauty parlor, then walked her down two long halls to her apartment. They also had taped a "Welcome Home" sign on her door. I planned to remove it later. It just felt like a taunt to Mom, who we had led to believe this situation was temporary. We opened her door, and Dad escorted her into the living area. She looked around and commented on the furniture, the art placement, the flowers, and her favorite quilt and teddy bear, given to her by my father, on the bed.

"It's lovely," she said, shuffling through the apartment with her walker. She looked tired, so I asked if she'd like to sit in one of her new chairs. As she lowered herself gingerly, I showed her how to work the recliner since she really needed to keep her legs elevated when possible. Because of her cardiac issues, she suffered terrible edema in her lower extremities. She shot me her notorious Mom look, and for a second, I thought she might be getting back to her old snarky self. (Snarky was one of her favorite words. She wore the badge with pride and even sported the word on her license plate many years earlier.) Dad sat in the recliner next to her, reaching for her hand as the ever-dutiful husband. Noble and I sat down in my grandmother's chairs at the card table, which I had covered with one of her vintage tablecloths. I checked the flowers to ensure they had enough water, then took two sodas from the refrigerator and offered them to both parents. Mom eagerly accepted hers, though she couldn't open the bottle by herself. My father rejected his, so I handed it to Noble. I felt I was playing hostess. In reality, I was trying to suppress my sadness that she likely would never leave this place. And it would never be "home."

Around four-thirty, one of the medical techs knocked on the door, introduced herself, and asked Mom (whom they would later call "Judge" with great respect) if she was ready to go to the dining room for supper. She looked at the clock and said, "I never eat this early!" The med tech explained dinner service started at four-thirty and ended at six. Mom shot my father a scowl, yet he just patted her hand.

"We'll join you," he said. At least he understood she was afraid to go by herself.

Around five, we escorted her to the dining room and found a table that would accommodate all four of us. I looked at the table next to ours, trying to identify what was being served. It seemed fine – pasta with red sauce, a salad, rolls, and chocolate cake for dessert. We opted not to eat but encouraged Mom as she did so, reluctantly.

"How is it?" I asked hopefully.

"About the same as hospital food," she said, putting down her fork. I encouraged her to keep eating, but she shook her head. Then she said, as she'd done many times before, "You know, since I was a little girl, I've never been able to eat when I'm upset." I nodded, then picked up her fork and handed it back to her. "Please, Mom?"

She took the fork and launched into her cake. "Mom, you never would have let me get away with that," I said with a smile.

"I never would have put you away," she said sharply. I felt like someone had punched me. Noble patted my knee under the table before I got up to refill her iced tea.

Spent from emotion, I looked at my watch and told her we needed to get home to let out the dogs. She nodded, mouth full of cake. I leaned in to give her a hug and told her I'd see her the next day. Noble, too, gave her a hug. As we stood up to leave, my father said he'd walk us out. I could see the look of panic on Mom's face, but he assured her he'd be right back. Once outside, he shook Noble's hand, gave me a brief hug, and thanked us both for all our hard work. I was glad he recognized all that we had accomplished. Then he handed me a check, reimbursing me for what I spent to outfit her apartment. It didn't remove the emotion from the day, but it made me feel heard. For a moment, anyway. He returned inside and spent the next two hours with Mom. When he called later, upset, and said she had begged him to spend the night since the bed was big enough. He gave some lame excuse about that being against the rules (it wasn't). He simply didn't see any resemblance between himself and the same-aged residents. Spending the night in an assisted living facility, even with his wife in a lovely apartment, was not something he ever would entertain despite many future months of her begging.

Dad programmed all our numbers into her phone and left the legend in plain sight. By nine that night, she had called twice, asking when she would see me next. I promised I'd stop by the following evening and join her for dinner. She sounded so lonely; my heart tightened. I wasn't sure how this was going to work out if she didn't try to make the best of it. But then, what would I have done in the same position? I had no way of knowing.

I, too, had lost my appetite, so I drank a few glasses of wine, which only exacerbated my weepiness. Noble listened patiently as I agonized over the day, finally suggesting we go to bed and find something mindless on television. I fell asleep quickly and awoke with an emotional hangover from the tears, yet I knew I needed to get to my office. The day felt unusually long, but I got through my meetings with minor distraction before heading toward Mom's facility to sit with her at dinner. When I arrived, Dad was already there, sitting protectively close to her like Greta sits next to me. I pulled up a chair, Mom greeted me with a smile, then turned her attention back to my father. Her table mates were nice enough, though two were in wheelchairs and barely verbal. I wasn't sure how she would make friends here.

And so it went for the weeks leading up to Thanksgiving. I spoke with her at least once, if not twice, each day and at least three nights during the week, and I sat with her (and my father) at dinner. She seemed to be settling in, as much as one could hope, though she begged Dad on every visit to go home. Every time, he told her, "Maybe soon." It would never happen, and we both knew it, but it was the humane answer, as much as it was a bald-faced lie.

Noble and I had planned to have my father over for Thanksgiving, yet it was too soon and too dangerous to bring Mom from the facility to our home. We might not be able to return her without emotional trauma. So, we joined her for their Thanksgiving luncheon before coming home to finish preparing Thanksgiving dinner. At least they served ham as an option; eating turkey twice in one day seemed excessive. Our own dinner was as enjoyable as it could have been, given our somber moods. Other than my first honeymoon, this was my first Thanksgiving without Mom at the table. I felt her absence keenly, yet I did what I could to keep everyone entertained. My father ate stoically, then left after he finished his pumpkin chiffon pie. Before settling in for the evening, I called my daughter, who, as always, was having dinner with her father's family, to wish her a Happy Thanksgiving. I kept the conversation brief for fear I'd break down. I didn't want my emotional weight to become a burden for her.

That weekend, Noble noticed a strange, painful spot on the second toe of his left foot. Because of years of football injuries and a few accidents on his parents' farm, his feet were already damaged. This toe bowed up at an odd angle, causing it to rub against the top of his shoes, but this didn't look like a regular abrasion. We treated it with antibiotic ointment for the next few days. It just became more inflamed, so he made an appointment with his primary care doctor for the next day. Having almost lost a leg to a staph infection following knee surgery in college, Noble knew to take this seriously. After being seen by three different doctors in the same practice, each of whom offered a different diagnosis, he grew more frustrated.

Three days later, the toe was more swollen, discolored, and an oozy wound had opened up. It was the nastiest thing I had ever seen. He called his primary care doctor again and was told to go directly to the emergency room. Once we arrived at Arlington Memorial and the emergency room physician examined his foot, she immediately put him on an IV drip. This either was staph or MRSA. Both were life-threatening to him. The problem was the hospital didn't have a podiatrist on call. One parent at Noble's former school was a podiatrist, so we called him and sent a picture of Noble's foot. He spoke with the emergency room physician, and they agreed he needed to be transported to Medical City, where the podiatrist had privileges.

For the second time in two months, I followed an ambulance carrying a loved one to the hospital, frightened beyond words that whatever this was might take Noble from me. I called my father en route to the hospital. He told me not to make a big deal out of this because it was probably treatable. So much for a sympathetic ear. I told him I probably wouldn't see Mom for a day or two, depending on the situation, but I would call and check in. He asked me not to burden her with my "sad tales of woe." Interesting.

Throughout our marriage, I had never known Noble to complain, and this situation was no different, yet I could see the fear in his eyes as the attending physician examined his toe before telling us he needed to be admitted. Once he was moved to his room, still connected to the IV, we held hands and prayed. That evening, his podiatrist–Dr. B–came to examine him, then said he needed surgery the following day to irrigate the infection, pack it with antibiotic beads, and stitch him up… hoping to save his toe. He would biopsy the tissue to ensure we weren't dealing with MRSA. I couldn't contemplate that possibility because one of my dearest friends, Darrell, had died from the same just two years earlier and much too young.

I stayed with Noble as long as I could, then told him I'd be back the next day for his surgery. Covering him with a quilt I had brought from home, I kissed him gently before leaving. I cried the entire way home and once there, did what one should never do: I started Googling. I didn't like any of what I read.

The next day, I worked from home for a few hours before going back to the hospital. Though I told my father Noble would undergo surgery later in the day, he never showed up to offer support, but a close friend did, thankfully. Dr. B told me if they were in surgery any longer than thirty minutes, it probably meant they couldn't save the toe, but he would let me know. I paced, sat, paced, and sat some more for the next forty-five minutes, convinced of the worst. Just then, Dr. B came to the waiting room and said the procedure had gone well, the toe had been spared. But Noble would have to remain in the hospital and, once released, would need to see an infectious disease specialist for further treatment.

For the next four days, my schedule was a blur of going to work, checking on Mom, visiting Noble, and trying to sleep. I also stayed in touch with Noble's family to apprise them of his status. I think my father may have visited him once but didn't stay for long. Finally, they discharged him with a walking boot and a referral to an infectious disease specialist in Mansfield. We already had an appointment scheduled the following day.

I was relieved to have Noble home but concerned about his continued treatment. Dad drove us to the specialist and joined us as the doctor explained that Noble would have to be on a peripherally inserted central catheter (PICC) line for the next six weeks. The PICC line provided a daily tidal wave of antibiotics to his system to ensure the infection would be conquered. While we had planned to go to Santa Fe for New Year's, we knew that wasn't realistic. Yet another plot twist neither of us could have anticipated.

A week before Christmas, I began making plans for how best to celebrate as a family amidst all the unexpected changes we had just weathered. Before going into the hospital, Mom had all but finished a Christmas quilt for Dad but could not hand stitch the binding. She asked that I bring it from her home so she could try, but she couldn't even thread the needle, so I brought it to my house to finish the work. I knew Mom wanted to have something to give my father. He was unsure what to buy for her, so I found and purchased a human-sized teddy bear she could cuddle when lonely. He thought that was a good idea. Then I told him we needed to bring Mom to our house for dinner. Again, he argued it wasn't a good idea because there was no way he could transport her easily from her apartment. This time, I doubled down and assured him Noble and I could handle it. He continued to reject my suggestions until I finally told him I would take responsibility. She did not need to be alone on Christmas. Eventually, he relented.

Presents all wrapped, house decorated, appetizers prepared, and Christmas dinner underway, we awaited my father's arrival. Around four-thirty, he rang the bell, then brought in a few presents to place under the tree. His plan, he said, was for us to celebrate with Mom, have dinner, take her back to her apartment, and then we could have "our" Christmas. That idea didn't settle well with me, but I didn't want to risk a tantrum, so I just nodded. I accompanied him to her facility where we found her dressed in an elegant gold top I had loaned her for the occasion, a pair of black yoga pants, and the special shoes she now needed to wear to accommodate her edema. She had brushed her hair and applied makeup. She looked beautiful, and I told her as much. She smiled. I followed behind as Dad guided her down the hall, out the front door, and to his car. So far, so good. Once settled in, we headed to our house. Noble met us to guide her out of the car, steady her on her walker, and help my father as they navigated the curb. The dogs were outside, and the moment we entered the house, they were jumping at the patio door, but I needed her settled in the living room before I allowed them inside. They, and the cat, were delighted to see her and showered her with love (and hair). She relished the excitement.

I was in hostess overdrive mode, so intent on making the evening perfect that I couldn't sit still. After sampling the appetizers and ensuring everyone's glasses were replenished, I brought the presents they had for one another, our presents for Mom, and a present I had purchased for Mom to give Noble from under the tree. She opened the soft lounging suits I had purchased and handled them as if they were made of spun gold. I fought back tears. Next, she opened a picture I had found and framed of her and her best friend, Kay, who had died one month earlier from Alzheimer's. Her death had affected Mom deeply. I wasn't sure if this gift was a good idea or not, but she hugged it to her chest and proclaimed it "so very thoughtful." The picture was a black and white of the two of them in 1953, high school seniors who co-edited their high school newspaper. They both looked young, beautiful, and ready to take the world by storm.

Finally, I gave her a box holding a boar's hairbrush–a suggestion from my father–so she could fix her rapidly thinning hair without damage. She seemed to appreciate it. Then, I handed Dad the large gift bag with Giant Teddy, and he handed it to her, helping her open it. She laughed and sat Giant Teddy in her lap. That's a picture I will always cherish, though it was hard to see her shrinking frame so diminished behind Teddy's fluff. Finally, I handed Dad the box in which I had wrapped the Christmas quilt. I couldn't wait to see his reaction, especially since it had taken me two full days to complete the binding. He opened it, nodded, gave Mom a kiss, and put it back in the box without comment. Without recognition, though he had to know it was I who had completed her project. Deep down, I knew my finishing the quilt was more to illustrate my commitment to salvaging this strange holiday than making him happy, but his flat affect hurt my feelings.

Presents opened and prime rib resting on the cutting board, Noble began carving while Dad and I helped Mom from the living room, up the step, and into the dining room. I had borrowed her Lenox Christmas China for the occasion and complemented the service with my sterling silver flatware, crystal goblets, a floral centerpiece, one of her Christmas tablecloths, and red linen napkins rolled in gold pinecone rings. She pronounced the table "beautiful," saying I always had displayed a knack for decorating. I kissed the top of her head before bringing the side dishes from the kitchen. Noble and I gave one another a quick hug. He whispered things were going well, and he hoped I was happy. I bit the inside of my cheek and gave him a wane smile. It was as good as it was going to get.

After saying grace, we started eating. I had hoped a home-cooked meal would entice Mom to eat a bit more than usual, but she just picked at her food. I couldn't tell if it was the emotion of the day, her recognition that her life would never be the same, or just that her stomach had shrunk in the past few months, but I encouraged her to eat a little more so she could have chocolate cake for dessert. That did the trick! I was trying to lengthen our visit as long as I could, but once she finished nibbling some of her cake, she said she was tired. Though only seven o'clock, I followed Dad as he drove her back to her apartment. Once we got her settled, I gave her the biggest hug I could manage and told her I'd see her tomorrow before leaving Dad to have a few private moments with her.

Thirty minutes later, he was back at our house, slightly teary but ready for us to have "our" Christmas. I poured myself a glass of prosecco, and we exchanged presents before he declared he was "wiped out" and needed to get home. Arming him with leftovers Noble had packed up, we escorted him to the car and wished him a Merry Christmas. He hugged me and, this time, held me close for a minute, whispering, "You done good, kid." That was the best gift of all. He took it back the next day.

Noble's son from his first marriage was arriving the following afternoon from his mom's house in Oklahoma City, so I got up that morning to ensure all his presents were wrapped and under the tree. Early afternoon, I went to a friend's house–just two streets over–to enjoy some wine and exchange our presents. I had talked to Dad that morning to see if he was okay. He had slept in and admitted to feeling a bit down. I understood. He planned to join Mom for lunch, reluctantly it seemed. I said I'd visit her the next day.

Returning from Tina's house, I put the lasagna in the oven and tidied the house while Noble went to the train station to pick up his son. We had planned to have our "official" Christmas celebration the following evening; this was his "welcome home" meal, as requested. I was happy to comply. We had just finished our late dinner when Dad called shortly after nine. He sounded unwell and said life didn't feel worth living anymore. I tried to draw him out, carefully. He said he felt he was dying, that it was as if he was being tormented from within. Worriedly, I asked him to explain.

"I just feel like shit, Suzanne, okay? I feel like I'm being, I don't know, punished," he snapped. I heard him take a sharp intake of breath.

"What can I do, Dad?"

"Nothing. Just nothing matters anymore. I need to go," he said and hung up.

My instinct told me something was very wrong. While prone to self-pity, my father had never sounded like this, at least not to me. I remembered him telling me, some twenty years earlier, that if he ever were diagnosed with a terminal illness, or he felt he had lost his quality of life, he planned to take the matter into his own hands and die on his own terms. While that concept didn't align with my beliefs, they clearly did with his. I told Noble I needed to get to his house. I'd be home soon.

Within five minutes, I was at Dad's door, which was locked (and he hadn't given me a key). I rang the bell several times, nothing. I knocked on the door. Nothing. I called from my cell, nothing. Again, I pounded before he opened the door, his face red with fury.

"Why the hell are you here?" he shouted. I said I was worried because he sounded desperate on the phone.

"All I wanted was to take a fucking shower and go to bed!" he yelled. I blinked back tears.

"I was just trying to help you," I said.

Before I knew what was happening, my father wrapped his right hand around my throat, squeezing with all his might, then shoved me backward with a force I didn't think he still had. Fortunately, I didn't fall off the front step.

"Leave. Me. Alone!" He went back inside, slammed the door, and locked it. I heard him yelling on the other side.

I got in my car and sat for a moment, trying to gather myself, before returning home. Noble met me at the door. By now, angry marks had appeared around my neck. Quietly, I told him what Dad had done, and I saw his face darken with anger.

"Let's just leave it alone for now," I said as he embraced me in a tight hug. "I don't want to ruin the rest of the evening."

Good girl, compensating.

Chapter Thirty-Six: Free Falling (Part Two)

The next morning, I awoke to an email nasty gram from my father, accusing me of violating his privacy, preventing him from getting a good night's sleep, and behaving like a lunatic. He finished the email by writing if I ever pulled that kind of "stunt" again, he'd call the police and then he'd call Noble, in that order. I didn't respond. We didn't speak for days. I couldn't make sense of the situation, but at a minimum, his accusations felt like projection on his part. I also began worrying about his mental health, so I left a voicemail for his psychiatrist. He never returned my call.

We celebrated New Year's Eve quietly and greeted 2020 with our hearts hoping for a better year ahead. My father, having returned to some semblance of normalcy, dropped by earlier that evening to share champagne and ring in the year. Maybe things will get better.

"We plan, God laughs." That adage of Mom's certainly fit the year ahead.

I returned to work, and Noble had just two more weeks on his PICC line before his treatment was finished. Mom appeared relatively stable and had made a few friends at her facility. Dad spent his days, at least as I understood it then, visiting her and seeing his bevy of doctors. We all, as it seemed, had settled into our "new normal."

Mom's birthday was at the end of January. I had made plans to visit friends in San Antonio the week prior. I desperately needed to get away, and with everything under control at home, I thought a long weekend would be just the thing. I didn't tell Dad where I was going, just that I was going out of town for the weekend. The weekend was as relaxing as it could have been given the guilt I felt about "running away," but it gave me some time to process all I was juggling. Three days after my return, Noble's toe had exploded with infection, and he made an appointment with Dr. B the next day. We weren't sure what to expect. Noble called on his way home from Dr. B's office to tell me he was scheduled for amputation surgery the following day. Mom's birthday.

Just fuck.

I had to make an important presentation that morning on the other side of Fort Worth. Unfortunately, there was no way I could cancel at the last minute without it becoming a political issue at work. We already were in chaos mode, and I had taken my share of time away from the office to attend to family matters. So, I promised Noble I would be at the surgery center before the procedure started. My father had agreed to drive him there but wouldn't stay.

As was usually the case, the committee before which I was to present was running behind schedule. I fidgeted, watching the clock. My presentation would take at least twenty minutes, and with any committee meeting in academia, the ensuing discussion could go on forever. When it finally was my turn, I clipped through my PowerPoint, stopping for questions, and navigated the ridiculous commentary efficiently and effectively. Once dismissed, I made my way to Mansfield as quickly as I could. When I arrived, the receptionist told me Noble was getting prepped for surgery and that I wasn't allowed back; I needed to stay in the waiting area. My best friend, Margot, met me there, and together, we waited. I thought I had failed him.

His surgery went well, and after his anesthesia had worn off, the nurse told me I could pull my car around and wait for someone to wheel him outside. I helped him get into the car and handed him a bottle of water. What he really wanted, he said, was a Whataburger. His spirits were good, and his eyes, despite what he had just endured, twinkled as they always did. Thanks to the nerve block his anesthesiologist had administered, he wasn't yet feeling any pain.

After stopping at Whataburger, we got to our house. I let the dogs outside before settling him in bed with his meal and the remote control. I was slated to be at Mom's by five for her birthday celebration, and I still needed to pick up flowers and a few miniature Bundt cakes. Nearly hyperventilating, I arrived in her room just after five o'clock–Dad came in a few minutes later with her favorite pizza, as planned. I took the dishes and silverware I had brought in a picnic basket and arranged them on the table, put her flowers where she could see them, and arranged her modest gifts on the counter. Dressed in the same outfit she had worn at Christmas, she looked positively regal and, to my surprise, ate three generous slices of pizza. It was the happiest I had seen her in a long time.

Once she had blown out the candle on her cake and we cleaned our plates, she opened her presents. She had become more forgetful in the last few weeks, so I recommended Dad buy a journal and a nice pen so we could document our visits for her subsequent review. She loved the journal and immediately opened the luxurious lotion I had given her — her favorite, hard-to-find scent — and thanked us profusely. I apologized but told her I needed to return to my patient. Thankfully, she understood.

Noble's foot was healing nicely, so I could return my focus to work, visiting Mom, and checking in on my father. He was still experiencing unpleasant cardiac episodes. His erratic heartbeat caused such fatigue that he didn't have the energy for even the most mundane tasks. In early February, his cardiologist referred him to yet another specialist in Dallas who recommended a pacemaker. They scheduled his surgery for the following week. Again, Noble and I drove him there. I waited while his surgeon performed the procedure and met him back in his room. They kept him overnight for observation, but the surgeon said all had gone well and that the pacemaker should help resolve most, if not all, his issues. If only it could be that simple.

Noble had made sure Dad's refrigerator and freezer were well-stocked with frozen dinners (Dad's favorite), sandwich fixings, and other staples he would need for the next week since we didn't know what his strength level would be. Surprisingly, he seemed fairly spry when we picked him up from the hospital. He was convinced he had been "fixed."

Yet, he wasn't really. But we wouldn't know that for a few weeks.

By now, COVID-19 had gone from being a virus sweeping through China to a genuine threat in our own backyard. One of my local friends had been admitted to the hospital in early February with pneumonia. She died a few days later, and it was subsequently attributed to the coronavirus. A former employee, who had resigned to start a business and had taken a quick trip to New York, also showed up positive. Despite her relative youth, she was deathly ill. No one knew what we were up against, yet the world had changed before our eyes.

The week before Spring Break was to start in mid-March, Mom had begun coughing a deep, phlegmy cough. I contacted Mom's primary care physician and asked her to check on Mom. I was worried the cough wasn't responding to the over-the-counter medications being administered by the med techs. The next day, Noble had gone to see Mom and was there when Dr. H examined Mom. The doctor concluded that Mom had bilateral pneumonia and needed to be taken by ambulance to the emergency room. He called me at work, and I left immediately, first calling my father, then calling Margot, who talked to me the entire drive to the hospital. My mind couldn't help entertaining the worst: what if Mom had COVID? There was no way she could survive it in her weakened state.

By the time I arrived and met Dad in the parking lot, Mom already had been admitted to the ICU, yet again. Noble was with her in the room, sitting in the corner as the nurses connected myriad monitoring devices. She looked grayer and frailer than she had even a few days earlier. Dad moved a chair so he could sit close, and Noble stood so I could take his seat. It was time for him to get home, since the dogs hadn't been out for hours. I thanked him for staying with her. Mom weakly waved goodbye. She knew I was there, but she only had eyes for my father. As usual.

I stepped out and asked the nurse about Mom's prognosis. She said the doctor had not yet seen Mom, but she was fighting two fronts: pneumonia and her A-fib. Once again, it was out of control. After returning to Mom's room and sneaking a peek at the monitors, I could see that her pulse rate and oxygen were dangerously low, though her blood pressure was elevated. The nurse had connected Mom to oxygen through a nasal cannula, but Mom kept fidgeting with it. I offered her the apple juice I had procured from the nurse, and she drank it thirstily. With nothing left to do, I said my goodbyes and headed home for the evening. They were still holding hands when I left.

Fortunately, I had brought my laptop home with me, not knowing how long Mom might be in the hospital. As COVID took hold of the Dallas/Fort Worth area, employers–including mine– were issuing "work at home" orders. For many, this move created further anxiety. For me, it was a relief. At least I'd be able to stay close to both parents and help navigate, as much as was possible, their medical challenges. Initially, Mom's proved the most difficult. While her pneumonia was being well-managed, her A-fib wasn't responding to the myriad medications the team administered. Her cardiologist told me she'd need to stay in the ICU until both conditions improved. Noble and I took turns visiting. He brought her milkshakes and malts...anything to put some weight on her delicate frame. I came to her room one afternoon to find her sitting on the edge of her bed, her marigold gown partially opened in back, and I was horrified by what I saw. She was as thin as a concentration camp prisoner, every bone in her back visible. I helped her get back in bed, worried she would fall. That was the last thing she needed.

About five days into her ICU stay, Dad called to say he had experienced what felt like a cardiac event while at the grocery store. He was home, so I told him I was on the way. When I arrived, he was in his favorite recliner, quite pale and clammy to the touch. I suggested we call his primary cardiologist, and surprisingly, he agreed. I dialed Dr. V's number, explained what I could, and handed the phone to Dad. Their conversation was brief–Dad articulating what he was feeling, then responding with a series of "okays" and "all rights." He hung up and looked at me dejectedly.

"Well, the good doc said if I'm not feeling any better by tomorrow, I need to go to the emergency room where they will admit me for evaluation," he said, taking a sip of his Scotch. "I guess we'll see."

The next morning, I called to check his status. He hadn't slept well, which was now common, and his heart rate was all over the map. He said he felt weak and shaky. I told him to get his things together. I was on my way.

"I have things I have to do first," he said. I didn't understand what was so important that he'd put his health aside, but I relented.

"I'll pick you up at two," I replied. He agreed.

When we got to the hospital, he said he wanted to visit Mom first, so we took the elevator to the cardiac ICU and slowly, very slowly, walked to her room. As always, she was happy to see him–like my dogs, who act upon my return as though they hadn't seen me for years…even if I had only been gone for an hour. He told her he wasn't well, and her face immediately contorted with worry. "I'll keep you posted," he promised, bending down to kiss her forehead. She clutched his hand. He placed his other hand on top and gave her a squeeze. I watched from the doorway, then told him we needed to go.

"If I can walk to the emergency room, I think I might just be okay," he said. I took a breath for courage and said, "No, Dad, that's not how this is going to work. Dr. V said you needed to be admitted, so we're getting you admitted." We made our way slowly to the ER, where he was immediately put in a temporary room awaiting Dr. V's paperwork to admit him. He showed up a few hours later, examined Dad, and said he needed an emergency procedure–

angioplasty–the next morning. Already in his own marigold hospital gown, Dad just nodded, then thanked Dr. V for seeing him.

"Tomorrow, then. Try to get some rest tonight," Dr. V said before heading on to his next patient.

Once again, it took several hours for the medical team to find my father a room. It was past the time he could have anything to eat, though he could have apple juice. Like Mom, Dad had lost weight and looked as fragile as I had seen him, but he seemed optimistic that the angioplasty would "fix" him. By nine o'clock that night, after I had complained several times that we shouldn't have been kept waiting so long, a nurse wheeled him to his room in the cardiac ICU, across the hall and just a few rooms down from Mom.

Two elderly parents in the same cardiac ICU, with COVID lurking around every corner, are a lot to process. Dad wanted to visit Mom, so I accompanied him to her room. She became concerned when he told her about his procedure the next day. I watched as her monitors began beeping. I guess he felt he needed to apprise her of his situation, but it wasn't helping hers.

Dad had given me his key so I could put his newspapers and mail in the house, and I vowed to monitor things. After finally leaving the hospital that night, I dropped by their house to check mail and ensure a few lights were on. I looked at the chaotic dining room table, covered with piles of paperwork and his various checkbooks, and found a notebook with what appeared to be instructions to me regarding bank accounts and other assets, as well as their locations. There were briefcases in his upstairs office, the notes directed, in which I would find various documents and savings bonds. The precious coins he collected were in a box in his office closet. At least I knew what I might need to manage at some point. Heading upstairs, I noticed an envelope atop of pile of other mail, so I sat down to take a look.

It was a thank-you card from Judy for the wonderful Valentine's Day celebration, the Carolina Herrera perfume, and the five-thousand dollar check he had given her. "I look forward to spending it together!" she wrote. "Love, Judy."

Bile rose in my throat. Apparently, she was back in his life. Yet, he was still seeing Linda. Doing the mental algebra: he was cheating on Mom and cheating on Linda and cheating on Judy. No wonder his heart was failing. Irony?

I drove home furiously and told Noble what I had found. Nothing surprised him anymore, he said. Time would prove that statement false.

The next morning, I pulled my mood together and arrived at the hospital a few minutes too late. Dad's procedure was moved up, and he already was in the operating room. That was the first day the hospital imposed new restrictions because of COVID. I had to check in with a clerk in the lobby, then have my temperature taken before receiving a mask and getting clearance to proceed to his floor. Drinking fountains already had been covered with plastic to prohibit use, and signage throughout the hospital directed visitors to keep a distance from others and to make use of the newly installed hand sanitizing stations. It was surreal. The world had changed overnight.

I went to see Mom. She was weak and drowsy and kept falling asleep, her breathing labored. I held her hand for a few minutes before heading toward Dad's room to await his return. About twenty minutes later, two orderlies wheeled Dad's gurney into the room and lifted him to his bed. I covered him with the quilt I brought and offered him some water. Eyes closed, he just shook his head. He was still groggy, so I sat quietly, texting Noble that he was out of surgery. Next, I received a call from Dr. V, so I stepped into the hall to keep from disturbing Dad. He told me he couldn't complete the angioplasty. Dad's arteries were fully blocked and would require bypass surgery immediately. He didn't perform this highly specialized procedure, he said, but had referred my father to a cardiac surgeon who would evaluate him the following day.

Meanwhile, he said, Dad needed to rest. I decided to head home and get some rest myself. Who knew what the next few days would bring?

When I returned that evening, Dad wasn't in his room, so I walked across the hall and found him with Mom. As had become habit, he was sitting by her side, holding her hand. They both looked up and greeted me with wan smiles. Seeing them in matching gowns, each looking as fragile as the other, brought a lump to my throat, but it was quickly dislodged as I remembered the card from Judy. We had eaten Valentine's Day lunch with Mom at her facility. Did he really leave from there to celebrate with his second mistress? My anger rose like acid reflux, burning as I worked to tamp it down. Now wasn't the time for a confrontation, yet I had a difficult time making eye contact with him.

Mom's nurse came into the room and said they would transfer her in two days from the cardiac ICU to the rehabilitation unit upstairs. The duration of that stay would depend upon her progress. She handed me a stack of forms to complete. The next day, we were informed Dad would undergo bypass surgery the morning after they moved Mom. It was all too much to process, yet they both were relying on me. I couldn't let them down.

Noble and I returned to the hospital the afternoon Mom was to be moved. I persuaded the nurse to let us all have dinner together before they transported her, and might they give us until seven? After a few calls, she agreed, so Noble left to pick up dinner for four at our favorite local restaurant. He thought we all needed some comfort food. Because of his scheduled surgery, Dad couldn't eat after six, so we somberly finished our meals–to the degree any of us could–by five-thirty. From there, we made idle conversation about the news coverage we were watching, mostly about COVID, until the nurse came with a wheelchair to take Mom upstairs. I saw, again, the terrified look in her eyes — akin to those of a cornered animal. In many ways, we would soon learn she was. I took Noble's hand and guided him out of the room so my parents could have a few moments alone.

The walk from her room to the elevator felt like a death march. The four of us processed slowly, solemnly, sadly, together. When we reached the elevator bank, we all said our goodbyes to Mom…they felt permanent somehow. I gave her the biggest and longest hug I could offer, and she asked that I keep her informed about Dad's wellbeing. I squeezed her hand, promising I would. Noble hugged her next, then it was Dad's turn. I couldn't bear to watch, so I turned my back, wiping the torrent of tears from my cheeks. As the elevator dinged, I forced myself to turn around and watch as they wheeled Mom in, then blew her a kiss as the door began closing.

"You okay?" Dad asked. I merely shook my head.

"I'll walk you to your room," I said. Noble told me he'd be waiting in the lobby.

We got to his room, and once he climbed into bed, I covered him with his quilt. His surgeon said they would begin prepping Dad at seven, and I told him I'd be there by six-thirty. I pulled a chair close to the bed, having so much to say yet unsure where to begin, so I asked how he was feeling about his surgery.

"I guess we'll see," he said. "Apparently, it's the only option I have."

"Dr. N is highly regarded," I told him, taking his hand. He looked up at the ceiling, his eyes brimming with tears.

"This is not at all what I expected," he said.

"Me neither."

"I've had a good life," he said, wiping his eyes. I had hoped for more, but he left it at that.

"Did you say everything that needed to be said to Mom?" I asked. What I meant was: Did you apologize for breaking her heart again and again, for betraying her, for lying to her, for giving the best of yourself to others instead of our family? He nodded. I was certain he hadn't.

"You need to be rested for tomorrow," I said, standing to leave. I needed to get home to my safe place, where I could unleash all my complicated emotions. I leaned down to give him a hug and told him I loved him, recognizing that might be my last chance.

"Suz?" he asked as I walked to the door. I turned around in time to hear him whisper, "I'm proud of you for all you're carrying." I bowed my head, nodded, then blew him a kiss before leaving to find Noble. That was the only time I could remember my father offering me praise.

The morning arrived quickly. I hadn't slept well, so my morning preparations were a blur. I arrived at the hospital, checked in at the lobby, had my temperature taken, donned my mask, and headed up to his room. My plan had been to spend the day working at the hospital, so I was laden with my laptop bag and a tote carrying a shawl, a notebook, my phone charger, and a bottle of water. At exactly six-thirty, I stepped into his room quietly and heard him chatting on the phone. He saw me step around the curtain and quickly ended his call with, "I love you too."

I knew it had to be Linda. My anger returned, and this time, I couldn't contain it.

"You look nice," he said as I sat down. An offering, of sorts, I suppose.

"Who was that?"

"Just a friend," he answered, "Wishing me well."

"It was Linda, wasn't it?"

"She's not a morning person, but she set her alarm just for me," he said, smiling. Well, I did too! I decided to leave it alone. For the moment.

"How nice."

He said he had slept well, but he didn't ask about my night. I drank my coffee, and we waited for the orderly to bring him to the pre-op. Not surprisingly, I had little to say. Shortly before seven, two burly men entered the room with the gurney and helped get Dad settled before transport. I asked if I could come to the pre-op. They nodded, so I followed.

Once there, a surgical nurse took his vitals, as well as a blood sample, to ensure he was stable enough for what would ultimately be a ten-hour procedure. The surgeon wouldn't know what needed to be done until Dad's chest was cracked open and he could identify the blockages. For a moment, though, it seemed the surgery might not happen at all based on Dad's red blood cell count, which was just south of normal. This was a concern, the nurse said, because he would require transfusions, anyway. Coming into surgery at a deficit created additional challenges for an already complicated procedure. Eventually, Dr. N looked at the readings and deemed my father strong enough for them to proceed.

Because his would be open-heart surgery, they had to prepare his chest. I decided it was best to give Dad his privacy, so I gave him a quick hug, told him I loved him and I'd see him sometime that evening. The nurse had my phone number and said she would call throughout the procedure with progress reports. I asked if I could set up my laptop in his room and wait. She said I could work in the cafeteria, but not in his room. Because of the new COVID protocols, I couldn't have anyone–including my husband–wait with me, so I elected to return home–just two miles away–and work while I waited.

But first, with my coffee cup refilled, I thought I'd go upstairs and visit Mom. We hadn't yet spoken that morning, but I was sure she was up and probably finishing breakfast. I stepped into the elevator and pressed the button for the sixth floor. When it opened, I was greeted by two employees staffing a wide table. They asked what I needed, and I said my mom was a patient and I'd like to see her.

"Oh, we're so sorry, but because of COVID, no visitors are allowed."

"But, she's my mom! My dad just went into open-heart surgery. I just want to see my mom!" I could feel my lower lip quivering.

"We understand, but we must abide by the new rules. No exceptions." There was no point in arguing. While disappointed, I appreciated their abundance of caution. No one could have predicted the toll COVID would take in the coming weeks, months, and years. At least they were keeping Mom safe.

I came home, made another pot of coffee, and set up my laptop to get some work done. I couldn't concentrate. Around nine, the nurse called and said Dad's procedure was underway. Close to eleven, she called and said, based on Dr. N's assessment, Dad would require four bypass procedures–a quadruple bypass. I became alarmed. How long would it take? She said at least seven more hours. Maybe longer. He was eighty-three. Could he survive that?

Around lunchtime, Mom called, sounding almost manic. She hadn't slept well, she didn't like the nurses, and could I come and get her out of there? I assured her she was there to get strong enough to return to her apartment.

"I just feel," she stammered, searching for her word, "kerplunk." This was a word I hadn't heard, but I sensed what she meant. I told her I'd talk to the nurse.

"No! I want to get out of here! I need to see Dad!" I told her he was in surgery and that the surgical team was providing regular updates. He would be okay, I said, but he'd be in the operating room for several more hours. She started to cry. Honestly, my nerves already were shot, and I was exhausted. I tried to remain patient, told her I loved her and was proud of her courage, then hung up. Next, I called and spoke to the nurse on duty, suggesting they give Mom something to calm her down. I felt guilty doing so, but I knew her agitation would only trigger her A-fib. I couldn't have both parents staring down the barrel of death on the same day.

Shortly before five, Dad's nurse called and said they were wrapping it up, which would take another hour, all had gone well, and he'd be back in his room within the next hour. I arrived just after six and, unfortunately, missed meeting Dr. N by a few minutes. Dad was still sedated, but his eyes were open. I sat down and squeezed his hand. They attached him to a battalion of monitors. His chest, still stained with iodine, sported what looked like a zipper from just under his clavicle to well below his sternum. For a moment, I forgot my deep-seated anger and focused on the person lying before me: a fragile old man who had averted death. I think I was grateful. I think.

He wasn't conversant, obviously, and the nurses had said his anesthesia could take a few days to wear off, so I kissed his forehead gently and said I'd be back tomorrow. He squeezed my hand before I left. That night, I drank a fair amount of wine, called Margot, and cried about the stress of it all. She listened thoughtfully and finally said, "Well, it sounds like you're handling it, honey." Of course, I was. Did I have a choice?

Late the next morning, after checking on Mom, I dressed and returned to the hospital to see Dad. He was sipping some juice when I entered the room, still slightly groggy and looking quite disheveled. I smoothed his thinning hair into place and moved a chair close to his side. His voice was raspy from having been intubated for nearly ten hours, so I nattered away about the weather and my pets and a project I was trying to complete for work. He seemed remote…lost somewhere I couldn't reach. I began asking questions to draw him back to reality.

"So, I guess you and Judy are seeing each other again?" I prompted. He nodded.

"Why? After she broke your heart?"

"I missed having her in my life," he whispered.

"But you're also involved with Linda?" He nodded.

"Dad, why? I don't understand!"

"I can't explain it." He started coughing, holding the pillow they had given for this very reason close to his chest. I asked if he needed water, and he shook his head.

"I'm afraid they're taking advantage of you," I said gently.

"They wouldn't do that."

"Do they know about each other? Judy and Linda, I mean." He shook his head.

"I don't know what to say, Dad, but this all seems so terribly wrong. For everyone!"

He looked over at me, exhaled, and closed his eyes.

"I've tried to stop, Suz, I really have. I've tried to cut it off with both of them, with all of them. But then, I relapse, I guess. I just can't quit. I just can't."

At the moment, I was too tired and too conflicted to understand what he had just admitted. I would, years later, but not while sitting next to him in the cardiac ICU, with my lonely mother confined upstairs in the rehab unit. He fell asleep, and I returned home to my husband.

Good girl, gob smacked.

Chapter Thirty-Seven: Shrinking

By the time my father was discharged from the hospital, some five days later, the world already had changed. Stores had been depleted of many of life's basic necessities: food, paper products, bottled water, and beyond. Other than those businesses deemed essential–hospitals, doctors' offices, banks, and grocery, liquor, and hardware stores–cities, including ours, were completely shuttered. Protective masks were in short supply; news of COVID's spread and its corresponding death toll dominated the headlines.

On the day he was to be released, and once masked and cleared to enter the hospital, I walked briskly to his room to review discharge instructions with him and the cardiac nurse. We were told he needed to see his primary cardiologist within the week to evaluate progress and given a lengthy list of potential complications that would require emergency attention. Mostly, she said, he wasn't cleared to drive for at least a month, and ideally, he should not leave his house except for doctors' appointments because he was too weakened to survive COVID. I already knew that.

I gathered Dad's belongings while the nurse completed the paperwork. She said an orderly was on the way and directed me to where we could meet Dad with the car. Now dressed in regular clothes, I could see how much weight he had lost in just over a week. He looked emaciated, his color still hadn't returned, and from head to toe, he simply looked gray.

Once again, Noble had stocked Dad's kitchen with food we would prepare for him, as well as his favorite frozen dinners and pot pies he could prepare for himself. I had organized the newspapers and mail and had made sure his bed was nicely made. We helped him from the car and guided him inside. The short walk fatigued him, and he said he'd like to lie down. I tucked him in and put a bottle of water on his nightstand. Was he hungry? Could I bring him anything?

"I'm fine for now," he said, reaching for his flip-phone. Inwardly, I cringed. I knew he was desperate to check for texts from his girlfriends. I had seen plenty of their exchanges while he was in surgery. Yes, I checked.

"Let's give Mom a quick call," I proposed. "I know she'll want to hear that you're home safely."

"I'll call her later," he said. "Could you turn off the light? I think I need a nap." I did as he asked, and then we left.

Now that we had toggled quickly to fully remote work and begun using MS Teams to communicate, the College was operationally back on track, if differently. I got home just in time for the first of three consecutive meetings that afternoon and was happy for the distraction–grateful for some semblance of normalcy in my completely chaotic world. For the next few weeks, I spent my days navigating meetings, deadlines, checking on Mom, shuttling Dad to doctors' appointments, and ordering whatever we needed through Amazon. Truth be told, I was thankful for COVID only because it allowed me to be home and, therefore, close to my father during his convalescence. Noble gallantly braved the infected world as needed, masking up and shopping for groceries and liquor a few times per week. Occasionally, we would drive to the parking lot across from Mom's rehab room window, six floors up, and wave to her as we spoke by phone. One of her nurses even helped coordinate a few visits via FaceTime. Mom looked about the same physically, but she sounded more confused. We still did not know when she would be discharged.

By late April, Dad had been cleared to drive and was visibly relieved he no longer needed to rely upon us, though he said he was grateful for our support. I spoke to him daily and visited four or five times per week, checking his refrigerator for supplies and sitting with him while we watched ABC Nightly News. The stronger he became, the testier his demeanor. Once again, I found myself sidestepping potential landmines. My one concern, though, beyond his health, was his procrastination regarding the paperwork needed to establish me, as designated in their wills, as the beneficiary of their varied accounts. He had promised to complete the process even before Mom first went into the hospital. Knowing now there were other women in the mix, women who surely were focused on his money, the subject felt more urgent.

One evening, I carefully introduced the subject and asked, with every bit of tact I could muster, if there was anything I could do to help him do as he had promised. He shot me a look, took a sip of his Scotch, cleared his throat, and said gruffly, "I'll get to it when I get to it." I was confused. Had he changed his mind?

"But, Dad, I thought the whole reason we spent an entire summer putting all the legal instruments into place was so we wouldn't have to worry about it!" I said, my voice rising despite my better efforts.

"I'm not worried, Suzanne," he said flatly. "It's my money. I'll handle things as I see fit."

And there it was. In his mind, he had been fixed. He wasn't about to cede the power he believed he wielded over me in the form of my promised inheritance.

"It isn't about the money," I said sharply. He looked at me, raising his eyebrows, then sneered.

"Then what is it about, dear daughter?" I fought back angry tears, feeling reduced to a petulant child.

"You said you wanted to make sure you didn't leave me a mess to clean up!"

"Well, I'm still here, so I guess I haven't, have I?" He took another sip of Scotch and popped a handful of peanuts into his mouth.

"Whatever, Dad. I need to go. Talk to you tomorrow."

"Leaving in a huff, are you?" I had no response.

Once again, he failed to keep his word. I shouldn't have been surprised or disappointed, yet I was both.

On April 29, I was awaiting Noble's return from an elderly neighbor's home. Having taken on a few handyman jobs in the neighborhood, he had agreed to help repair and paint her dilapidated siding. I had wrapped up all my meetings for the day, so I was sitting on the patio with my dogs while watching the songbirds at my feeder. My cell phone, which had been faithfully by my side for the last six months, rang. It was the rehabilitation hospital calling. Hopefully, with good news.

The discharge nurse was on the other end of the line, wishing to provide an update on Mom. I sat up straighter, eager for information. Yes, the plan was to discharge my mother in the next two days. Wonderful! This was positive, right?

"Here's the situation, Ms. Groves," she said, pausing. My spine tingled. "Your mom's been evaluated by our doctor here, as well as her own doctor from the assisted living center," she continued.

"And?"

"We're recommending she be placed on hospice care," she said gently.

I inhaled sharply. "Why?"

"Their mutual assessment is that she has six months, maybe less, to live," she said flatly.

I couldn't breathe. I began to shake.

"Ms. Groves? Are you still there?"

"Yes," I said, my throat tightening. "What do I do?"

"We've been in touch with the medical director at your mom's place," she said. "She'll be able to provide you some suggestions."

"So, so, um, when can I see my mom?"

"Probably the day after tomorrow," she said. "We want to make sure she's stable enough to transfer. I'll need you to fill out some paperwork…"

"Yes, I know. Do Not Resuscitate orders for transport, right?"

"Yes, ma'am." I told her that once I knew precisely when she was to be discharged, I would arrange to pick up her things and sign the paperwork then.

I had only been off the phone for five minutes, my head in my hands, when Noble came out to the patio to find me sobbing. Between hiccups, I told him that Mom had been given an expiration date–for God's sakes, like she was a gallon of milk or something– and by my calculations, that meant the end of October if she lived the full six months. He reached down to give me a hug. I pushed him away.

"I can't," I said. "I need to call Dad."

With our dogs on his heels, Noble unfurled the garden hose and began watering the plants along our fence line. I dialed Dad's number; he didn't answer. I dialed his cell phone; again, no response. I texted him to call me as soon as he could. It was, after all, a Wednesday. I surmised he was likely with Linda, as I had learned that was one of his two preferred days for visiting her. Emails and all. Yes, I had looked.

About ten minutes later, he called from his cell. I hadn't stopped crying, but with my voice breaking, I told him what the rehab nurse told me. That Mom had maybe six months to live, that we would need to find a hospice provider, that this isn't what was supposed to happen, not at all!

"Well, it is what it is," he said stoically. "I'm sure you can get this all handled."

"I'll make some calls tomorrow," I said, trying to calm down.

"Okay, then. Just keep me posted. Talk to you later," he said, ending the call.

I'd like to think it was my imagination, but he sounded as relieved with this news as he had when I informed him that his own mother had died. I wanted to be wrong.

Just then, Noble walked toward me with something in his hand.

Remember the gold shrimp earrings Mom had loaned me for sorority rush? Several years later, to her great dismay, she lost one of them. When Jack and I went to St. Maarten in 2005, I found an identical pair and bought them, to her great delight. Like the original pair, they were her go-to earrings, which she wore almost daily. She had kept the orphan earring in her jewelry box, which now belonged to me.

After they moved from the house that would become mine, the backyard had become overgrown and had to be practically razed once I moved in. Once Noble and I were married, we dug up old flower beds, created new flower beds, and essentially transformed the backyard. Our two German Shepherds had worn a trail in the grass that now was not much more than packed dirt. We spent every evening on our patio, and Noble watered the grass and garden every evening.

Yet, on this day–the day I was told my mother wasn't expected to live beyond October–something unimaginable happened. After rolling up the hose and turning off the water, Noble was walking back to the patio when he saw something gleaming on the packed dirt in front of him. He picked it up, holding something he'd not seen before, and brought it to me for inspection.

There, in my hand, was Mom's lost gold shrimp earring, mangled and worn, but there just the same. A chill passed through me, and I looked up at Noble with tears in my eyes.

"I'll be right back," I said, dashing into the house. I pulled Mom's jewelry box from my closet and found the orphaned earring, then jogged back outside.

"You're not going to believe this," I said, handing him the intact earring.

He shook his head in wonder. I didn't know what to make of it…there was no reasonable explanation. Not one. The following day, I showed my pastor, and she said, simply, that it was God's way of letting me know that soon my mother would be made whole.

Between meetings, I spent most of the following day on the phone, speaking with the medical director and attending physician at Mom's assisted living facility to figure out what hospice entailed and how to select the best provider. As it turned out, the doctor was on the board of one of the recommended options, so I assumed that meant Mom would get the best care from them. I called and cleared my choice with Dad. He said to do whatever I thought was best. With Mom due to be transported the next day, I went to the facility and signed all the necessary papers to begin hospice care the moment she arrived. I called Mom that evening and told her how thrilled I was that finally, after six weeks, we'd get to see her tomorrow!

"Has it really been that long?" She sounded sleepy and confused, her voice wistful, as if she was a small child.

"It has, Mom, but you did it!" I said, trying to sound buoyant.

"Will Daddy be there?" she asked.

"Of course, Mom, Dad and I and Noble will be there to greet you," I said.

"But what about Daddy?" It took me a moment to realize she was talking about her own father who died in 1990.

"We'll all be there," I said reassuringly. "See you tomorrow!" I hung up the phone, feeling every inch the liar. Yet, if it comforted her, was it wrong? My stomach roiled.

The next day, around noon, I had arranged to meet one of Mom's nurses in the circular driveway outside the hospital and transport her belongings back to her apartment. From there, masked and cautious, I went to the grocery store for flowers, drinks, and snacks, which I took to her apartment. Around two, Dad and Noble joined me, and together, we waited outside for the call that medical transport was underway. By two-thirty, we were greeting her as the driver helped her from the wheelchair, then steadied her on her walker. Everyone was masked, yet it didn't disguise her joy at seeing Dad. Noble and I paved the way, holding open the door and escorting her back to the apartment she hadn't seen for nearly two months.

She moved more slowly and cautiously than she had before, yet we eventually made it the short distance to the apartment and helped her sit down in one of her two leather recliners. Dad took the other seat and reached out to hold her hand. Once again, she only had eyes for him. Noble took a seat at the table while I busied myself getting her a Coke and an orange.

It was déjà vu, but this time, the clock was ticking.

Things had changed, though, since she was admitted to the ICU in March. Because of COVID protocols, residents were seated only two per table for meals, and visitation was limited to one family member per day. The facility had made a special exception for us to be together for her return. I tried to explain the pandemic and what havoc it was causing, but she continued staring into Dad's eyes, holding his hand. He gave me a sharp look and shook his head, but I proceeded anyway.

"Oh my. Just like in 1916," she said, shaking her head. "That's when my grandparents died. Two days apart. My mom almost died, too." I nodded. "She and my aunt were orphans," she continued, then began coughing a raspy cough. I knew the stories and the history. I merely listened as if it were the first time I had heard about it.

"I don't want you to be an orphan," she said.

"I don't either, Mom. That's why you must take care of yourself." Noble got up from his chair and took my hand.

"How's Daddy?" I looked over at my father. He shook his head ever so slightly.

"Same as ever." That was all I could say.

Safely settled and warmly welcomed by the med techs who dropped in to say hello, I knew there wasn't much more we could do for Mom, so I told her I'd see her the next day.

"We'll coordinate, okay?" Dad said. It wasn't as though he had a work schedule to juggle, but I chose simply to nod and say, "Just let me know." I embraced Mom in a tight hug before moving toward the door. Noble leaned down and kissed her cheek. We left as my father was unbuttoning his shirt to show Mom his surgical scars. She ran her hand softly down his chest and said he looked like a warrior. I noticed her tender, if not childlike, expression. Despite everything, she loved him the most. My father basked in the light of her adoration.

Over the coming weeks, the visitation schedule became the subject of great tension between my father and me. After his visits, he would call and tell me all the things hospice was doing poorly, and would I please call and set them straight? After my visits, I'd often call him and cry…I couldn't bear to see her withering away. He would tell me to stop being melodramatic. One evening, after a particularly difficult visit during which I needed to change her soiled diaper, I stopped by his house for a glass of wine and reassurance. He offered the former yet deprived me of the latter.

"I don't know what you want me to say, Suzanne. It is what it is."

I couldn't contain my anger. "You know, Dad, here's the thing: she's my mom!"

"Yes, dear daughter, and she's my wife," he responded matter-of-factly. "Dear daughter" was not a term of endearment.

"I've never known life without her," I said. "And the idea of losing her breaks my heart. You've been married before! You all didn't meet until you were in your late twenties!"

"So?"

"So? I'm looking for you to at least acknowledge…something! I only have one mother!"

"And?"

I couldn't stop myself.

"You've had...you have...so many women. If she had been so important to you, you would have given her the attention, the loyalty, the respect she deserved...that you vowed to give her!"

He stared at me with such contempt, I thought I'd turn to stone.

"That's enough, Suzanne. I think it's time for you to go."

And so I did. For the next few weeks, our only communication was via text and related solely to Mom's care. Until his next health issue.

Good girl, coping.

Barely.

Chapter Thirty-Eight: Training for the Marathon

Now that he believed his heart was fixed, my father decided he would click through his list of other ailments and get those addressed, too. His behavior reminded me of the person who replaces their flooring and then decides the rest of the house should also be remodeled. I suppose he was hoping to be "marketable" when he found himself widowed. I'm sure he had begun evaluating his prospects while continuing to play the role of long-suffering husband to all who would give him an audience.

In early June, though, his plans were thwarted. Despite having met with specialists to diagnose his enlarged prostate and inguinal hernia, and receiving green lights to proceed with corresponding surgeries, he still wasn't feeling "right." He called one afternoon, sounding breathless, and said he had just returned from the grocery store and was thoroughly depleted of energy.

I suggested he make an appointment with his cardiologist. He said he already knew the problem, as verified by Google. "I just feel like I'm dying," he said, not for the first time. I couldn't help wondering if this was a carefully crafted play on my sympathy to draw me back into his web. "It's my mitral valve. It needs to be replaced."

"Why don't we let Dr. V make that determination," I said impatiently.

"I have a two o'clock appointment on Friday," he snapped.

"Fine. I'll take you," I said. "See you at one-thirty."

Three months into working remotely, I had developed as close to a new routine as I could, given so many personal variables. When

Mom's facility wasn't on lockdown because of COVID cases in the building, I visited her between video teleconferences. When visitation was prohibited, I stood outside her window so we could chat through the screen. Like the rest of the country, Noble and I found a respite in our evening binge-watching. Before we cuddled up on the couch, though, I made sure to text or call my father. Lather, rinse, repeat. Unlike so many others, Noble and I were blessed that as spouses and best friends, we actually enjoyed one another's company. Our confinement was our happiness, much to the chagrin of my father.

When I arrived to chauffeur him to his cardiologist appointment, he shuffled slowly to my car, so I got out and walked to the passenger's side to hold the door. He sat down gingerly and fastened the seatbelt before I gently closed the door. I could feel his mood already.

"How're you doing?"

Silence. Did he hear me?

"Did you get some sleep?" I asked.

"No," he grunted.

I turned on the radio to catch Terry Gross on NPR. I'd always fantasized about being a guest on her show because she knew how to draw out the very best in people. I wished I had that magic touch with my father. Periodically, I'd look over to find him staring stonily ahead. As was so often the case with him, I fought the urge to make small talk, but the silence was making me uncomfortable. He could at least try, couldn't he, to be cordial?

"So, last night, Noble and I found a wonderful new series we really like," I began.

"Good for you," he barked. Ah…I was beginning to realize what was bothering him, and it had nothing to do with his heart–at least, not physically. My guess was that either Judy or Linda had somehow disappointed him…maybe both. He used to take out his romantic frustrations on my mother. Now, it was my turn.

"I'm not sure what's bothering you, but please don't take it out on me," I said, taking a detour to avoid what I knew would be traffic congestion ahead.

"Why are you going this way?" he demanded.

"Because I'm the one driving. I know what I'm doing."

"Sure you do."

I turned up the radio, and he started to cry. Oh, geez. I handed him the bottle of water I had packed. He shook his head. I placed it back in the cup holder.

"You can't possibly understand how I feel," he whimpered.

"Then please tell me," I said cautiously, trying to keep focused on traffic.

"I'm tired of sleeping alone, watching TV alone, eating alone. At least you have Noble."

"Yes, I'm very blessed," I said flatly. Did he actually resent my happiness, such as it was amidst the pandemic, a high-pressure job, and caregiving my aging parents?

"Did, um, did something happen that you'd like to talk about? You know, with…?"

"Stay out of my fucking private life. Please!" he spat.

My lifelong relationship with my father had never been easy–it always felt like three-dimensional chess. The game, it seemed, had changed yet again. Clearly, I didn't understand the new rules. I clenched my jaw and pulled into the parking lot.

"Let me drop you off here," I said, maneuvering into the circular drive in front of the entrance. "I'll park and meet you in the lobby."

He pulled the requisite surgical mask over his face and slowly exited the car. I parked and walked swiftly to meet him. When we arrived outside the cardiologist's office, we had to sign in and have our temperatures taken before they admitted us inside. The nurse stopped me and said I would not be allowed in. I looked at my father.

"She's my medical power of attorney," he snapped. "She has to be at this appointment." Months earlier, I had begun carrying the folder with all my legal instruments to every medical appointment, so I showed her the appropriate form. She nodded and allowed me to join my father in the waiting room.

While Dad fidgeted, I pulled out my phone and began checking work email. Though there was nothing requiring my immediate attention, the task alone grounded me in my reality because I couldn't understand my father's. Finally, the nurse called us back. I smiled and thanked her as my father shuffled forward.

His weight alarmed me. He was down to one hundred and fifty-seven pounds from his "healthy" weight of one hundred and seventy pounds. He looked at the number and grimaced. "See?" he said, pointing at the digital display. "Something's wrong." I nodded and patted his back.

Once inside the examination room, the nurse asked the standard questions: "What brings you here today? How are you feeling? Have you noticed any changes since your last visit?"

"I feel like shit, okay?" Oh, boy.

"He's been complaining of lethargy and weakness," I offered carefully. She took his blood pressure while he glowered at her. I made a note of the reading. It seemed unusually low.

"Please come with me so we can run a quick EKG," she said, beckoning him to follow. "You can stay here," she said cordially. I smiled.

Dad came back to the room, and I waited for him to offer some information. Instead, he sat down with a grunt, but nothing more. Finally, Dr. V came in and Dad perked up.

"Please," I thought, "Please, please, please don't ask him how he's doing."

"Hi there! So, how are we doing today?" Shit.

"Well, I don't know. How are we doing?" Dad asked snidely. Dr. V sat down and reviewed the nurse's notations on his tablet. Thankfully, I suppose he had grown accustomed to my father. Maybe all his patients were jerks...who knows? He didn't seem disturbed by Dad's rudeness.

After Dad gave Dr. V a full rundown of all his symptoms and the diagnosis he had produced from his Google searches, he said, "It's simple, doc. It's mitral valve prolapse. I need mitral valve replacement surgery." He sat back with a satisfied grin on his face, both hands lifted in a gesture of "duh."

"Let me take a listen," Dr. V said, putting his stethoscope on Dad's chest, then he sat back on his stool.

"Everything sounds pretty good to me," he said, typing something onto the tablet. "And your EKG looks good too." I could see Dad getting agitated.

"Then why the hell do I feel like hell?" he demanded.

In my handy file, I always kept a current list of my parents' medications, just in case. And despite being routinely underestimated by my father, I, too, was proficient with online searches. I told Dr. V while I was clearly not a physician, I noted one of the medications that might be contributing to his lethargy. "I'm just wondering," I said. "I see the dosage was increased at his post-op visit with you, so maybe if the dosage were decreased, or if he stopped taking it altogether, might that help?"

My father looked at me with an expression of surprise. I smiled and shrugged.

"Very good idea," Dr. V said appreciatively. "Let's give that a try and see how things go over the next week or two. Will that work?" Dad, however, continued to push his perceived mitral valve prolapse, and Dr. V reiterated he would re-evaluate my father in two weeks. We had been dismissed for now.

I walked slowly with my father to the lobby, then told him I'd pull the car around so he didn't have to walk too far. He didn't object to my route this time, so we drove in peace until we reached his driveway.

"Good call on the medication," he said. "But you might have run that by me first."

"I wanted to wait to hear what Dr. V said," I replied. "I did some research, though, and it seemed to make sense."

"You're not a doctor," he said, unfastening his seat belt. "Thanks for driving me. Talk to you later." I watched his hunched frame slowly inch toward the front door. I waited to see if he would turn around and wave. He didn't.

Two weeks later, we repeated the visit to Dr. V. This time, though, Dad said he felt a little better energy-wise but still felt a strange flutter in his chest. Still? The "flutter" was news to me. I didn't know what to believe–was this sensation real or was this the one symptom that would convince Dr. V to refer him to one of the specialists in Dallas? Honestly, don't we all know how to say what a doctor needs to hear so we can get the prescriptions we think we need?

After some good-natured verbal sparring (was it?), Dr. V listened to my father, reviewed his vitals, and said, "While it's not my professional opinion that your issue has anything to do with the mitral valve, I think you'll be happier hearing that from a specialist at UT Southwestern. Here's a referral," he said, handing my father a piece of paper. "I hope this works out the way you want."

All of Dad's prior procedures, other than the quadruple bypass, had been performed at UTSW. He trusted the institution and its practitioners completely since "they're the best of the best," as he fervently believed. At the time, anyway.

And they are among the best, but that doesn't mean they can perform miracles. Sometimes, "We plan. God laughs." Sometimes, shit simply happens.

After an initial consultation, the cardiac valve specialist agreed to admit Dad in mid-July for a procedure to repair his leaky mitral valve. IF that was the issue. Unlike any other person I've known, Dad was as enthusiastic about surgery as my dogs about car rides. No fear, no anxiety, just excited to be going somewhere new. An adventure! My dogs, however, weren't eighty-four years old.

As had become custom, we picked Dad up and put his overnight bag in the back. He and Noble kept up a steady chatter while I sat in the backseat, playing Words with Friends on my phone. I had packed my laptop, a cashmere shawl, a bottle of water...all my standard wait-in-the-hospital accoutrements these days. Noble dropped us off at the emergency room, as the doctor instructed. We donned our masks, waited to be cleared once our temperatures were taken, checked in at the desk, completed all the necessary paperwork, and then waited for his name to be called. The emergency room was quite busy, with several people hacking up their lungs (or so it sounded). I pulled my mask tighter to my face and offered Dad some of my hand sanitizer. COVID was still raging.

We were finally called back, but it would be another three hours before a room became available, even though his doctor already had scheduled his initial procedure for the next day. Naturally, Dad grew more impatient and looked to me to intervene. He already had changed into his marigold hospital gown, denoting him as a cardiac patient, so he let me take charge. I had grown tired of this shade of yellow, which I had seen way too much the past four months; it just intensified his grayish pallor. After repeated calls to the doctor's office manager, who patiently told me they were doing everything they could, we finally were escorted to Dad's palatial room with a view overlooking downtown Dallas. Imagine a marriage of the Four Seasons with a teaching hospital. It was lovely, even with the blinking monitors to which he had been connected and the ubiquitous antiseptic scent.

The nurse–a lovely young woman with an effervescent smile–handed Dad a menu and asked him to make a selection for his dinner that evening, before six, of course. He beamed up at her and began doing what he does. I booted up my laptop in disgust. Amazing how quickly he could perk up when a pretty woman was in his midst. "Will you be taking care of me?" he asked sweetly.

"I'm sure going to try," she responded, squeezing his arm.

"Good luck with that," I thought.

The honeymoon quickly halted when Dad was informed he could only order what was on the heart-healthy menu. He argued he wasn't on a heart-healthy menu, thank you very much, and he should be allowed to have what he wanted.

"You're having a cardiac procedure tomorrow," the nurse cajoled. "Just following doctor's orders." Dad tossed the menu to the floor.

I picked up the menu and suggested he have some salmon ("won't be good enough") or maybe some grilled chicken ("I had chicken last night") or possibly the sea bass with some green beans and salad ("doesn't sound terrible") or even the vegetable stir-fry with rice ("no way"). He settled on the sea bass. Shortly before Noble was scheduled to meet me outside, the doctor dropped by to discuss the imminent procedure, accompanied by three of his med students. Dad sat up, delighted to have an audience, and proceeded to share with them his entire medical history. "I'm a bit of an anomaly, you see," he offered. Understatement of the century.

Once they left, I told him I'd see him in the morning and urged him to get some rest. He had his trusty flip phone by his side. I knew how he would spend his evening. I gave him a quick hug before heading toward the door, loaded down with my laptop bag and tote. He already was plugging his phone into the charger.

We arose early the next morning so I could get showered, dressed, and ready to head toward UTSW. Noble insisted on driving me since I had developed a bit of a phobia about highway driving, understandable to anyone who's had a few close calls on our notoriously treacherous thoroughfares. He dropped me off and asked me to keep him apprised of Dad's procedure and to alert him when I was ready to come home. "Thank you, oh gallant sir," I said, giving him a quick peck.

"Call me 'Jeeves,'" he said, eyes twinkling as he tried to emulate a British accent. Giving him a mock salute, I watched him pull out of the drive, wistfully wishing he could keep me company. Alas, COVID protocols.

Though hungry and caffeine-deprived, Dad seemed upbeat when I greeted him. I unloaded my things and sat on the spacious couch, then turned my attention to CNN. As had become normal, the headlines were bleak. "Are you sure this is what you want to watch?" I said, trying to keep things light. He ignored me.

Twenty minutes later, his doctor came in to review the day, which would begin with a transthoracic echocardiogram (TTE) to confirm the mitral valve prolapse and measure its severity. While they would moderately sedate Dad, he wouldn't go under general anesthesia until the actual mitral valve repair, likely later in the day. "Any questions?" he asked. I looked at Dad. He looked at me. We both shook our heads. "Okay, then, transport will be here in a few minutes. I'll see you in the lab." Sure enough, Dad was wheeled away shortly thereafter. He had given me his watch, his partials, his wallet, and his phone for safekeeping.

First, I called Mom to let her know they had just taken him back for a diagnostic procedure. She was flustered and couldn't follow what I was telling her. All she knew was he was in the hospital. I assured her he would be fine and that I'd call her later with an update.

Then I had to peek. Of course, I did. I powered up his phone and saw he had called Mom once last night and once this morning. But he had been on the phone with Linda and Judy, alternatively, most of the evening, and both had sent texts expressing their deep love and concern for his well-being. "I'll bet," I thought. I wondered why he didn't bother deleting the messages. Did he know I would look? Did he want me to see that despite my protestations (not that they mattered), he was still carrying on like an untethered frat boy?

Twenty minutes later, the orderly returned my father to the room and helped move him into his bed. The doctor approached me with two of his med students.

"We encountered a bit of a problem," he said, looking over to my father, who struggled to sit upright. He was a tad loopy.

"It seems there's a blockage in his esophagus," he began as his students took notes. "We couldn't get the tube past it, so I'm afraid we're at a standstill until we can identify the source of the blockage.

One of our gastroenterologists will be here shortly to review our next steps." I saw my father's face turn red.

"You've got to fucking be kidding me," he growled.

"Dad, you have been complaining of a frog in your throat for a while now," I offered. The doctor leaned in with interest. "Is that true?"

"Yes, for a few months now. We thought it was from his intubation during his quad bypass." He tilted his head thoughtfully, then glanced at his students.

Dad folded his arms like a petulant child.

"He had an endoscopy last year," I said. "I can give you his GI's information. Maybe you can get a copy of the films for a baseline?"

The doctor agreed that would be helpful, so I pulled up Dr. A's information and wrote it on a sheet from my legal pad. He patted my father's leg (a very brave move on his part) and said he'd follow up later. My father was seething.

"What a load of bullshit," he said, pounding the mattress with his fists. I knew better than to say anything, so I left to find a nurse and ask if he could have anything to eat or drink. She consulted his chart and shook her head. "Not until we know what happens next."

Apparently, the GI lab was fully booked, so my father wouldn't have any diagnostic procedure until the following day. At least he could order some food...from the heart-healthy menu. I went to the cafeteria and bought myself a baked potato and an iced tea and a bottle of root beer for him. I thought that might bring him a smile. It didn't.

This was Day Two. As his situation unraveled, Dad would spend the next thirteen days in the hospital while varying teams of doctors played the medical version of whack-a-mole, treating whatever they identified as being more emergent than his leaky mitral valve. I spent all but two of those fifteen days with him, working and participating in video meetings while also running interference between the teams of doctors, asking questions about their theories based on my Google medical doctorate. Several seemed impressed by my inquiries, but I was simply trying to keep my father alive. He was losing weight and growing weaker–physically and emotionally–by the day. Meanwhile, Noble was doing his best to keep Mom from a complete breakdown, visiting her daily between his own projects and shuttling me to and from Dallas. We both were exhausted and overwhelmed. I feared Dad wouldn't survive the ordeal. I wasn't sure we would, either.

Raised by parents who swore by contingency planning, I had to know what I was dealing with in terms of his personal affairs–financial, I mean. I didn't expect what I would find. I thought I knew everything. My concern was trying to get things sorted in preparation for the worst-case scenario. Isn't that what I had been taught?

The fourth night Dad was in the hospital, I drove to his house, took the mail from the box, and let myself in. The air was still and musty. Breakfast dishes sat in the sink, waiting to be put into the dishwasher. I turned on the lights and walked first to their bedroom. The bed was made, but Mom's side was still covered with old issues of Sports Illustrated and the most recent newspapers he had read. It was as if stuff had displaced her in so many ways. I sat on his side of the bed and opened the nightstand, finding a Valentine's card from Linda along with a ridiculous Beanie Baby bear and a small box of chocolates. She had signed it with, "I love you," in penmanship that only could be described as juvenile. What adult dots their "i's" with a smiling face? She did, apparently. Pathetic.

Next, I ventured upstairs, peering stealthily around each corner and expecting Dad to jump out of the shadows at any moment. "Stop being ridiculous," I told myself. I opened the door to his office, turned on the overhead light, and sat at his desk, taking in the various scraps of paper with notes and phone numbers. I started the computer and waited for it to boot up while opening his desk drawer to examine the contents. There I found two grainy pictures, likely printed from his flip phone: he and Linda, topless and smiling, and Linda straddling him backwards on what I assumed was her couch. The photo had captured more than I wanted to see. I recognized my father's hands on her thighs—wedding ring still in place—as her head was thrown back in presumptive pleasure. I closed the drawer and saw, beneath his desk, a penile pump with a towel and some lubricant. I gagged. This was how he was spending his time?

With the computer now "alive," I opened his mailbox and entered Linda's name in the search bar. The screen lit up with hundreds of emails from the last four years. He had saved everything. It only took me a few minutes to realize they had been carrying on for years, and he clearly was besotted—and possessive—while she continued serving other male clients. He didn't like it. She didn't care. That was the price, I deduced, for her to continue "seeing" him. He would have to wait his turn, though she did, of course, "love" him. As did her mangy dog, as suggested by the pile of cards she had sent to his P.O. box (really?) signed by her with, of course, "hugs from Harry." I went downstairs, opened one of his mediocre bottles of wine, poured a stout glass, and headed back upstairs. I had to learn more. Did I, though?

I opened his photo file and was appalled at his cache. Some women I recognized, others I didn't. All were nude, displaying enormous breasts and shaved vulvas. And these were older women he obviously knew. Another file contained images he had saved from whatever porn sites he frequented. These women were young and obvious professionals. I wondered how much he paid to access these sites.

Returning to his mailbox, I found seductive correspondences with Van, planning and then thanking her for the intimacy they shared in 2018. I found a few relatively bland emails to and from Judy, mostly about how the Dallas Stars had been playing on any given night. Yawn. Then I found emails he had exchanged with his first wife, Karen, whom he'd divorced some sixty years prior, suggesting how nice it would be if they could see how "our old bodies might work together now. I assure you, I've learned a lot since then. I have references." He inserted a smiley emoji.

I pushed the chair back and took a swig of the marginal wine. He had divorced the woman for cheating on him while he was at a training conference in Alaska, and he still wanted to go to bed with her, some six decades later? I continued perusing their correspondence and stopped cold when I saw a message indicating he had offered to send her money. His ex-wife? What?

In that email, he waxed eloquently about how honored he was to have the means to give to so many charities each year–he delineated them all in a show of largesse, I suppose. It was obvious he was trying to impress her with his philanthropy. Fair, I guess…maybe? But what I read next turned my blood to ice. He was especially proud, he wrote, to have been able to help pay for two of his "friends'" grandchildren to attend college.

Breathless, I shut the computer down. The same man who didn't provide so much as a dime for his one and only grandchild helped two "friends" with their grandchildren's college tuition? I took another gulp of wine. I couldn't process any of this. So, I headed downstairs and sat at the dining table to rifle through his checkbooks. There were several.

Oh, how these women prospered in the glow of my father's obsession. By my rough calculations, blurred somewhat by his mediocre wine on my empty stomach, he had written checks for close to one-hundred thousand dollars to his mistresses over the years, not to mention loans to bail the "professionals" he sometimes bailed out of jail. I had seen enough for one night. I could resume my reconnaissance tomorrow. But I had to get home. I was due to go back to the hospital the next morning.

I awoke with a migraine, which didn't surprise me, given the combination of red wine and extreme emotion the night before. After taking my medication, I soaked in a hot bath and sipped my black coffee, hoping the combination would enable me to face another day at the hospital. I was mostly silent on the way to Dallas.

Noble periodically touched my knee as he drove. I felt in a fog as I mentally rewound all I uncovered at my father's house. All of that, right under Mom's nose. My father was definitely brazen, banking on the fact that she would see none of it because he managed the finances, and she was too infirm to climb the steep stairs to his office. I thought of her alone in her apartment and my most recent visit. Now in a wheelchair, she rolled back and forth anxiously, asking what she had done that was so bad that we locked her away like a prisoner. I now realized my father wanted her out of the way so he could do as he wished, with no accountability. My heart tightened, and my eyes welled at this epiphany. Yet, here I was, doing all I could to help him survive this current medical crisis. I convinced myself I was doing it for Mom. She wouldn't survive without him, even as they lived apart.

My father was in the bathroom when I got to his room. I set my bags on the couch and hollered, "Good morning!" He shuffled slowly to his bed while I plugged in my laptop.

"Nothing good about it," he grunted. He looked gaunter than he had the previous day, and I noticed he hadn't finished his breakfast.

"Are you hungry? Would you like something from the cafeteria?"

He shook his head.

"Something to drink?"

"Nothing's going to help," he said. "They're killing me here."

"What do you mean?"

He started to cry. I was frozen in place.

"This morning, I weighed one hundred and forty-five pounds," he said. "I'm wasting away, and they're not doing a goddamned thing besides running tests. I just need to get out of here."

I didn't see that happening. In my view, he was too weak to come home.

"Well, let's see what the doctor says," I responded, booting up my email. He turned up the volume on the television so we could listen to CNN.

A little while later, one of his many doctors, a youngish resident internist, came into the room with his gaggle of med students, so Dad muted the television. I moved my laptop aside, put my surgical mask back on, and stood to greet them.

"Good morning," he said, introducing himself once again. "Based on some tests we've run, we'd like to take some x-rays today," he said.

"I'm here for my mitral valve," Dad barked. "Why do I need x-rays? When are you people going to listen to me?" I looked nervously at the doctor, who took a deep breath.

"We need to look at your bone density," he said calmly. "So, we're going to take some x-rays of your hips and back." Honestly, my father had been complaining of discomfort in both areas, but I attributed it to his having been bedridden for a week.

"Whatever," my father said. "I just hope I don't die first."

"Quit being grumpy, Dad," I cajoled, trying to ameliorate the tension.

"One of the radiology techs will be by shortly to take you to x-ray," the doctor said. "Do you have any other questions?"

"Yes," Dad barked. "When can I get the hell out of this place?"

"I'm afraid I can't answer that just yet," the doctor responded flatly. "We need to know what we're dealing with here."

"You're dealing with ME!" Dad shouted. "So, DEAL with me!"

I walked out to the nurses' station with the team, thanking them for their patience.

"I think he's just scared," I said. "Do we have reason to be worried?

"I don't know yet," he said. "That's all I can tell you."

I returned to his room, feeling as though we had fallen down Lewis Carroll's rabbit hole. None of this made any sense, despite my incessant Google searches. I had run out of questions to ask. I returned my attention to my emails, and Dad drifted off in a nap.

After his heart-healthy lunch, which he ate reluctantly, I went to the cafeteria to find something of my own. Returning with a salad and iced tea, I placed a piece of chocolate cake on his side table.

"I thought you could use this," I said, handing him a fork.

"I guess it doesn't matter anymore," he said, taking a large bite. "I'm going to die, anyway."

I tried to lighten the mood. "Aren't we all? You know my favorite quote, right? 'Life is uncertain. Eat dessert first!'" I grinned. He looked at me up and down as if I were an alien.

"I think you need this more than I do. You're getting too thin," he said, pushing the cake toward me.

Admittedly, I had lost a few pounds throughout this ordeal, but any time he mentioned my appearance or my weight, something lurched inside. I didn't want to be held to what I now knew were his standards for attractiveness. I just smiled politely. "Noble doesn't seem to mind."

Two hours later, an orderly came to take Dad to x-ray. Once again, I powered up his phone, not looking for anything in particular but curious, nonetheless. He had spoken to Mom after I left yesterday and once again early this morning. His time seems to have been devoted primarily to Linda–two calls plus about ten texts last night, two calls and no texts this morning. He spoke with Judy between calls with Linda. I suppose she wasn't much into texting. I shut off the phone and reconnected it to the charger, feeling oddly hurt rather than angry. I sat with that for a few minutes, sipping my cold coffee. I concluded while I was the one devoting my time to his care, they were the ones receiving his favorable attention. In turn, they offered him a type of comfort my presence obviously didn't. I had to wonder how long they'd persevere if he dismissed them the way he dismissed me. But then, he was paying for them, so there's that.

Just before the orderly escorted him back to the room, I straightened his bed, plumped his pillows, and procured an apple juice from the patients-only refrigerator by the nurses' station.

Anything to be helpful. Of course. He was agitated when he arrived, as he was when he departed, grouching that all of this was a waste of his time. Not knowing what to say, I asked if he'd like to watch CNN or something else.

"I don't care."

I took the remote and powered on the television. Anything was better than his petulance.

An hour later, his internist and two other residents entered the room. I turned off the television and stood to greet them. Dad sat up straighter in his bed.

"Well, I'm afraid we're looking at something we didn't expect," the internist said. "From everything I'm seeing on the x-ray, combined with your bloodwork, I think we may be dealing with multiple myeloma." WHAT?

My jaw dropped.

"How could you possibly have determined that?" Dad bellowed. I sat down abruptly as my legs began shaking.

"Your bones look like Swiss cheese," the doctor replied stoically. "When we consider that along with your fatigue, unexplained weight loss, low blood cell count, kidney damage, and joint pain, that's the diagnosis we have at the moment."

"At the moment?"

"The only way to conclusively diagnosis multiple myeloma is through bone marrow," he replied calmly. "I'm afraid it's a painful procedure but necessary before we can begin exploring treatment."

I looked at Dad, who had begun to cry.

"Assuming my father wants to undergo the procedure, when is the soonest it can be done?" I asked.

"Possibly tomorrow, but more likely the following day," the internist responded. My father put his hands over his face. I told the team I would discuss this with Dad, and we'd let them know.

But before they left, Dad said, "I'll do it," wiping his eyes. "What choice do I have?" The internist nodded and made a notation on my father's electronic health record.

"We'll let you know when it's scheduled." I walked them to the door, trying to maintain my composure, and thanked them for their thoroughness, even though the news was devastating.

"Dad, whatever this is, we can get through it," I offered gently.

"I'm not so sure about that," he said somberly.

"So, not to be indelicate, but if this is what we're facing, I think we need to talk about you possibly going to live with Mom."

"I don't disagree," he said, which frightened me even more. "Go ahead and find out what that would require."

The one moment I had hoped for his righteous indignation, I received his compliance instead.

"While we're discussing the hard stuff, there aren't funds in the trust account to cover things that, um, might be needed if, you know, the situation heads in the wrong direction," I said quietly. I hated myself for focusing on practicalities, but I was the product of my upbringing.

He picked up his phone, called one of his brokers, and asked her to transfer money into the trust. "That should more than cover anything that might be needed," he said. I told him I needed to get some air, but I'd be back in a few minutes.

Grabbing my phone and my purse, I left the hospital, walked to the parking garage, and found a private spot where I could smoke a much-needed cigarette. I sobbed. Multiple myeloma was a death sentence. I remembered Dad saying, decades earlier, that if he ever received a terminal diagnosis, he reserved the right to take his own life. I believed him then, and I knew he'd do it now if this was his diagnosis. I called Noble, and once he answered, I could barely speak. He waited until I could choke out the words "multiple myeloma," and all he could say was, "Oh, fuck." Indeed. I told him I'd be ready to come home in the next hour or so.

When I returned, Dad's eyes were closed. He was clutching to his chest the overpriced stuffed bear I'd bought a few days earlier in the gift shop. That image alone captured the enormity of this development and its impact on my father. I would never forget that moment of fragility, regardless of what drama lay ahead.

Dad opened his eyes to see me watching him from the chair by his side. "Are you okay?" he said, obviously noticing my reddened eyes. I nodded. "You?"

"It is what it is." God, how I hated that sentence.

"Have you given the nurse your dinner selection?" I asked.

He nodded. "Beef tips."

"I always liked beef tips day in elementary school," I offered hopefully.

The nurses had just changed shifts, and his new nurse on duty was, thankfully, one of his favorites. Maybe she could help lift his spirits. But that night, I noticed his reticence. Normally, he flirted with all but the male nurses. We chatted for a minute, then Noble texted to let me know he was waiting in the parking lot.

"Dad, Noble's here so I'm going to leave for now, but I'll be back in the morning, okay? Can I get you anything before I go?" He motioned me over and gave me a long, urgent hug, which I returned as if it was our last. "I love you, Daddy," I whispered in his ear before leaving.

My husband was waiting for me in the parking circle with an ice-cold martini sitting in a Yeti in the drink holder. The minute we pulled away, I began to cry. Despite myriad complicated feelings about my father, and so often having cursed him for what he had done to our family, this was not the way I wanted him living his last days. He seemed defeated, yet I knew from my research–not to mention friends who'd had cancer–that if he was in fact riddled with multiple myeloma, he would have to summon some semblance of strength for the fight ahead. In my heart, though, I knew he wouldn't. Not on his own, anyway.

When we got home, I refilled my drink, took my dogs, and retreated to the patio to watch the hummingbirds at my feeder. I rocked in my rocker compulsively, self-soothing behavior that wasn't working. I called Mom to check in. I told her Dad was still in the hospital, but they were taking good care of him. I couldn't bear to tell her the truth, and with her dementia worsening, she wouldn't have understood, anyway.

Noble wanted me to eat something. But as had become normal, I had no appetite. As he sat down in the rocker next to mine, I stared at the bird feeders, trying to conjure some way I could help Dad through all of this. An idea emerged, so I grabbed my phone and reluctantly called Linda. She didn't answer but responded via text, asking, "How's your father?"

I responded he wasn't doing well, and without giving any specifics (because honestly, I didn't feel she deserved them), I suggested he needed a friend and a big, hearty, "Hell, yeah...you can do this" vote of confidence. I left it at that, putting my phone on the side table and hating myself for what seemed like a betrayal–yet again–of Mom. Yet I tried to justify it by telling myself, and Noble, that if she could coax him to a path of optimism, it would have been worth it. Wouldn't it?

After another fitful night, I arrived at the hospital late the next morning, exhausted and anxious about how I would find Dad. As it was, he had eaten a substantial breakfast and was talking to his original doctor–the interventional cardiologist–when I arrived. I greeted him and my father with as bright a smile as I could muster, then asked how everyone was doing today. The cardiologist had learned Dad was to undergo a bone marrow biopsy early that afternoon and wanted to intervene. Based on his and one other doctor's analysis, his belief was that we weren't looking at multiple myeloma at all. If, however, my father wanted to undergo the painful procedure, he certainly would support it.

I looked at my father, who just shook his head and rubbed his eyes. I could feel his rage about to erupt. And so it did.

"You people," he began, "don't seem to have a fucking clue what you're doing! You've damn near killed me, you know that? This morning, I weighed one hundred and forty-two pounds–I'm lying here, withering away, why you all dick around trying to figure out who's right. You know who's right? I'm fucking right! All I wanted," his voice caught, and he coughed, "all I fucking wanted was for you to fix my mitral valve. Nearly two weeks later, and nothing's been resolved. You people," he concluded, "don't know what you've done to me."

"So, if I'm understanding correctly," I began carefully, "there's clearly something wrong, but you can't figure out what? Is there any way he can still have the mitral valve procedure?" I saw my father shift uncomfortably in his bed and could tell his hips must be hurting–that, or he was simply annoyed. Probably both.

"Let's step outside," the doctor said. I looked at Dad with a shrug and said I'd be right back.

"Here's the situation," the doctor began. "I'm sorry for the way this might sound, but your father is eighty-four years old. He's lived a long life–longer than most. In fact, he's exceeded his life expectancy for someone with his health issues. We just don't feel it's in his best interests to proceed with anything invasive at this time." Because we were both wearing masks, I couldn't interpret his expression, though I sure as hell could understand his intent.

"Wouldn't that have been the right assessment, then, before putting him through two weeks of torture?" I asked, my eyes welling with angry tears.

"We really didn't have any way of knowing, but now he's just too unstable."

"So, where do we go from here?" I asked, already realizing how Dad would respond to the news.

"Home," he said. "We'll get him ready to be discharged tomorrow. Do you have any other questions?"

"I guess he just goes back to his primary cardiologist, and we take it from there?"

"That would be my best suggestion at this point."

"Thank you, doctor." For nothing, I wanted to add. Yet I was trying to keep my composure.

I returned to Dad's room, and he looked up at me expectantly. I shook my head.

"They're going to prepare you to be discharged tomorrow," I said, just as a nurse entered with a modest bouquet and a greeting card she handed to Dad. He opened the envelope, read the card, and smiled.

"Well, that's not like her at all," he said with a chuckle, placing the card under the stack of magazines on his bedside tray. I cocked my head, waiting for elaboration. He offered none, so I dove in.

"Linda, yes?" I said, sitting on the couch. He nodded.

"I reached out to her last night," I said, "via text." His surprised look was priceless.

"You needed something I guess I couldn't provide, so I told her you needed cheering up."

"Well, thank you," he mumbled.

"Here's the thing, Dad. You have no idea, no idea at all, what it cost me emotionally to do that," I said firmly. "But I did it anyway because I didn't want you giving up hope." He thanked me again. I left to go find a cup of coffee, which my shattered nerves clearly didn't need, yet it gave me a moment to recalibrate from all that had just transpired. I also knew he was eager to text Linda.

The next day, Noble and I returned to Dallas for the last time, stopping at the Crate & Barrel outlet store on the way since we thought we were running early. No sooner had we begun paying for our purchases when Dad called my cell, demanding to know where we were. I told him we were about five blocks away and would be there shortly. When we pulled into the circular drive at the hospital's entrance, he was waiting in a wheelchair. The orderly was standing behind the cart with Dad's belongings. Once Noble and the orderly helped him into the passenger's seat and placed his bags in the back, I asked how he was feeling.

"Same," he grunted. "I weighed one hundred and forty-one pounds this morning."

"Have you had lunch?"

"Yes." I decided not to press any further. Noble caught my eye in the rearview mirror and offered a weak smile. I shook my head in frustration, but at least we were on our way home.

After a thirty-minute trip during which Noble tried, unsuccessfully, to engage Dad in conversation, we pulled into his drive, then helped him into the house.

"I need to pee," he snapped.

Noble went to the car to get Dad's belongings. I sat on Mom's chair, fidgeting. Dad came into the living room and demanded to see his mail.

"I sorted it for you," I offered. "See the box by the fireplace? That's what I thought was junk mail, but you can look through it if you'd like." He nodded.

I brought him the stack of what I considered relevant mail, and he immediately began flipping through the envelopes. I didn't tell him that during his hospital stay, I also had taken the key to his post office box and checked it a few times to find statements for a few of his investment accounts, several cards from Judy, as well as a "thank you" card from some woman in Colorado for his twenty-thousand-dollar contribution to her son's cub scout troop. A search on Facebook indicated she was one of Judy's friends. I couldn't understand why he would have parted with that much money for a woman he ostensibly didn't know. Of course, I couldn't ask, though. And why would he have financial statements sent to a post office box when Mom was entitled to know how much money they had in total? Just two more of his many secrets.

Noble sat on the couch, and we watched my father quietly. The room felt chilly, yet the temperature was too warm for my comfort.

"Dad, do you want me to turn the air conditioner up?" I asked. "It feels warm in here."

"It's just you. I'm fine," he said, continuing to flip through the mail.

"Can I get you anything? Water? A Coke, maybe?" He shook his head.

"I think I'm going to lie down," he said, getting up slowly from his recliner. "Thank you for bringing me home," he said, nodding at Noble.

"We'll be over later with dinner," I offered. "I made a king ranch casserole." This flavorful concoction of shredded chicken, mushrooms, cheddar cheese, Rotel tomatoes, and golden mushroom soup layered with corn tortillas had proven curative to so many of my friends over the years. I always followed Mom's recipe. I hoped it would encourage him to eat.

"Thank you." I walked over and gave him a hug. He responded weakly. He shuffled into the bedroom, and we left for home.

"He doesn't look too good," Noble said as he opened a beer.

"No, he doesn't," I said, then poured a glass of wine before calling Mom. I assured her he would be okay, that we would take good care of him while he was convalescing.

"I need to come home," she demanded. "I can take care of him!" She was now fully bound to her wheelchair and couldn't toilet herself, relying instead on the help of the residents' assistants.

"Mom, it's your turn to be taken care of," I said softly. "We've got this. As soon as he's strong enough, I know he'll come see you." She made me promise. I did so, reluctantly, since I didn't know what the next few weeks would bring.

Good girl, gassed.

Chapter Thirty-Nine: The Weight of the Wait

For the next month, Noble became Dad's valet, of sorts, running his errands and managing his laundry while I assumed the roles of nurse, companion, and cheerleader–both of us doing what we could to help restore his physical and mental strength. Every evening, after I had concluded my day's video meetings and assignments, I went to his house to prepare his dinner, have a glass of wine, and keep him company while we watched the evening news. That COVID was still wreaking havoc was a blessing, only because I had the flexibility to drive one mile in either direction and see both parents as often as possible.

During the first week or two, I didn't think he would make it. His body was weak, and his spirit seemed defeated. Getting out of bed exhausted him, and I routinely emptied the plastic urinals next to his bed. Some afternoons, Noble arrived to find Dad bundled under the covers and sound asleep–the house uncomfortably warm. His myriad prescriptions were arranged like infantry soldiers on the kitchen counter, with Post-it notes in front of each to remind him what to take and when. I routinely asked if he wanted me to drive him to see Mom. He said he didn't want anyone to see him in his condition. I had hoped that meant the mistresses too.

He needed a new primary care physician, so I found a gerontologist who happened to be taking new patients, even as she was in her late seventies herself. Dad had never been seen by a female doctor, and while reluctant, he agreed to an appointment. She reminded me of my younger mother, had Mom been a physician instead of an attorney and judge. She was tough, direct, and would not be manipulated by my father. When she couldn't immediately diagnose why he couldn't seem to gain weight, he dismissed her as "worthless," but he wasn't in the position to find another doctor. Secretly, I thought she might just give him the metaphorical kick in the pants he needed to get stronger. Surprisingly, it worked. Within another few weeks, he was back to driving, grocery shopping, and visiting Mom.

Among other things, I would later learn.

The first week in October, I began having severe stomach problems–inexplicable pain that failed to respond to any of the over-the-counter medications I tried. Some days, it was so bad, I couldn't force myself to eat. I knew, of course, it was internalized stress: the countdown had begun to Mom's projected "expiration date." Yet, at the conclusion of every visit by one of her hospice nurses, her prognosis was good. She wasn't physically declining as the result of her congestive heart failure–there, her vitals were stable. The dementia had taken over, though, and while she always recognized me as "Suz," she had difficulty communicating her thoughts.

On one of my Saturday visits, she could tell I was visibly upset. Earlier in the week, I had a few conversations with my father, during which I tried to convince him to end his relationships with Linda and Judy.

"You have Noble," he said, "You have companionship. Why shouldn't I" he asked, defensively.

"Because Mom needs you. Because she's your wife."

"The woman I married is gone, Suzanne. She's never coming back. I deserve to be happy."

"So does she," I rebutted.

After that discussion, I went home and booted up Google, doing a search to see if Linda's listings (and corresponding reviews) on the various sex-for-pay websites were still active. They were. The next evening, armed with screen shots on my phone, I returned to my father's, and after we each had a drink, I broached the subject.

"Dad, you know that Linda's still advertising her services, right?"

"Not possible, Suzanne. I bought out her business." What? How much did she snooker him for this time?

"Doesn't look that way. Here. Take a look." I handed him my phone after launching the same Google search. He scrolled through the listings and returned the phone to me impassively.

"You need to stay out of my personal life. Get it?" He stood up, ready to escort me to the door.

"I'm just trying to protect you, Dad. Do you think these women would have anything to do with you if it weren't for your money?"

"Goodbye," he said, going to his bedroom and closing the door.

I was still reeling from this exchange when I visited Mom, and she asked what was wrong. I shook my head. She asked about Dad, but I told her we weren't speaking. She anxiously crab-walked her wheelchair around the living room, nearly running over my feet a few times, while wringing her hands.

"Why aren't you speaking?" At this, I shouldn't have, but I did–I unloaded, telling her about Judy, about Linda, about my concerns, and about my anger that once again, others were getting the attention we deserved.

"Well, Suz, I've learned to live with it, so you might as well, also."

"I can't." I began to cry.

"He is your father," she said. "You can decide you don't want anything to do with him, but I promise you, you'll regret it."

I didn't bother to tell her any time I challenged or upset him, he dangled his estate and its potential division under my nose. He never realized I wanted his loyalty, affection, and praise above anything else.

"You'll regret it," she reminded me.

"So, have you seen Mom and Daddy?" she asked, peeling the wrapper from one of the miniature chocolate bars I brought. She was referring, of course, to her parents.

"I haven't, no," I said calmly. "I'm not sure where they are right now, and they're hard to get a hold of."

I couldn't wait to leave, as was now generally the case, yet I needed to keep visiting as much as possible. Soon, I wouldn't be able to have even the most nonsensical conversation with her. I couldn't have known how much I would miss our unspoken connection that had remained, despite thoughts that couldn't be communicated or understood.

In early November, our hospice provider contacted me to say Mom had been approved for another six months; no changes were needed. After calling my father, who seemed ambivalent about the update, I mentally reset the clock and began focusing on the holidays. Of course, I invited Dad to join us for Thanksgiving and Christmas dinners. Of course, he begrudgingly agreed to join us for both. We knew, though, that Mom wasn't stable enough to join us for either. I did what I could to maintain the peace with him while managing my own grief. Though still alive, Mom had begun to fade. My therapist called it "anticipatory grief" because I knew how Mom's story would end–I was watching it unravel before my eyes. Any time I tried to discuss my sadness or concerns with my father, though, he simply responded, "You're not God," or, "It is what it is," or, worse yet, "You need to take care of yourself." Hadn't I always?

We rang in 2021 joyfully, hoping for a better year ahead. Yet, COVID had rebounded, so it appeared this new year wouldn't differ dramatically from the last. Protocols at Mom's facility vacillated, depending on how many residents or employees had contracted the virus. While I ensured Mom was vaccinated and boosted, she was still as susceptible as the rest. Noble and I took great precautions to minimize our own exposure to avoid infecting her.

I can't say the same about my father. While he wore masks in public, I also knew from his clue-laden texts he met Judy periodically for dinner, and I'm sure he had resumed his weekly visits with Linda too. I also knew, from peeking into his refrigerator on my less frequent visits, that someone else was bringing him meals and baked items. We had reinstated our "tradition" of hosting him for Sunday night dinners, sending him home each week with several containers of leftovers. We never really enjoyed it, but we did spend our entire day shopping and tidying up and preparing delicious food, anyway. He, however, always left right after finishing. I was sure his girlfriends received more praise and favor for their efforts.

As I became more anxious about Mom's deterioration, he grew more passive-aggressive in his interactions with me. In early March, Noble's son came for a quick visit. Dad was keen on seeing him, so we invited Dad for Sunday dinner. I had just gotten braces, so my teeth were quite sensitive. At my bonus son's request, I whipped up an enormous lasagna, which I knew I could eat comfortably. The house smelled divine thanks to all the garlic and herbs in the sauce. The table was set, and we awaited my father's arrival. From the moment he entered the house, he was bent on discounting me at every turn. I showed him my teeth and said they already were getting straighter. He said it was my imagination because they couldn't possibly move that fast. We began talking about March Madness, and I shared my hopes that Texas could advance beyond the first round. He said that was ridiculous. I countered that Texas had won the Big Twelve conference title, so we had as good a chance as anyone. He argued Texas had NOT won the conference and I should know the facts about my own alma mater. At this, I looked over at my bonus son and husband. They both shifted uncomfortably in their seats before retreating to the kitchen for another helping of lasagna.

I asked my father if he'd like anything else, but he was still chewing methodically, so he just shook his head. I refilled my wine and did the only thing I knew would salvage the situation. Once Noble and his son returned to the table, their plates re-loaded, I mentioned that my father had played baseball on the farm team for the Saint Louis Cardinals. I asked if he regretted not being pulled up to the pros.

Boy, how the atmosphere changed. He lit up, cleared his throat, and began telling his stories. I asked encouraging follow-up questions. My bonus son feigned interest, and Noble asked relevant questions. Soon, the room felt lighter, or maybe, it was just my third glass of wine. Inside, though, I was seething. How dare he treat me so disrespectfully in my own home?

Now that he had put on some weight and was riding the exercise bike I gave him regularly, his health seemed to be continuously improving. So much so that in April, right before his birthday, he decided he would move forward with the procedure to fix his inguinal hernia. I cautioned it might still be too early, given what had happened last summer, and was it necessary?

"You're not a doctor," he countered roughly. "I don't need your input." I imagined he would need our help, though. Yet, I never heard him discuss the subject again.

In between preparing to return to my office in early July, after nearly seventeen months of working remotely, and visiting Mom as often as I could manage, Noble and I began planning how we would celebrate our fifth anniversary in June. We decided we would spend a few days in San Antonio, then head down to the Gulf Coast to spend a few more days on the beach. Nothing fancy or exotic–just a chance to get away, but not so far that we couldn't come home the same day if an emergency arose. We had our pet sitter lined up and were eager to have some fun for the first time in nineteen months.

When I told Dad where we were going, he simply grimaced. "Well, that doesn't sound very romantic," he said snidely. "Wouldn't have been my choice."

"Dad, you of all people should know romance is what you make of it," I volleyed. I failed to mention that at least we weren't sneaking around.

"Well, I hope you have a nice time."

And we did, though we wished, in hindsight, that we had spent the entire vacation in San Antonio. Port Aransas' beaches were unusually windy and filthy, and the surf was laden with jellyfish. That said, we still enjoyed being alone together, though I slept with my phone under my pillow…just in case.

I called Dad once we were home to let him know we were safe. He was characteristically dour. I asked how he was doing, and he barked, "Not well." So, I asked him to expound, and he told me to "leave it alone." Two days later, I received a cryptic text from him: "I'm going away this weekend. Please, no questions. I need this!" I slammed my phone on the bed. Of course, he would respond to our anniversary getaway with a hint that he, too, had something planned with someone. I didn't respond. Clearly, he resented our happiness, so he would do what he did best: masterfully antagonize me so my focus would return to him.

Though I was still itching to find clues in his house that might indicate where he was and with whom, I ignored my curiosity and spent the weekend trying to quell my resentment instead. He texted on Sunday he was back, and I replied I hoped the getaway served him well. I didn't actually mean it, but it seemed the most dispassionate response. Tuesday evening, when I stopped by to drop off his favorite cookies I had made, I noticed a small slip of paper flutter to the ground when I unlocked and opened the door. I pretended to ignore it, but I knew exactly what it was: his famous "trap" to see if someone had opened a drawer or door. At that moment, I realized he likely had left something salacious for my discovery. I was glad to have adhered to my inner voice that echoed his words, "Leave it alone."

Two weeks later, I received a call from Mom's facility that once again, she had fallen and, while pretty bruised, she was otherwise all right. These types of accidents were happening much more frequently because she forgot she needed her wheelchair and would try to get out of bed on her own. She already had lost all control of her bladder and bowels and was having difficulty feeding herself because she couldn't remember which utensil to use. After a lengthy discussion with the facility's medical director, during which she recommended Mom be moved to the memory care unit, my father and I concluded it would be in her best interests.

The memory care unit was full of patients who resembled those in the movie Awakenings, but for the fact they would never emerge from the fog of dementia. After my father and I toured the locked-down unit and inspected what would be her new room–significantly smaller than her apartment–I signed the papers and scheduled the date for her transfer. In the parking lot, I cried–shoulder-shaking, gut-wrenching tears. My father just looked at me stoically. "It's for the best," he said.

"They're zombies, Dad. I don't want to see her like that!"

"She's no different. It is what it is."

I had grown to despise that phrase. While to some, it seems pragmatic, to me it just seemed apathetic.

We had measured the new room and determined Mom's current queen-sized bed wouldn't fit comfortably, so Dad volunteered to find a twin bed that would be better suited. The plan was to move her that Friday, just three days before their fifty-eighth wedding anniversary. I told Dad the best approach would be to let Noble and me move everything but her queen-sized bed into the apartment while he kept her company. We didn't know how this change might agitate her. He felt strongly we couldn't possibly complete the move in one day. Noble and I knew better.

That Friday morning, we arrived with plastic bins and garbage bags to make the move easier, and Noble borrowed a dolly from the maintenance crew. Dad and I already had told Mom she was moving to a more manageable room in a unit with more hands-on care. We didn't feel the need to mention it was for residents whose minds were scrambled with the static of dementia. She just nodded like an obedient child while wringing her hands in her lap. Once my father arrived, he sat with her while we began boxing and unloading things in the new room. We went back and forth for the next three hours, hauling her possessions while getting suspicious stares from the memory care residents. I arranged her artwork, made her bed, and hung her clothes–essentially, a reprise of all I had done nineteen months earlier when she first moved into her apartment. With everything transferred except Mom and her quilt, Noble and I went to her room to let them know we were ready to move.

She looked at my father anxiously. He held her hand while she rolled herself out of the room, down the long hall, through the dining room, down another long hall and, finally, to the passcode-protected doors leading into the memory care unit. She blinked as we entered the small parlor, noticing the vacant-eyed residents sitting on couches and chairs around the large television, then looked at Dad with fear in her eyes. He squeezed her hand. We kept walking until we opened the door to her new room. I must say, it looked nice–as nice as it could, anyway. My father nodded approvingly. Noble then left to return the dolly to the front office and begin loading items that wouldn't fit into her new space into the back of my SUV.

My father and I stayed with Mom until she said she'd like to take a nap. Anymore, she slept most of the day, so I gave her a hearty hug and let her know how very much I loved her.

"You're the best daughter in the entire world," she said. "I don't deserve you."

"Well, you're stuck with me," I said, subtly wiping away tears. "I'll see you tomorrow."

I stood in the hall while my father said goodbye. Then we walked through the facility and headed out the front door to the crippling heat of July in Texas.

"Well, we got it done," I said. "In three and a half hours, no less!" I couldn't help taking a moment to be right.

"Yes, you did," he said, moving in to give me an awkward hug. "You done good, kid."

"Do you want to go to dinner on Sunday night? Just the two of us?" That was the day before their anniversary.

"Sure," he said. "Tex-Mex?"

"Sounds fine."

I watched him amble to his Mazda, noticing the more pronounced stoop in his posture as he carefully opened the door. I felt a pang of regret that I hadn't done more to smooth over our relationship. I was doing the best I could, though, to maintain my sanity amidst the ever-changing landscape of my family.

We had an uneventful dinner that Sunday, and when he dropped me off at my house, I gave him a tight hug and told him I loved him.

That was the last time I ever saw my father, not quite four months before he died.

Good girl, giving up hope.

Chapter Forty: Letting Go

Over the twenty-six months Mom was at the assisted living center, there was extraordinary turnover among the residents' aides–not unexpected given the combination of the obscenely low pay these employees typically receive and the exhausting effects of the pandemic on all healthcare workers. She had as many wonderful caregivers as she had apathetic ones. Even in her cloud of confusion, though, she innately knew who really cared about her and responded accordingly. A few months before we moved her into memory care, a new aide named Lakeesha was assigned to Mom. She was a lovely young African American who delighted in hearing the stories Mom could still tell.

I appreciated Lakeesha because she seemed to understand the toll Mom's rapid decline was taking on me, so she gave me as much care and comfort as she freely offered Mom. She also provided candid commentary–often unsolicited–about some of the other aides who became impatient with Mom's difficulties in communicating, or her bedwetting, or her wandering through the facility in search of…something. Mom was particularly intrigued by the "secret tunnel" and would repeatedly ask my father, my husband, and me if we had seen it. I wondered if her tunnel was some type of metaphor for imminent death and her journey to Heaven. It was, in fact, the long hallway leading to the memory care unit.

As we were completing plans for her transfer, I asked the medical director if Lakeesha could still care for Mom once she had moved. They assured me that would be possible. Besides fashioning her room to feel as similar as possible to her apartment, I wanted Mom to have at least one constant in her new environment. I was pleased she would continue to receive such supportive and attentive care.

She had only been in her new room for a few weeks when, during a call with my father, he began waxing eloquent about how wonderful Lakeesha was and how much he appreciated her being so gentle with Mom. I emphatically agreed, saying she was quite a blessing at a difficult time in Mom's journey and that we, too, were thankful for her kindness.

"I think she's the kindest, most generous and loving person I've ever known. You know," he said with his wry chuckle, "if she weren't so young and didn't have a huge boyfriend, I'd probably ask her out."

She couldn't have been over than twenty-five, tops. How did he know she had a boyfriend, much less that he was huge? My stomach churned. Was he serious, or had he lost his mind? Or both? I listened to him recount tales of computer problems and hours on the phone with the no help desk, but I was seething inside. I concluded the call as quickly as I could then sat down at my laptop to compose and send an email outlining just how his words about Lakeesha made me feel–his statement about asking her out was inappropriate, and did he really think it right to make a play for my mother's best caregiver? Moreover, what about me? I've been nothing but kind and loving toward both parents. Couldn't he see that? I pressed "send" and poured a glass of wine.

The next morning, his response was waiting in my inbox. "You really thought I was serious? YOU have a problem. Not me." In that moment, I knew I had had enough and needed, finally, after fifty-six years, to set some boundaries with my him. I didn't speak to him for the next week, though I did text him a few days later about arriving at the facility to find Mom slumped in her wheelchair against the wall, unresponsive to my words or my touch. I couldn't tell if she was heavily medicated or just having an episode of some sort, but I truly thought she was days from death. "Quit being so melodramatic!" he texted in response. I left that one alone.

A few days later, I received a call while at work from the facility's medical director. As with any time someone called from there, my heart seized up–what bad news awaited? In this case, she said she was on the speaker phone along with the facility's executive director.

"Is Mom okay?" I asked.

"I'm sorry, I should have led with that. Yes, she seems to be doing fine," she said. "We have another issue we need to discuss with you, though. Do you have a few minutes?" I said I did.

"We've received a formal complaint from one of your mom's aides about some inappropriate behavior by your father," she said calmly. I shook my head in disgust.

"Let me guess. Lakeesha?"

"Yes. She said your dad showed her an email exchange between the two of you, and it made her uncomfortable. She also said he stands too close to her, almost hovering, and when she was in my office telling me about everything, he looked in the window and tapped on it to wave goodbye on his way out. She's asked to be removed from the memory care unit."

"Just shit," I said. "Sorry. Honestly, this is shocking, but not surprising, given my father's history. I just hate that this happened."

"It's not your fault, obviously. But we wanted to talk with you before we speak with him. We're going to ask that he meet with us. Do you want to be there as well?"

"No, absolutely not," I said. "But you can conference me in by phone. Just let me know. Again, I'm just so sorry."

"We'll be back in touch."

Three days later, she called to let me know my father was in the executive director's office and said she'd call back shortly for the discussion.

"Hey, it's Marleen," she said when I answered. "I'm here with Chris and your father. Do you have a minute?"

"Yes, of course. Is everything okay?" I asked, playing dumb.

"Mostly, but we wanted to include you in a discussion about the aide who has asked to be removed from your mom's care. She said your father had behaved in a way that made her uncomfortable, so we wanted to address that."

"Let me see if I have this straight. You're telling me Mom is losing, I'm guessing Lakeesha–her very best caregiver–because of my father's inappropriate behavior?" I could only imagine my father's stony expression as the conversation continued and was glad I wasn't in the same room.

"Yes, I'm afraid so," she said. My father remained silent.

"I don't have any words to justify my father's behavior or actions," I said coldly. "All I can do is apologize and let you know how much we appreciated the care she provided to my mother. Is there anything else?"

"They still can't get your mother's laundry right!" my father thundered. "Do you know they haven't washed her clothes in almost a week?"

"No, I wasn't aware of that. Marleen, can you please investigate the situation?" She promised she would.

"Well, if there's nothing else, I need to get back to work," I said. "Again, I'm so sorry you had to make this call, but while I'm shocked, sadly, I'm not surprised. Please let me know if anything else comes up. Have a good afternoon."

After hanging up, I knew I had reached a point of no return with my father. I no longer wanted to be privy, in any form or fashion, to his chauvinistic attitudes towards women, whom he only saw as objects to meet whatever needs he had in the moment. Whether it be sex, companionship, admiration, cooking, housekeeping, or, in my case, caregiving–he wanted what he wanted, when he wanted it. He had perfected his skills of manipulation, often in the form of what I learned to be gaslighting, to have his way.

We didn't speak for nearly two months after that conference call, not just because of his response to my email about Lakeesha and the corresponding humiliation with the facility's leadership, but because of a letter he mailed our family attorney. The week following the call, I was in a meeting at work when the attorney called me, so I stepped out of the conference room, concerned about what he had to say.

"Just got a letter from your father," he drawled. "Who the hell are Linda and Judy?"

I moved out further into the hall so my conversation wouldn't be overheard.

"Um, why?"

"Well, it seems he wants to leave them both a bunch of money." I asked how much, and he read me the letter.

"They're his mistresses," I said frankly. "I can't believe he'd do this."

"It's not like him to mail a letter instead of calling for an appointment," he said. "And besides, he can't do this, as we discussed when we drew up the wills and other documents a few years ago."

"What do we do?"

"We just ignore it," he said. "Don't worry."

After hanging up, I immediately called Noble and told him about my father's letter.

"What a son of a bitch," he said.

"Here's what I think," I said, pacing through the hallway. "He knew Trip would alert me. He did this to punish me for calling him out about Lakeesha." I was furious.

"I'm pretty sure you're right. Just leave it alone. Your father loves nothing more than to feed on your emotions like a big, yummy steak," he said. "Because that's what narcissists do. Even to their own daughters."

"Pretty much," I responded.

The day before my birthday in late August, I received a card from him in the mail. I asked Noble to open it the next morning, as I feared it would be another of his nasty grams. My father prided himself on always selecting the perfect card to match his sentiments, often underlining specific words for emphasis in green ink from his favorite felt-tip pen. He always signed cards to me with either "DoD" (for Dear Old Dad) or "Daddy." This card was a generic birthday card, the kind one might give a co-worker or neighbor, and he signed it "Your Father." Enclosed with the card was a check for one thousand dollars. I put the card and check in my desk and sent him a quick text to thank him. "Enjoy," was his response. When the day's mail arrived on my actual birthday, another, more sentimental card waited which he had clearly purchased and had Mom sign. It looked as if a toddler had gotten hold of a pen and scribbled. She always had such perfect penmanship. I cried when I saw her attempt at a signature. That was my first birthday spent without seeing either of my parents, though I visited Mom the following day. I waited for two months to deposit the check from my father because I wanted him to know I didn't need his money. Petty, I know, but it was important to me I send some type of message. How he interpreted it, I'll never know.

As fall began, I was much busier at work, and by the time I could get to Mom's facility for a visit, she usually was ready for bed. As with most dementia patients, she suffered from "sundown syndrome"–her cognition declined as evening approached. This made it nearly impossible to converse with her, so my visits became less frequent. Noble filled in the gaps, visiting her in the early afternoons. She always told him had she met him first, well, I'd be out of luck. She deserved to have been married to a man with a heart as kind as his, yet she never seemed jealous–even before she became sick–of my happiness, just wistful that her romantic fate had not been better. Over the next two months, she had a few more falls, another urinary tract infection, and a stomach virus. After every discussion with the medical director, I texted my father to provide him with updates. Based on my conversations with Marleen, it was apparent he was visiting less and less frequently, which gave me cause for concern–from a distance.

One evening, I called to ask how he was doing.

"I'm dying, Suzanne. That's how I'm doing."

"I'm sorry to hear that, Dad. What's going on?" He said it was his heart and nothing could be done about it.

"Is there anything I can do to help?"

"No!" His voice sounded more gravelly than usual.

"Well, okay. Let me know if you think of something." I hung up without telling him I loved him.

Thanksgiving was fast approaching, and with all that had transpired between us, I told Noble I just couldn't bring myself to invite my father to celebrate with us. It was his favorite holiday, and while I didn't want him to be alone, I couldn't bear the thought of putting up pretenses when we all felt otherwise. Instead, we made plans with my best friend, Margot, and her husband at their home. I didn't know when the right time would be to tell him we had other plans, or if I even needed to do so. I assumed, somewhat passive-aggressively, that in the absence of any discussion about the holiday, he would know.

The first week in November, Mom's current hospice provider called to inform me they would not recertify her-certified for six more months of hospice care because her congestive heart failure had not materially worsened. By this time, she had exceeded the life expectancy estimated by thirteen months. "She won't get any better," the hospice rep said, "but she isn't showing signs of significant decline at this time."

I called Marleen and asked if it was possible to have Mom approved for hospice care because of her dementia. She gave me the contact information for a provider in the memory care space. After obtaining all the necessary information from them, I called to let Dad know what I was doing. "I know you'll handle it," he mumbled.

"How's everything?"

"No changes, Suzanne. Still dying." We exchanged a few more cordial words before disengaging. I immediately phoned his cardiologist to ask for clarification.

"He says he's dying," I told Dr. V.

"Not to my knowledge. I just saw him last week. His vitals were stable. I saw nothing that concerned me." I thanked him and hung up. That was the evening of Monday, November 8.

As part of my job, I was tasked with writing various messages from the college's chancellor to our employees, including the annual Veterans Day tribute. I sought to bring more than a Hallmark-card sentiment to these missives and took great pride in creating something poignant each year. Usually, I forwarded the Veterans Day message to my father, with a note thanking him for his service. This year, I didn't. He wouldn't have cared, and I didn't want to be rebuffed.

That night, Noble and I had eaten dinner and settled in to watch a movie in front of the fire. I had begun drifting off, as I so often did, when our home phone rang. It was about ten-twenty. Caller ID showed it was my father. I jumped up, startled. He never called this late, back when he still called. My only thought was that something had happened to Mom, yet the facility was under direct instruction that when she passed, I was to get the only call so I could drive to my father's and give him the news in person. I looked at Noble nervously before answering.

"I'm looking for a Suzanne?" a male voice asked. It wasn't my father.

"This is she," I said, my throat tightening.

"I'm Officer Vega with the Arlington Police Department," he said.

Oh God, what had my father done now? Did he have another car accident, worse than the one he'd had the previous December?

"Yes?"

"We're here with your father," he said. "I'm sorry to tell you he's passed."

"WHAT?" I screamed. "WHAT?"

"He's passed."

"We're on our way," I said, shaking so violently I could barely hold the phone. I ran to our bedroom to change clothes, grabbed the closest jacket I could find, and we sped to Dad's neighborhood.

Using the clicker to open the security gate, we arrived to find two police cars, an ambulance, and a fire truck in front of his house. I ran inside, with Noble on my heels, to find three police officers waiting for me in the front parlor.

"What happened? Where is he? I want to see him! What happened?" I tried to move past one officer, but she held up her hand.

"It wasn't supposed to be this way," I said, sinking into one of Mom's chairs and putting my head in my hands. "It wasn't supposed to be this way. Oh, God, I'm so sorry. It wasn't supposed to be this way." I was crying so hard I could barely breathe.

"May I get her some Kleenex from the bathroom?" Noble asked one of the officers. She said she'd bring the box to me.

"I don't understand," I said finally. "Why are you here? What happened?"

"We received a call just after ten from someone named Linda, who said she was concerned about her elderly friend because she hadn't heard from him in a few days," the officer replied. "She said his front door was usually unlocked, but when we got here, it was locked. Fortunately, the side door by the garage was unlocked. When we arrived, we found him in the bathroom."

"How did he die?" I couldn't believe I had just uttered those words.

"We're guessing he had a heart attack," the female officer replied.

"I want to see him!"

"Ma'am, we can't allow that. It looks like he fell from the toilet. There's quite a bit of blood. Also, it appears he's been dead for a few days."

I began hyperventilating, rocking back and forth to calm myself down. Noble went to the kitchen, poured a glass of noxious wine, and handed it to me. Grateful, I took two big gulps.

The female officer approached with an envelope.

"Here, we found this," she said, handing it to me. They had already opened and read it before I arrived.

I opened a brief note, written with my father's favorite green felt-tip pen, and tried to read it without spilling my tears onto the page.

> *Dear Suzanne*
> *I have had a blessed, lucky, and wonderful life.*
> *My only regret is that our relationship (sic) could have been better.*
> *My heart has failed—mechanically and emotionally.*
> *I am leaving you with a nice inheritance. So, as my dying wish, I am asking you to be generous with it, especially to Linda, who has cared for me these past months.*
> *Take care of your mother—who is the only person I have known to accept me unconditionally.*
> *I Love You*
> *Sorry to leave you such a financial and physical mess.*
> *Daddy*

I folded the letter and returned it to its envelope before placing it carefully in my purse. I was too shocked to see it for what it was until several days later, when I realized this likely was a suicide note. The officers, though, said they saw no reason to send my father's body to the medical examiner, ruling it death by natural causes. They asked what funeral home we wanted to use. I provided the phone number, and after they called, we waited for another hour and a half before the transport vehicle arrived.

Needing air and a cigarette, I stepped outside to the front porch, sitting on my father's stoop to drink the disgusting wine and smoke. I alerted my boss, my best friend, Margot, and one of my most trusted team members. My boss told me to take all the time I needed, which would prove quite a lot.

I just couldn't wrap my head around the fact he was gone. I felt there was so much left unsaid, though I suppose I had expressed it with my distance. Narcissists, as I learned, greet any perceived confrontation with a full throttle character attack, and truly, I had had enough over my lifetime. Still, the thought of him dying alone, no matter how it had happened, filled me with a feeling I can't describe. Not quite guilt, not quite sadness, not quite pity, not quite anger–just pain.

The funeral home van pulled into the drive, and I stood up to greet the two employees as they brought the stretcher through the foyer and back to the primary bathroom. Sitting down in Mom's chair, I started shaking once again. A few minutes later, they came back through the foyer, Dad's body covered with an American flag since he was a veteran. His date of death would be November 11. Veterans Day. Once they loaded him into the van, I approached slowly, tears pouring down my face, and reached in to touch his leg, which was bent at a strange angle and cold to the touch.

"I love you, Daddy," I whispered. We watched as they wound their way down the street. When I went back inside, the female officer handed me a folder with resource information for victims and survivors. I thanked the two remaining officers, both of whom gave me a hug.

"Let your memories be a comfort to you," the female officer said. How I wished that could have been true. Though he was gone, the saga wasn't yet over.

Good girl, grieving.

Chapter Forty-One: It Is What It Is

I awoke the next morning with a pounding headache and then was hit with the thunderbolt realization that the previous night had really happened. My father, for whom I had such complex and confusing emotions, was gone–his body lying in the morgue at the funeral home–cold, dead, alone. No more words were left to say, no more arguments to be had, and no more games to be navigated. It was over, yet I was ill-prepared for the heavy cape of shock interwoven with grief that seemed to suffocate me.

But so much work needed to be done. That was my early salvation. The funeral home called to schedule a meeting to discuss my father's arrangements. I set it up for two days, hence, drank some coffee, smoked about ten cigarettes, and then got ready to go to his house and start trying to determine where to start. Noble went earlier than I to clean up the blood in the bathroom, eager to be of service. When I got to the house, I tentatively walked into the primary bedroom. His bed was unmade, a brown banana peel languished on the floor by the wastebasket, and it all just smelled like death. I peered into the bathroom and tried to imagine how he had fallen before slapping the thought from my mind. I didn't need to envision that.

Bringing a large box of trash bags, I thought we could begin with the basics first: sorting all the trash. There was a lot. It became obvious quickly that my father really could not care for himself or the house, yet his ego prevented him from calling me for help. I cried, feeling punished for finally asserting my boundaries, even if that meant getting disinherited. It wasn't about the money...it was never about the money. I had shown I was willing to walk away from all of it. I wondered if he noticed, and at some deep level, respected me for it. I'll never know.

On his dining room table, overflowing with financial statements, bills, and magazines, Dad had kept a notebook listing all his accounts, the people he wanted me to contact upon his passing, and instruction as to the location of his coin collection and some savings bonds. He had shown me this long before he died, so I knew to look for it and had already seen it when he was last hospitalized. The coin collection, he had written, was in his office closet, and the savings bonds were in one of his three briefcases, also in his office. He already had told me the combination for the Samsonite briefcase so mentioned, but his note indicated keys also could be found in his top dresser drawer. Of course, I already had examined the contents of these briefcases while Dad was in the hospital and knew precisely what they contained–some of which I didn't want to see–but our primary mission that morning was to pull valuables from the house. Noble was cleaning out the refrigerator, so I headed upstairs.

First, I looked in the closet for the box of coins and stamps. They were missing. I looked in the corner, where the briefcases had been sitting for years. They, too, were gone. I went to the media room, which they used as a storage facility, thinking he may have moved them. Not there, either. I opened his vertical filing cabinet that, while chock full of folders, didn't contain the briefcases. Panicked, I ran downstairs and into their closet. It had additional storage in the crawl space. Nope. I had to get out of there, so I grabbed my phone and coffee, and went to sit outside on their back porch. I needed more information to make sense of the situation, so I called the Arlington Police Department and asked to speak with someone about the night before.

The records keeper could not have been more accommodating, telling me what time Linda had called before the first responders were dispatched to Dad's house. I then told her there were important items missing, items my father wouldn't have given away, and I had my suspicions. She forwarded me to a detective. I shared my concerns, and he opened an investigation.

"Do you think your father could have given her these things?"

"No way," I said, taking a sip of coffee. "Absolutely not."

"Do you want to proceed with charges?"

"I want you to talk to her." He said he would investigate it.

We spent the next two days at the house, sorting through every piece of paper on the dining table, in and on his desk upstairs, and through the piles stacked methodically on his office floor. I left each day with bags to bring to our garage. We arranged to have an industrial shredder take care of what we didn't need once I was clearheaded enough to organize everything. That would take nearly a month.

On the third day, Noble was outside loading up my SUV when a neighbor named Kara from two doors down introduced herself and asked if everything was okay. Noble explained my father had passed, and that Mom was in a memory care facility. She offered her condolences and graciously asked if she could be of help. Noble requested her number in case we needed help with the homeowners' association (she was on the board) as we prepared for an eventual estate sale. We had to leave to meet with the funeral director. I was exhausted and likely filthy, but I didn't care. He told me about meeting Dad's neighbor and said he had her number.

I had an epiphany. I texted her, introduced myself, and asked if there were security cameras at the gate to the community. She said there were not. I then asked if they kept logs about who came and went to each house in the neighborhood. Every home had a unique code, either programmed into the clicker or used on the keypad to protect access to the community. She said logs were, in fact, kept. I asked if she could pull the log for my parents' home for the full week in which Dad had died. She promised to get back to me as quickly as possible.

My father's last wishes were quite specific: he wanted to be interred at Dallas/Fort Worth National Cemetery. As a decorated officer, having been awarded the Bronze Star for his service in Vietnam, plus two additional Medals of Commendation for his exemplary service, he would be entitled to a distinguished military service. I shared this with Karen, our funeral director, who seemed disappointed I didn't want to watch her full video about all the service options available to us. I knew his urn needed to be green–his favorite color. She asked if I was planning a memorial service, and I told her I wasn't. Truth be told, there was no one to invite, other than his one friend from his brass trains group, who I cared to meet. Obituary? I told her I'd write it that evening and email it the following day. After I filled out the contract for his cremation, transport to National Cemetery, and her time coordinating with them for his military service, we left. Noble asked how I was feeling. "Numb," I replied quietly. The entire process was surreal and navigating it mostly alone–though Noble did everything he possibly could have to help–weighed heavily on me. I was so angry at the mess my father had left me and the things he had asked me to do, I struggled to breathe. Eating was entirely out of the question.

When we got home, I settled into the couch to shake off the day. My phone beeped, showing a message, and there it was: the gate log Kara had procured and attached. I put on my glasses so I could read it clearly and gasped. His gate code had been used the Monday I had last spoken with him then four times on the night police found him dead: the first, just before 9. The second and third entries were "authorized access" around ten-fifteen, then Noble and I around 10:30.

I hollered for Noble to join me; he was trying to give me space.

"You are not going to fucking believe this," I said, shaking with anger. "Holy shit."

"What?"

"Linda was there," I said, standing up to pace. "She was there before nine, but didn't call the police until eight after ten? What the ever-loving fuck?"

"Makes a pretty strong case that she took the briefcases, doesn't it?"

"While my father lay dead on his bathroom floor, she took the time to grab the briefcases and the coins, leave, lock the door, drive home, and then call the police? Are you fucking kidding me?"

"You need to call the detective with this information tomorrow, baby. Try to breathe."

I jogged to my desk to grab Dad's flip phone, bringing it back to the living room before powering it on. I found a text from Linda's husband, of all people, on the day before the police called us from Dad's home, thanking my father for his generosity. Linda's mouth was sore and swollen, he wrote, but the dental procedure went well. Let us know, he continued, if there's anything you need. Otherwise, he wrote, she'll plan to come visit you tomorrow. That would have been Thursday. I also noted several inbound calls from her cell, but no outbound calls from Dad's.

Shit! Her husband was in on the grift, too? I looked through one of Dad's checkbooks and saw he had written her a check in late October for twenty thousand dollars. I sat motionless at my desk. When we were drowning in hospital bills from Noble's staph infection and subsequent surgeries, my father never offered to help, and we never asked. Yet, here he was, paying for dental work for his married mistress, with her husband–who should have been able to pay–thanking Dad for the help. All my father's harangues over the years about the importance of sound financial planning in case of an emergency–of his diatribes about my financial irresponsibility–and here he was, funding medical bills for his sixty-five-year-old, married girlfriend. I was seething and began hating him all over again.

Except you're not supposed to hate or disparage the dead, right?

The next morning, I called the detective, then emailed him the gate log. With Noble back at work and before heading back to my father's house for a day full of sorting, I took out the list of people Dad wanted me to notify. Coffee in hand, I first called his best friend from college. Next, I called Barry, his one genuine friend from the brass trains group with whom he had lunched weekly for years. He was deeply saddened and spoke at length about how much he admired my father and his military service. I responded cordially. I had never met Dad's cousin Alice, but hers was the next call. We spoke for at least thirty minutes, and she couldn't have been kinder, also indicating how proud Dad was of all my accomplishments. Clearly, she had no idea of his secret life. It wasn't mine to share with her.

Next, I was to call Judy, Van, and Linda. I didn't need to call Linda, but the other two calls were difficult to make. I was surprised by how old Judy sounded. Her voice sounded hoarse and more unsteady than I would have expected from a seventy-six-year-old woman. I told her my father had passed, and she expressed her condolences. Then, I told her what their relationship had done to me and to my mother and asked how a good, God-fearing Presbyterian could have carried on for so many years with a married man? Did her son know? She seemed taken aback and could only apologize. Finally, I needed to call Van. One of her grown sons answered, and when I introduced myself, he said she'd have to call me later. I left him my number, just in case. As it turned out, her younger son called me back first, and in a strange turn of events, we became quite good friends, talking frequently over the next few months about my father, his mother, and how strange the whole thing seemed to be. Van called the next evening, with both sons in the room, and I shared the news my father had passed.

"He was truly something," she said. "I'm sorry to hear that, but I know how proud he was of you and your daughter."

"Thank you." I had learned we both were bragging fodder for him, especially with his girlfriends. That is, when he wasn't denigrating me for all the supposed hurts and wounds I inflicted on him. Yes, I read all of those emails in the subsequent weeks.

"I know you were quite special to him," I began slowly, "But I need to let you know that in 1978, when my mother read one of your letters to my father, it broke her in ways that could never be fixed. And I can't possibly forgive you for destroying my family."

There. I finally could say what had tormented me for decades.

"I don't know what to say," she offered.

"I promised I would call you, and I've done so."

"If you're ever in the area, I'd love to meet you," she said. I grimaced.

"Have a nice evening." I hung up the phone. I was counting on her apparent senility to excuse my cold response.

Having made the calls, I knew I was in the proper headspace to write Dad's obituary. Free of any sentimentality, I wrote a straightforward piece that I filed, without his picture, the following day. That evening, I received a message from Linda via Facebook messenger, saying she was so sorry about my father's passing. "We were wondering," she wrote, "if you have a memorial service planned." Interesting. The obituary had not yet been published. She knew. My suspicions were confirmed.

"You have a lot of fucking nerve," I responded. "But by writing 'we,' you just implicated your husband, too." She didn't respond. "I want my father's things back." To this day, she hasn't responded. The detective followed up only once to say she wouldn't return his calls. Truly, there were bigger issues in Arlington that needed the APD's attention, so I let it go.

For the next several days, I spent most of my time at their house, coordinating with an estate sale company and a realtor–one of our friends–to plan the disposition of their household and home. I already pulled the items I wanted to keep but kept telling myself to be judicious in what I kept because their things are not them.

The first week after Dad's passing, I couldn't bring myself to visit Mom. Even with her dementia, I knew she would see something was wrong, and I didn't know how to tell her. The second week, Noble and I went to see her on a Saturday. Sitting in the leather recliners, we watched her roll herself nervously around the room like a caged animal. Finally, she pulled right up to me and peered into my eyes.

"How's Dad?"

I looked at Noble, who shut his eyes and nodded.

"Mom, I don't know how to tell you this, but Dad's gone," I said, choking back tears. She blinked a few times, then rubbed her forehead.

"What? Where did he go?"

"He died, Mom. He died two weeks ago. I'm so sorry." I wiped my eyes. She looked up at the ceiling, then turned her glance back to me.

"But what about Dad?"

"He passed away. They think he had a heart attack."

A few moments passed before she began shuffling her wheelchair around the room again, chewing her bottom lip.

"Did I like him?" I didn't respond.

"I don't think I liked him."

"No, Mom, I don't think you did."

Good girl, spiraling.

Chapter Forty-Two: Foreign Ground

One of life's greatest truisms is that so many of the things most annoying about a person leave an unexpected, unfamiliar, and jarring chasm once they're gone. For fifty-six years, I knew how to navigate my father's tantrums and directives at Christmas, always trying to find a way to turn his bitterness into something reasonably palatable—at least, survivable—for the rest of the family. Yet, between his death on November 11 and my daughter's college graduation on December 18, my emotions were so fragmented that Christmas simply felt burdensome in a way my exhausted self couldn't comprehend. I bought and wrapped gifts in a fog; decorations, though, were sparse. We assembled and illuminated our Christmas tree, yet I couldn't bring myself to unwrap and hang ornaments. All I added was Mom's prized angel from Germany—older than I—and the star Dad had made from a stationery box some fifty-eight years earlier. Normally, I spent weeks making homemade raspberry and blackberry jam for friends and family, as an homage to my grandma. It was too hard. I wanted to feel joyous, yet I felt uncomfortably untethered. I didn't know how to do Christmas without the constraints that bound us all, unhappily but traditionally.

I did the best I could. It had to be enough because it was all I had.

A few days after Christmas, I fell ill with what most probably was COVID, though two PCR tests were inconclusive. Spending New Year's Eve and New Year's Day on the couch, bundled in blankets and racked by body aches, wasn't how I wanted to transition to what I hoped would be a better year, yet I was more concerned to learn Mom had tested positive. I couldn't visit her. She wouldn't have known, anyway. Her memory had evaporated like a puddle of water under the relentless Texas sun. Just before Christmas, Noble had gone to visit, and she greeted him with a smile. "Hi, Danny!" she had said, eyes glistening. Danny was her first love, some seventy-eight years before. Noble didn't correct her.

After taking a few days off to fully recover, I returned to work in early January. The two-week break had helped me begin the agonizing process of trying to heal, yet I still felt off balance, buffeted by my ever-changing feelings about my father, our relationship, and his absence. Having hired an estate sale company to help clear their house of their possessions we didn't want to keep, I tried to focus on the practical matters at hand, including lining up a realtor so I could put my parents' house on the market. The process exhausted me, but I was doing what my parents expected of me: to briefly fall apart, then get on with it. "You've got five minutes," as Mom always said.

Unlike other organizations for which I had worked, my current employer honored MLK Day as a holiday, so I spent that Monday in my home office sorting through boxes of paperwork and letters I had brought from my parents' home. When I got to work the next day, January 18, I felt better than I had in months–not quite myself, if I'd ever be that person again–but able to laugh with my colleagues and focus on a few new projects.

I had intended to visit Mom on my way home, but I knew by the time I would arrive, she would already be ready for bed and besides, evenings were the worst time to see her given her advanced dementia. So, I drove home, chatting on speakerphone the entire way to Margot, then came into the house, poured a glass of Merlot, and began sharing my "normal" day with Noble. He listened patiently for the next ten minutes until my cell phone rang. My caller ID showed it was someone from the med tech staff at Mom's facility. I remember hoping she hadn't fallen again. I answered the phone as Noble silenced CNN.

"Hi, Suzanne, it's Mimi," she said. Mimi was one of my favorite med techs.

"I'm here with your Mom," she continued.

"Okay," I intoned.

"I'm sorry to tell you, she's passed."

"She's what?" I began trembling.

"She's gone, honey. I came into the room to check on her, and she had already passed."

I began sobbing and fell to the floor. "Are you sure? Are you completely sure?"

"Yes, I'm sure. I'm just so sorry. We all loved the Judge."

I needed Mom. The thought of her dying alone, maybe wondering if she had been forgotten, filled me with such remorse, I couldn't forgive myself.

"She knew you loved her," Noble said as I sat on the couch, burying my head in my arms. "And," he said quietly, "she didn't die alone. God was there. She wasn't alone."

After the first week of paralyzing grief, I put my energy into writing Mom's eulogy, which was the most important piece I've ever produced. I wanted to ensure her tenacity, her ferocity, her talents, her accomplishments, and her character were beautifully captured. The day of her service was a cloudless, crisp day. My daughter had flown in from Nebraska and was ready, if needed, to read the eulogy were I unable to get through it. The chapel filled with a few of her former colleagues, members of her quilt guild, and many of my closest friends, who sat rapt as I told Mom's story with nary a dry eye in the room.

In the reception that followed, several of the guests said they had no idea just what an exceptional life Mom had led. Of course, I left out the tough stuff about a lifetime of betrayal by my father and the irony that she–like Dad–had succumbed to a failing heart in the end. Hearts can only endure so much disappointment before they literally break. The world had broken Dad's heart because nothing and no one ever was enough to make him feel appreciated, if not idolized–one hazard, I suppose, of narcissism.

In turn, he broke hers. And mine.

Grief, unto itself, is a complicated, harrowing journey. Its five purported phases are neither chronological nor linear, and often, each might arrive unexpectedly over the course of a day. The path to forgiveness is harder, though. Having forged a close relationship with Jon, Van's son in Olympia, I found something as close to understanding as I could allow myself. And these conversations, along with those with my pastor and my therapist, helped me begin seeing my father as an individual who was deeply tormented by desires never satisfied, self-loathing masked as superiority, and his belief that the world should bow to his wishes because he said so. His mental illness as a narcissist, combined with his sexual addiction, became the proverbial crosses Mom and I would bear. My struggle to forgive him centered upon my sanctimonious belief that he preached "decisions," yet clearly made choices that devastated our family. He knew what he was doing, didn't he? Or was his addiction too powerful?

"I have to ask," Jon said recently, "Do you have any happy memories of your father?"

His question hurled me into a jarring slide show of my fifty-six years with Dad. I thought about him teaching me to play catch in the backyard. Those sessions usually ended with mutual frustration, but at least he tried. I remembered family road trips through the Deep South and up Highway One from Los Angeles to Yosemite, where Mom and I had his undivided attention–though briefly. I remember his graciousness in paying for my first wedding and serving as the proud host of "the best party (he had) ever thrown." I couldn't think of many others.

"It's easier to remember the bad memories," I confessed, my voice painfully catching in my throat.

"Why do you think that is?"

"Because when I remember the few happy memories, where there was no subtext, no strings attached, no 'gotchas,' it hurts too much because I wonder, why couldn't there have been more? Our family's happiness wasn't his priority."

Often, the truth doesn't just hurt–it tortures.

My father died in 2021 and I've only begun processing the loss, not so much of him but the idea of him. I had hoped–longed for, really–the chance to achieve some semblance of closure while he was still alive, or at least to be assured of his love and approval. Until I finally had to distance myself from him, four months before his death, I wanted nothing more than to be a Daddy's Girl. I needed to see the full magnitude of myself, what I had achieved, and the very person I had become reflected back to me through his proud eyes. I craved a safe space where I could be honest about the lifelong psychological abuse I endured from him and the scars that, while invisible to others, nagged at me every day. I was desperate for an apology that would never come, for changed behavior that would never happen. I was sure, despite my life experiences showing otherwise, that he could change. That we would change. Does it do me any good to continue harboring these desires? Not really. When he appears in my dreams, which he does quite often, I never feel comforted. Instead, I feel haunted as if I'll never truly be free from him and his judgment. And I continue wondering, what's wrong with ME?

Being emotionally contorted and manipulated and gaslighted by a narcissist feels like living in the funhouse at a carnival. Yet, I didn't and don't see myself as a victim. Rather, I see my resilience, my strength, and my heart that remains open and trusting, not cold and hardened, despite lifelong trauma. So much of what I have accomplished in my life stems from my conditioned belief that love and approval must be earned, rather than given freely. I wouldn't trade any of my achievements, but I now see they don't define my worth.

What does? My loyalty, my character, and the good I try to put into the world each day to serve God. My father couldn't take that from me, not in life and absolutely not in death. People ask if I can ever forgive him for what he did to me and my mother. I've concluded that's the wrong question. If I can process at my deepest emotional and cognitive levels that he was powerless over his mental illness and addiction, forgiveness yields to compassion though he didn't earn it. But did he have to? Or is it simply enough to give him posthumous compassion going forward? I wish it had been different, I really do. But then, who would I have been? One thing is certain: I survived and will continue to thrive, no matter what.

Good girl, understanding.

EPILOGUE

"She's like quicksilver and stardust and the best Champagne," Mom had written about me to my father in 1966 when I was just sixteen months old. "You'll see."

On my fifty-seventh birthday, just seven months after losing Mom and nine months after losing Dad, Noble asked what I'd like to do to celebrate. I had copied this part of her letter, in her beautiful script, with an idea that I decided to execute that same day. We went to the local tattoo parlor, and I showed them what I wanted inked on the inside of my left wrist, telling the story of the letter she had written my father about me. My tattoo artist's eyes became misty as he adhered the decal with her words on my wrist. Thirty minutes later, I was branded with her love.

Through everything, I know I'm stronger than my struggles, more resilient than I knew, fiercely loyal despite my heartbreaks, and able to bend without breaking. Thanks to my faith and our loving God, I understand I'm not defined by where I've been, nor am I anywhere close to finishing my journey.

You'll see.

THE END

ACKNOWLEDGEMENTS

Writing, unto itself, may be a solitary exercise. But seeing a manuscript through to completion and subsequently getting it published is a team sport. From my first sentence to my final edit, I've been blessed to have been encouraged, comforted, and validated by people precious to me.

My husband, Noble Groves, worked overtime to keep me centered when memories and emotions became overwhelming.

My dear friend, Deborah Schall, listened without judgment and read without prejudice, assuring me this was an important story to tell. Thank you, Debbie, for your insights and support!

To JJ, my surrogate big brother, sounding board, cheerleader, and first reader, your encouragement, combined with your sense of humor and sensitive ear, helped me translate the stories I told you into a book that will hopefully help others. Thank you.

Fellow writer and dear friend, Gin Coleman, offered her discerning eye and generous heart as I worked to complete this book, giving me useful suggestions along the way in her lovely Southern drawl.

Linda Moore, one of my beta readers, gave me the gift of compassionate feedback enveloped by pragmatism as she provided suggestions which only enhanced the final product.

To my other beta readers, sharing your personal epiphanies inspired by my story reinforced my belief that we cannot heal what we're unwilling to acknowledge.

To "MEB," my phenomenal editor, thank you for your eagle eye and generous insights as I moved this book closer to the finish line. God certainly gave you exceptional talent, and I'm so honored you shared it with me.

I can't say enough about Reagan Rothe and my team at Black Rose Writing, who believed in this story and brought it into the light. Thank you, fellow Texans!

Finally, my therapist, Dr. Katharine O'Connor, gave me the emotional tools I needed not just to process many of the experiences described in my work, but to heal. Finally.

To all of you, thank you. Your support has meant the world to me on this transformative journey to understand.

About the Author

As an Air Force brat, Suzanne Groves relied on her imagination and innate curiosity to weather several early-life relocations. An avid reader from a young age, Suzanne went on to earn her B.A. in English from The University of Texas at Austin. She parlayed her degree into a successful advertising and marketing career, during which she received numerous national and international awards for creative excellence. The author of two books, Suzanne now writes women's contemporary fiction. When she's not working as the editorial director of a Dallas-based content marketing firm, Suzanne travels with her husband, works to keep up with her two perpetually shedding German Shepherd Dogs (and cat), and engages in literary shenanigans with her fellow authors.

Visit Suzanne at: https://www.suzannegroves.com

Other Titles by Suzanne Groves

We Need to Talk

Communicating Through Difficult Situations in Four Easy Steps

Suzanne Seifert Groves

Note from Suzanne Groves

Word-of-mouth is crucial for any author to succeed. If you enjoyed *You'll See*, please leave a review online—anywhere you are able. Even if it's just a sentence or two. It would make all the difference and would be very much appreciated.

Thanks!
Suzanne Groves

We hope you enjoyed reading this title from:

BLACK ROSE
writing™

www.blackrosewriting.com

Subscribe to our mailing list – *The Rosevine* – and receive **FREE** books, daily deals, and stay current with news about upcoming releases and our hottest authors.
Scan the QR code below to sign up.

Already a subscriber? Please accept a sincere thank you for being a fan of Black Rose Writing authors.

View other Black Rose Writing titles at www.blackrosewriting.com/books and use promo code **PRINT** to receive a **20% discount** when purchasing.